T0194862

Two Lifetimes

From *Fear* to *Love*

Patti Henry, MEd, LPC

BALBOA.PRESS

A DIVISION OF HAY HOUSE

Balboa Press books may be ordered through booksellers or by contacting:

Balboa Press
A Division of Hay House
1663 Liberty Drive
Bloomington, IN 47403
www.balboapress.com
844-682-1282

Because of the dynamic nature of the Internet, any web addresses or links contained in this book may have changed since publication and may no longer be valid. The views expressed in this work are solely those of the author and do not necessarily reflect the views of the publisher, and the publisher hereby disclaims any responsibility for them.

The author of this book does not dispense medical advice or prescribe the use of any technique as a form of treatment for physical, emotional, or medical problems without the advice of a physician, either directly or indirectly. The intent of the author is only to offer information of a general nature to help you in your quest for emotional and spiritual well-being. In the event you use any of the information in this book for yourself, which is your constitutional right, the author and the publisher assume no responsibility for your actions.

Any people depicted in stock imagery provided by Getty Images are models, and such images are being used for illustrative purposes only. Certain stock imagery © Getty Images.

THE HOLY BIBLE, NEW INTERNATIONAL VERSION®, NIV® Copyright © 1973, 1978, 1984, 2011 by Biblica, Inc.® Used by permission. All rights reserved worldwide.

Print information available on the last page.

ISBN: 978-1-9822-5713-2 (sc)
ISBN: 978-1-9822-5714-9 (hc)
ISBN: 978-1-9822-5715-6 (e)

Library of Congress Control Number: 2020920731

Balboa Press rev. date: 10/30/2020

To all my clients; you have taught me so much.
To my children; you have taught me so much more.
To my partner; you have taught me the most of all.

CONTENTS

Introduction xi

Part I: The Story

Chapter 1   Making Up a Story 1
Chapter 2   Momma Never Told Me 2
Chapter 3   Most People Run Away 10
Chapter 4   Bigger Than Religion 15
Chapter 5   Some Clarity 16
Chapter 6   Our Purpose on the Planet 21
Chapter 7   Conscious Choice 36
Chapter 8   A Twist to the Story 42
Chapter 9   We Are One 50
Chapter 10 The Bigger Picture: The Fifty-First Percentile 53

Part II: The Work

The Prework

Chapter 11 Garbage in, Garbage Out 65
Chapter 12 Resistances 70
Chapter 13 Deciding 76
Chapter 14 Thinking Differently 86
Chapter 15 The IS of Life 110

The Main Work

Chapter 16 Your Own Personal Dragon 135
Chapter 17 Ghost Drivers 137
Chapter 18 The Need to Grieve 150

Chapter 19   Forgiveness 168
Chapter 20   Where the Rubber Hits the Road 180
Chapter 21   Letting Go of Reactionary 183
Chapter 22   Taking Ownership 205
Chapter 23   Letting Go of Blame 210
Chapter 24   Step toward Your Fear 220
Chapter 25   Update Your Image 229
Chapter 26   Putting It All Together 234
Chapter 27   Step toward Love 238
Chapter 28   A Little More about Marriage 242

The Postwork

Chapter 29   Do Meaningful Work 252
Chapter 30   Walk in Integrity 255
Chapter 31   Have Adventures 258
Chapter 32   Give Back 260
Chapter 33   The Awakening Is Happening 263

Acknowledgments 267
Addendum 269
Recommended Readings, Links, and Movies 275
Index 277

INTRODUCTION

It is possible for us to live two lifetimes on this planet. The first one is full of pain and struggle; the second one is full of joy and freedom. The first one is run by fear; the second one is run by love. The first one is run by our wounded child; the second one is run by our authentic adult self. To get from Lifetime One to Lifetime Two, you must call forth your courage and walk down a scary, uncharted path in the dark woods. There is no other way. There are no shortcuts.

This book is about harnessing your fear to be able to go from Lifetime One, living in fear, to Lifetime Two, living in love. It chronicles how to move from an emotionally immature child to an emotionally mature, empowered adult.

When I speak at seminars, I start by singing, "What would you do if I sang out of tune? Would you get up and walk out on me?" Then I stop and stare at the audience and say, "Well?" Most people laugh and say they would sing along with me. I then tell them that I will try not to literally sing out of tune but that I am going to talk about ideas that are rather outside of the box that may sound out of tune. I warn them these ideas may clang their ears. At first.

I warn you too. Some of the ideas in this book may clang your ears. At first. That's because ideas outside of the box often put us on guard. They confront the way we think and may even lead us to *change* the way we think—which is scary. Why? Because it seems the most frightening word on the planet is *change*. We want it, we don't want it, we go toward it, we run away from it. Let's face it: change is hard. Yet the only constant in life is change. Strange, isn't it? That life is full of change, yet human beings are full of resistance to change.

So, try to keep an open mind as you hear ideas that collide with thoughts you may have had for a long time. Don't be afraid of the clanging.

It is rather like passing tones in music. When my son was younger and taking piano lessons, he, of course, had to go through the music slowly—at first. When he was learning to play the masters' works—Beethoven, Bach, Mozart—he would often come to a note that just sounded wrong. He would stop and say to his teacher, "I think it's written wrong." She would smile and say, "You will never learn to play the masters if you are unable to let yourself play the dissonant passing tones. These are the conflicts that have to be resolved in the piece. The melody is important, but the dissonance is also. It adds the depth to the music."

My hope is that this book, perhaps through its dissonance, will add some depth to your thinking and to your life.

My hope, too, is that it will help you shift from living in fear to living in love. This book, then, is about helping you harness your fear. Its goal is to walk with you, to encourage you, and to guide you on your journey from Lifetime One, being run by fear, to Lifetime Two, being run by love.

May it do just that.

Believe in the miracle of the second chance.
—Dan Zadra

The life you have led doesn't need to be the only life you have.
—Anna Quindlen

PART I

The Story

CHAPTER 1

Making Up a Story

We have to make up a story to make sense out of life.

That is, I think it's important for us to make up a story, or at least to find a story that works for us, to make sense out of the world. This helps us live—and not get stuck in extreme angst about the unknown. With our story, we are able to put to rest big life questions that have no definitive answers and get on with life.

Certainly there are big life questions that don't have definitive answers. Examples would be: Why are we here? What happens after death? Is there a God?

Now, there are a lot of people who will tell you they know the answers to these questions, but really, they are just telling you what they know they believe. You need to know what you believe. It can be different from what others believe. That is, you have a right to your own beliefs, your own story.

So, this is my story—the one I make up to put order into my world. This is my story explaining the purpose of life or what we are supposed to be doing while we are here on this planet. You do not need to believe what I believe. Take what you like and leave the rest, but again, you *do* need to know what *you* believe. Hopefully this book will help you question the "truths" that have been handed to you by others and let you figure out what is really true for you.

CHAPTER 2

Momma Never Told Me

I don't know about you, but there were certain things my mother didn't teach me when I was growing up. My father didn't teach me these things either. Now, to my parents' credit, they are almost 100 percent responsible for the civilization of me. They taught me to say please and thank you and to write thank-you notes when someone gave me a gift. I learned not to smack my gum and to always chew with my mouth closed. But the *big* life lessons somehow got left out. Now, of course, in their defense, nobody taught them. In reality, they got even fewer how-to-manage-life tools handed to them than were handed to me. And, let's face it, we can't teach what we don't know.

So, as a consequence, I have spent much of my lifetime being surprised, sometimes even shocked, when I bump into some amazing new level of understanding about something. Then in an instant, after my awareness has suddenly expanded, I think to myself, *It's so obvious! How could I not have known this?*

But it happens to me—does it happen to you?

When I do have one of those aha moments, I'm so excited! It's like discovering treasure. So I want to share some of the golden nuggets I've discovered, which maybe you weren't taught either. It turns out this treasure leads to understanding our purpose on the planet.

One nugget is this: there is a Point A in this lifetime and there is a point B as well. And in between Point A and Point B is a scary and uncharted path.

Point A ⟶ scary uncharted path ⟶ Point B

So here's my confession. For years I didn't even know there was a Point B. I thought Point A was all of life. But no. It's not. Point A isn't even that interesting—to tell you the truth. But most people live their entire lives there—because they don't know about Point B.

So, here's a general description of Point A, henceforth called Lifetime One:

- You are asleep.
- You are unaware of Point B.
- You feel like a child with no power.
- You are safe but at the price of living half a life.
- Perfection is the yardstick here; no mistakes allowed.
- There is a lot of striving for lots of money and lots of things.
- Winning at all costs is important.
- There is lots of anger, hurt, fear, depression, and anxiety.
- Addiction flourishes here.
- Relationships are miserable.
- There is a naiveté here, an unknowing.
- People are, in general, just not happy.

Elizabeth Lesser, the author of *Broken Open*, puts it this way:

I had been sleepwalking next to other sleepwalkers.
In the smug complacency of daily living,
we had all been asleep—almost drugged into a stupor.

That's Point A / Lifetime One.

3

Now here's a general description of Point B, henceforth called Lifetime Two:

- People are fully alive, fully empowered.
- The authentic adult self is present and powerful.
- Relationships are mutually satisfying.
- Money and stuff are no longer primary motivators.
- Cooperation abounds.
- People live fearlessly.
- People feel an interconnectedness with all beings.
- This is where wisdom lives.
- This is where love, joy, and peace live.
- This is where miracles abound.

Now, not to state the obvious, but Point B / Lifetime Two sounds remarkably better to me than Point A / Lifetime One. I just wish I had known about it sooner. I also wish I had known that I can live there. I'm here to tell you just that. *You* can live there.

I remember learning some of this in church while I was growing up. I was taught it through the concept of heaven. Belonging to a Baptist church, I was taught that after you die, you will go to heaven—where it's really nice. All the good stuff is there. However, in the meantime, I had to live on earth—where it really isn't that great because life is full of pain and suffering.

Now I believe the church misled me. Probably not on purpose—they just didn't know that Point B / Lifetime Two exists on earth. I now believe that Point B is a lot like the concept of heaven, where all the good stuff is. And that we can experience it right here on this planet. I'm not saying this to address what happens after we die. That's another discussion. I am saying it pertaining to how we live.

Let me put it in physical terms. Let's say Point A is like living in Chernobyl, polluted, as you know, by radioactivity from one of the worst nuclear power plant disasters in history. Point B is like living in Glacier National Park in Montana or some equally amazingly beautiful place.

The obvious question is *who* in their right mind would choose Chernobyl over Glacier National Park? Why wouldn't everyone just move to Montana?

Three reasons: either they don't know about Montana, or they have heard of this wonderful place called Montana but don't believe it is open to them, or they have some inkling it exists, but they do not want to go on any dark and scary, uncharted path to get there.

So, in this chapter, I really want you to understand that there is a Montana, a Glacier National Park, a Point B / Lifetime Two. I also want you to know it is open to you.

I remember an episode of *Candid Camera* from the 1970s where motorists were pulled over and told that Delaware was closed for the day. Naturally, they were quite in disbelief over this. They were then told, "Well, New Jersey is open—you could go there." This, of course, made for great comedy. What I'm telling you about, however, is no joke: Montana, Point B / Lifetime Two, is open to *you*. You can live a better life than you have experienced thus far.

Will you have to go down a scary, uncharted path to get there? Yes, in my story that I make up, you do. Will you have to be bold and courageous? Yes, in my story that I make up, you do.

However, the path is really just a puzzle that you have to figure out. To me, it just helps to know there *is* a puzzle—the same puzzle for everyone—and your charge is to figure it out. How to get from Lifetime One to Lifetime Two. So, take heart; you are not alone. You are not flawed because you haven't figured it out yet; *not knowing* is where everyone starts.

Part of the trickiness of the puzzle is to figure out how to go from asleep to awake—without even knowing you're asleep. It's like you are trapped in a box, but you don't know you are even in the box, until one day you bump into the wall. It's like Truman in the *Truman Show* living in an artificial world he doesn't know is fake.

So, you have a problem. To live at Point B, you have to wake up enough to even get your arms around the concept of *you are asleep*. Most people live unaware of Point B until at least their forties. I believe we can get aware of it earlier, however. And we must—so we can raise our children while we are awake.

But how?

I realize now that I was surrounded by this news of the existence of Point B my whole life—but I didn't recognize it.

For example, I knew all the fairy tales growing up. In every single one, the opening scene introduced the leading characters of the story: the princess and/or prince, the hero and/or heroine. Then the second scene was *never* "and they lived happily ever after." Oh no. First, they had to slay a dragon or some other fierce, wicked, evil monster. As a child, it was so scary. It seemed against all odds that this fierce, wicked, evil monster could possibly be conquered. But thankfully, it always was, and *then* came the happily ever after part. Surprise—fairy tales are the classic hero's journey, which has been told over and over again for thousands of years in thousands of different ways. Who knew?

Then in high school, I read *Siddhartha*, the story of the Buddha's journey to enlightenment. As a prince, he left the safe confines of his palace and ventured out into the world. He saw pain, suffering, and death, which were quite disturbing to him. Yet only through experiencing all of these things, and realizing how important the difficult path was in connecting him to his deeper feelings, did he reach nirvana, or peace—the state of perfect happiness with all that is.

Then I read Dante's *Inferno*. Same story. A person has to go through hell to get to purgatory to get to paradise. Hmmm …

I was also taught 1 Corinthians 13, the famous love chapter of the Bible: "But when completeness comes, what is in part disappears. When I was a child, I talked like a child, I thought like a child, I reasoned like a child. When I became a man, I put the ways of childhood behind me." Hmmm … the part versus the complete, the child versus the adult … another way to describe the two lifetimes.

And finally, I was raised with the Beatles, who cried out from the scary path, "Help! I need somebody!" This song outlines the difference between being young and not even knowing I need help to evolving into my mature self where I can, without shame, recognize my need for help and ask for it. Another way of describing the two lifetimes.

Of course I knew these stories, and they resonated with my soul, but I sure didn't know that they had anything to do with *me*.

It was everywhere, this message—but, clearly, I didn't know what it meant. Now I believe it means it is possible for us to live two lifetimes on this planet—one asleep and one awake—and that you can't wake up without confronting a fierce dragon on the scary, uncharted path that lies between the two.

I'm sure I did not teach this to my children, at least not clearly, because I didn't even know about Point B.

I did not teach my children that all the parts of this adventure called life—even the hard parts, the sad parts, the terrifying parts, the challenging parts—are valuable, sacred, and necessary to move you out of being asleep into being awake. I didn't teach my children that you must feel pain, suffering, loss, and even trauma to get there.

Nobody told me, and I didn't tell them these things:

You will fail miserably at least once in your lifetime—probably more.

You will feel despair. You will experience trauma.

You will cry ten thousand tears—and think you cannot recover—but you will.

You will feel friendless and alone.

You will make a *lot* of mistakes.

As Dr. Seuss says in his book about life, *Oh, the Places You'll Go,*
All alone!

Whether you like it or not, alone will be something you'll be quite a lot.

Nobody told me about all the alone feelings that would engulf me.

Nobody told me I would meet a dragon along the way from Lifetime One to Lifetime Two and that it would be large and scary. And I would be tempted to run away and hide in my safe castle. Nobody told me that there is no one who can conquer this dragon but *you*.

Significantly, too, nobody told me that all these experiences that feel really bad and scary are actually *good*. Doesn't sound good, doesn't feel good when you are going through them, but it's the path to wisdom, love, joy, and enlightenment—and it's the only way to get from Lifetime One to Lifetime Two. There are no airplanes that can fly you between the two destinations; you must walk the path. Alone.

Nobody told me that experiencing pain and suffering is the only way to diffuse their power over me. I wish they had.

It reminds me of a story about my first son when he was a baby. He was an incredible baby. We had a nanny for him who actually held him through all of his naps. He was such a calm, calm child who never cried. Really. He didn't cry. He was attended to immediately, and he was just happy.

When I was saying this to a friend of mine at the psychiatric hospital where we worked, he said, "He'll turn on you."

I said, "Oh no, I don't think he will! He's really so calm and happy."

He said, "It doesn't matter. He'll turn on you. They all do. They all go through the developmental stage of two. They all learn Mine! and Me! and No! They all feel frustrated and angry because they don't have the words to tell you what they want and need. *All* of them. Your child is not from Mars. He'll turn on you."

Then he added more gently, "I'm only telling you this so you won't be freaked out when it happens. If you know it's going to happen, it makes it easier." And he was right. My children did go through the developmental stage of two. And he was right: it did help to know in advance that it was coming.

So, it's the same thing with this going on the scary, uncharted path adventure. If you live long enough—and you don't run away—you will be pulled onto the scary, uncharted path. It helps to know in advance that this is going to happen. Does this happen to everyone? In the story I make up, it does. It seems that the Universe / God / Higher Energy / Quantum Physics or whatever it is wants *all* of us to get to Point B. We are constantly being pulled toward awakening. The Universe seems to give us opportunities, challenges, and encouragement, trying to push us down the path from asleep to awake. So don't be surprised when the scary dragon shows up. Recognize it and keep moving toward Point B.

So, if you are feeling in distress right now—lost, in despair, hopeless, and scared—I actually celebrate that. You have already left point A and are on your journey toward Point B. Trust me. It's not fun in the beginning, but you are moving in the right direction.

CHAPTER 3

Most People Run Away

Problem: People don't like to feel fear. Or terror. That's why most people run away when they get to the entrance of the dark and scary, uncharted path. Or they might run back out of the darkness after walking on the path a bit and coming across a very scary monster. They say, "What was I thinking?" and turn around and run back to Point A, where they go back to sleep. Don't let that be you.

For example, I've seen people who were in absolutely the wrong relationships for them. One comes to mind of a forty-seven-year-old female client who was dating a twenty-seven-year-old. My client was well established in her very successful career. She was personable, intelligent, and beautiful. Her boyfriend was a high school dropout who went from one minimum-wage job to the next. He had no money, so she paid for his apartment, gasoline, food, phone, and utilities. He, in return, lied to her, cheated on her, called her fat and other hurtful slurs, and took her car without permission, often leaving her stranded. When she finally broke off the relationship, she experienced the panic of being alone. Thus she went running back to what didn't work in the first place for another round of the same: settling for much less than what she wanted. She did this, of course, so she didn't have to face the fear of walking down that uncharted path by herself. She was terrified of being alone. So she decided to move back to Chernobyl. Fortunately for her, she chose therapy at the same time and was soon able to get back on her path: leaving Point A / Lifetime One—and the boyfriend—behind.

The thirteenth-century Persian Muslim poet Rumi said it eloquently:

don't go back to sleep.
people are going back and forth across the doorsill
where the two worlds touch
the door is round and open
don't go back to sleep.

Isn't it amazing Rumi was talking about the two lifetimes in the thirteenth century? He knew how important it was to wake up. Rumi and I are suggesting to you, then, that you don't go back to sleep, but instead, you walk through the door!

You are so worth walking through the door. Lifetime Two is so much better than Lifetime One. I want that for you.

Here is a story that my friend Bill Ferguson tells about his mother. As she got older, he and his siblings noticed that she was slowly losing her mind. She was then diagnosed with Alzheimer's, and it became clear that she was no longer safe to live by herself. She was doing things like putting her wet laundry into the oven to dry. So, the siblings decided the best thing was to put her in a home where they specialized in Alzheimer's and she would have twenty-four-hour care.

Well, his mother was *not* happy about this. In fact, she was deeply hurt. She felt betrayed. She was angry. She did *not* want to go. She did *not* want to leave her home where she felt comfortable and safe. She was depressed and despondent. She cried and cried and cried and begged to be taken home.

Then, after being in the home about a month, she met a man from down the hall who also had Alzheimer's, and they fell madly in love. They went everywhere together and talked for hours and hours. They introduced each other with "This is my sweetie," to everyone they met.

Then one night, they escaped. They walked out the door arm in arm and strolled down the street to a very nice restaurant, where they had the time of their lives. They ate, they drank, they danced and had so much fun.

Then the bill came. Which confused them. Of course neither of them had any money; they didn't have to pay for their meals at the cafeteria where they always ate. Luckily, the restaurant manager figured it all out, made sure they got safely back to the home where they lived, and was paid in full.

All this is to say they had five blissful, crazy-in-love years together before his mother died.

So, if his mother had known the joy that lay ahead for her, do you think she would have resisted going to the home? No, of course not. She would have been packing her bags, anxious to get there.

Similarly, that's what starting on the path between Point A and Point B is like. We resist it because we don't know the good that awaits us on the other side. If we did, we would have our bags packed and be anxious to get there.

That's the problem with trying to get to Point B. If a person's asleep, how can they know what it's like to experience the bliss of being awake?

I can tell you all about it. I can tell you it is the creme de la creme of life on this planet—that it's where your power is, your authentic self, your joy, love, and peace. I can tell you it's like living on a different plane. And I can tell you it's a place where you rarely experience fear.

But so what? It won't make sense to you until you experience it. And then you'll know what the heck I'm talking about. After all, how accurately can you explain an orgasm to a person who's never had one? What about natural childbirth? Falling in love? What it feels like to have a parent die in your arms? What it's like to jump off the high dive? Or have you ever tried to explain what it's like to have children to someone who doesn't have them? They say, "We have dogs. They're our children," and you think to yourself, *Yeah . . . it's different than that.*

There are some experiences in life that have no parallels. You just have to experience them to understand. Before you experience them, you think you understand, but after you experience them, you realize you didn't understand at all. The magnitude of the experience feels almost like another dimension. Like experiencing a whole new world.

And yet all the experiences described above are most definitely in this world. We just don't know them until we have had those experiences personally.

For example, I had a very close friend whose mother died many years back. When she called and told me, I was sad for her. I immediately sent her a sympathy card and asked about the funeral, which was in my friend's hometown more than a thousand miles away. Because of finances or my schedule or my children's schedules or whatever, I decided going to the funeral was out of the question for me. I sent flowers instead. I called my friend when she got back in town and asked her about it, again expressing my sympathies. I listened to her stories of her trip back home and how hard it was for her to be there without her mother being there too.

About a year passed. Then one day she said these shocking words, "It really hurt me that you weren't there for me when my mother died."

I was stunned. I thought I *had* been there for her! I was even a little irritated that she was hurt and that she was saying my efforts hadn't been good enough.

Then fifteen years passed, and my father died. The disorientation and brain fog that I experienced for at least six weeks afterward was indescribable with the words we have in the English language. When I came out of that fog and had access to my whole brain again, I called my friend and apologized for not being there for her more when her mother died. I completely understood what she was talking about on a level I could not have understood before I lost my own parent. It's the same as having Lifetime One experiences, asleep, or having Lifetime Two experiences, awake.

These two ways of experiencing life, asleep and awake, are so different that they feel almost like two different lifetimes. My goal, of course, is to rouse you from your sleep so you can get to the better life.

CHAPTER 4

Bigger Than Religion

This book is not about religion. The thoughts in this book are bigger than religion. They are universal, affecting Christians, Muslims, Jews, Hindus, Buddhists, pagans, agnostics, atheists, and everyone else.

The thoughts in this book are similar to the fact that we are all born and we all die. It doesn't matter what religion we are or aren't; we are all born and we all die. This concept is bigger than religion.

The concept of two lifetimes is the same. That is, it doesn't matter about a person's faith or lack thereof. It's true for everyone.

The Episcopal bishop John Shelby Spong, when speaking about religion, is also talking about the two lifetimes:

> That's what our faith is about, it's not about making you religious or moral or right. Our faith is about calling you to live, calling you to the fullness of humanity. We do not need to be saved; we need to become fully and deeply human. We do not need to be born again, we need to grow up.[1]

Our work, simply put, is just that: to grow up, to think like and act like an adult. This applies to all people in all faiths.

---

[1] John Shelby Spong, *A New Christianity for a New World* (San Francisco: Harper, 2001), 31.

CHAPTER 5

Some Clarity

Living two lifetimes in the same body?

Yes, not like a reincarnation lifetime but actually two lifetimes in the same body. Not like a born-again Christian lifetime either. Remember, the concept of two lifetimes has nothing to do with religion. It's bigger than religion.

The waking up, or awakening, leads people into a whole other dimension that they didn't even know existed. It is as if a person has been walking between two walls for years:

Then suddenly they reach a corner, and the walls are gone:

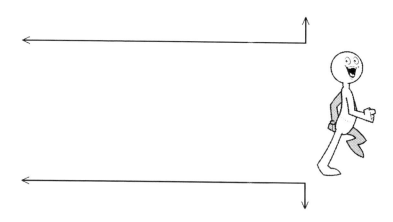

In an instant, a new, bigger world appears.

It's like what happened one December when my son was four years old. He came home from school quite excited because they had gotten a new boy in his class. He really liked him and felt he had made a wonderful new friend. When I dropped him off at school the next morning, I mentioned to the teacher that he seemed to click with the new boy in class. She looked a little puzzled and said, "Hmmm ... strange. We don't have any new boys in the class. They've all been here all year. I guess they just discovered each other!"

A new world. An exciting world. When I work with a client, I tell them that I know what I am saying will sound like I am speaking Chinese for a while, but if you keep coming back here, there will be a day that the lightbulb will go off, and you will understand. I liken it to the movie *Field of Dreams*. In that movie, the main character played by Kevin Costner plows down some of his cornfields in order to build a baseball field. He keeps hearing the haunting phrase, "If you build it, they will come." He wonders to himself, *Who will come?*

So, he builds it. It's a crazy thing to do—especially because he and his family are struggling financially—but he plows down his corn and builds a baseball field. And they do come: all of the great baseball players of the past who have already died. They come to his field—sort of like having a pickup game in heaven—and they play ball.

In the meantime, his brother-in-law is going crazy. He can't see the players. Other people can see them, and they are cheering at the games, but when the brother-in-law looks out, all he sees is an empty ball field in the middle of the cornfields. He tries to talk sense into Costner. He's anxious for him, scared, in angst that he is not taking care of his family. So much fear.

And then there is the moment. The magical moment when he *sees*. He looks out and can see all the players. He has, somehow, stepped into that next dimension and can see what Costner has been able to see all along. It's an awakening moment and the highlight of the movie.

This happens in my practice all the time. Clients call me up one day and say, "I get it! It all makes sense to me now!" and I high-five the Universe and say "Yes!" So exciting. One more person awake.

If you haven't seen the 2009 movie *Avatar* yet, I encourage you to find a copy and watch it. If you have seen it, I encourage you to watch it again. This movie is about the two lifetimes I'm speaking of: the humans representing being asleep, and the Na'vi—the blue people—representing being awake. The concepts I'm talking about here are visually reinforced in that movie.

In fact, there is a line in the movie that electrified me because it was so profound. It actually propelled me into writing this book. It was as if lightning struck me, and I became crystal clear what I needed to write.

The line is this: the Na'vi people believe we are born twice in this lifetime.

My belief is slightly different from that. I believe we have the opportunity to be born twice in this lifetime and that most people never get there. Most people never get there because they either keep their eyes shut and can't see the possibility or are too afraid to stay on the uncharted, scary path.

Think of what I'm saying: almost everyone you meet is still asleep. Almost everyone in every walk of life, in every job, in every marriage, in every religion. Hmmm …

But let me make this clear: this book is not about converting to a religion. As stated earlier, I'm not talking about being born again in a religious type of way. This born twice has nothing to do with Jesus or religion; it is more inclusive than that. However, moving from Lifetime One to Lifetime Two might actually feel like a spiritual experience—like being born into a new life. Addicts who get sober often explain their experience in this way: having a second chance at life or, in many ways, having a whole new life. Again, it doesn't matter what a person's religious beliefs are or not. This Lifetime Two is available to everyone. It is possible for *you* to awaken to a new world not dominated by fear.

The trick is you have to wake up to get out of your fear, and paradoxically, you have to get out of your fear to wake up.

That's how Second Lifetime is. It's tricky until one moment it's clear.

I can tell you all about it. I can tell you it is the creme de la creme of life on this planet—that it's where your power is, your authentic self, your joy, love, and peace. I can tell you it's like living in a different dimension. And I can tell you it's a place where you no longer experience fear.

But so what? It won't make sense to you until you experience it. And then you'll know what the heck I'm talking about. I have a plaque on my desk that says, "It sounds like English, but I can't understand a word you're saying."

This book may feel like that to you for a while. Keep reading. Eventually, I promise, it will make sense.

A fifty-year-old male client said to me recently, "I'm so weak. I'm *so* afraid I'll say something stupid or I'll hurt someone's feelings, and so I just sit there, feeling trapped inside my body. It's like my *self* is trapped inside of me."

Yeah, that's what I'm talking about: getting rid of fear so as to untrap yourself.

CHAPTER 6

Our Purpose on the Planet

In fact, in the story I make up, it's this untrapping of self that we are here to do. Untrapping ourselves so we can then join the healing force working toward peace on earth. It's moving from being part of the problem to being part of the solution.

If I had written the book *The Purpose-Driven Life*, it would have been very short. That's because I believe every single person on the planet has the same purpose: to wake up and move from Lifetime One to Lifetime Two. Every single person—including you.

Another way of saying this is: the purpose of this life is to evolve from being driven by fear to being driven by love. In other words, *your* purpose on this planet is to evolve from being driven by fear to being driven by love. We do this by shifting from letting our wounded child run our life to waking up our authentic adult self to run it.

Please reread the last paragraph. We have to wake up our authentic adult self.

Of course you've already grown up physically into an adult self. I'm talking about waking up our authentic, emotional adult self. For most of us, it may mean recognizing that we haven't done that yet. Remember the problem about Lifetime One though: we are asleep. We think we have already grown up. We do not think our wounded child—whatever that means—is running our life.

But he is. But she is.

Remember, it is a difficult concept to understand until you experience it. My very own grandmother once told me as I was explaining to her what this book was about, "Honey, most of the time, I don't even know what you're talking about. I just politely listen."

Oh.

So, I will do my best to use some words that make sense to you.

Lifetime One

There are many ways to describe Lifetime One:

asleep
run by our wounded child
lower-energy vibration
scared, ruled by fear
emotionally young
the yucky stuff
reactionary
defensive
blaming
victim
child
a feeling of disconnection
we chop wood, carry water

Let me emphasize: we don't even know that our wounded child is running our lives. We think our adult self is. That's the problem with Lifetime One: we don't even know that we don't know. The following are some clues to see if you are still in Lifetime One.

In Lifetime One, we believe someone else has our power. We believe we don't have choice a lot of times, that we *have to*, that people (usually our partner, sometimes a parent, sometimes a boss) "won't let us," that we are "not allowed to," that we will "get in trouble" if our wife/husband/boss finds out. We really don't know that we are in charge of our lives. We don't know that we have the power to create our lives any way we want. We don't know we can change things we don't like. We feel trapped. We de-self. We avoid conflict. We feel like a child with no power or options, and then we start acting like one. We people-please, trying to get others' approval. We do things without a real thought process—without even asking ourselves if what we are doing is really what we want to be doing. We are living our life sort of like a zombie. It sounds absurd, I know, but it's true nonetheless.

In Lifetime One, we get pushed around. We do things people tell us to do even when we don't want to. We say yes to things when the answer is really no and then have resentment and feel like a victim.

I honestly did not know that I was allowed to say no to things until I was almost thirty. I was taught that would be impolite. I thought if somebody asked me to do something, told me to do something, ordered me to do something, that I just needed to do it. That seems ridiculous to think a smart person in their late twenties did not know this, but I didn't. In fact, one time when I was doing a photo shoot, the photographer asked me if I would take off my shirt and bra for a couple of shots. I hesitated, and he said, "I won't take any shots of your nipples—just down to right above them. It would really, really help me out if you could just do a couple of shots." Sadly, I took off my shirt and bra! When I got home, I ran to my bedroom and cried, feeling so violated. My boyfriend was incredulous and asked, "Why did you do that? Why didn't you just leave? For God's sake, why didn't you just say no?"

Having been sexually abused since I was a young child, the honest answer was, "I didn't know that was an option."

So, too, it is with many people I work with at thirty, forty, fifty, sixty, even seventy years old. They are shocked to find out that *no* is an option for them. This inability to say no is one way to tell if you are still in Lifetime One being run by your wounded child. However, please note, you may be very effective at saying no in certain areas of your life but not in others. For example, you may be able to be very clear and directive at work yet have no power at home. That is, you may be able to say no to your colleagues at work—but not to your spouse.

Also, in Lifetime One, we stay in jobs where we are miserable, in relationships where we are miserable, and generally in a life where we are miserable. We put up with all kinds of things that feel bad to us—because we really don't know there is another way.

Marianne Williamson stated, "Your playing small does not serve the world." In Lifetime One, we may not be consciously playing small, but we are small. Our wounded child is in charge.

Lifetime Two

There are many ways to say Lifetime Two as well:

awake
run by our adult self
higher-energy vibration
love is predominant
no fear
nonvictim
nonreactionary
able to respond, response-able
at peace with all that is
adult
a feeling of connection with everything
the good stuff
a connection to love
we chop wood, carry water joyfully

In Lifetime Two, we are responsible for our lives—everything we are doing or not doing, thinking, and feeling. Everything. That is, we are responsible—response able. We are capable of responding to a stimulus rather than reacting to it.

We don't feel small. We don't get pushed around. We are living the life that we were born to live. We are in personal integrity. That is, our life is integrated: our thoughts are congruent with our feelings, which are congruent with our behaviors. We know our values, and our life reflects them. We are comfortable in our skin. We are not afraid. Life is good. Our relationships are good. We love our jobs. We live life with our arms wide open, wanting to take in as much of it as we can. If we don't like the way we are feeling, we take responsibility and change it. We are responsible to ourselves.

Lifetime Two is just hugely better than Lifetime One. It's where your power is. Where love is. And joy. And peace. It's where your voice is, where your boundaries are. It's where no fear is. Where happy is. Where empowerment is.

So here's an example of the difference: In Lifetime One, a problem is handed to you, which could be big or small. Your wounded child is in charge and says, "I don't know what to do!" and pretends there is no problem until it gets worse and worse. In Lifetime Two, you are handed the same problem, and your adult self says, "I don't know what to do, but I am smart and can figure it out." And you do.

A Word about God

Some people use terms saying Lifetime One is a disconnection from God, and Lifetime Two is a connection to God. Some use the word Jesus. No connection with Jesus versus a connection with Jesus. Some use the word Allah. I use the words *fear* and *love* most often because these words apply to all religions and mean more than religion. I also use the words *child* and *adult* as well, meaning an emotional child versus an emotional adult.

I have encountered many people in the world who claim to be connected to God, or to have a "personal relationship with Jesus," who are still run by fear. I then have to ask them to deepen their faith: If you believe an all-knowing, all-powerful God is in charge, why do you still have fear? If you have a personal relationship with Jesus, who came to the planet teaching love, love, love, why are you still acting unloving, reactionary, noninclusive, and so afraid? To these people, I say, "Try using the words *fear* and *love*: outgrowing your fear to live completely in the energy of love. Or try the words *child* and *adult*."

Actually, use whatever words work for you. The most important thing is to remember the good stuff is in Lifetime Two. That's the bottom line.

I have questioned whether or not a person needs to have a spiritual connection to God / Higher Power or whatever you prefer to call Divine in order to get to Lifetime Two. Since I personally feel a strong and constant connection to Divine, it's impossible for me to assess that question without that connection. This much I do know is true, however: I have always felt a strong and constant connection to God, but I have not always been an emotional grown-up living in Lifetime Two. I lived in Lifetime One with my wounded child in charge for many years. So, in the story I make up, having a connection with God is not sufficient to get to Lifetime Two. Is it necessary but not sufficient? I don't know, but I do know it's not sufficient.

I once worked with an astronaut who identified himself as an atheist. He, like so many clients I work with, came in needing to emotionally grow up. He needed to get out of Lifetime One and shift into Lifetime Two. He did this with no belief in God but with a strong belief in science and the cosmos. To me, that's a detail. Science and the cosmos are God in my opinion, so he, though an atheist, still had a strong connection to something bigger than himself. Again though, he had this connection while he was in Lifetime One as well as when he grew into Lifetime Two.

So, perhaps the connection gets stronger or deeper when one leaves Lifetime One behind and steps into his/her full adult self. However, though I see that often, I don't know that it is always true.

Again, I say it doesn't really matter. Having graduated from a Quaker college, I am most familiar with the Bible of all the holy books, so forgive me for using Bible verses for reference if that is offensive to you. I have read the Torah, the Qur'an, the I-Ching, the Bhagavad Gita, and the Book of Mormon as well. I have found amazing truths in all of these sacred texts. I am not saying one of these doctrines is better than the other. I am not saying one is less than another. I am saying, in the story that makes sense to me, it doesn't matter what sacred text you believe: Lifetime One and Lifetime Two exist in all faiths, for all people—even people who don't have any faith or whose faith is quantum physics.

The phenomenon is universal. Don't get stuck in the small stuff. To me, which sacred text a person reads, studies, and believes in is part of the small stuff. It's all small stuff except evolving from fear into love.

So, the purpose of this life is to *wake up*, to outgrow and transform the wounds of our childhood, to step into our authentic adult self, and to take hold of the life we were born to live.

Let's think about the story of Susan Boyle. Remember Susan Boyle? She was that incredibly frumpy older woman who anxiously stepped onto the stage at *Britain's Got Talent*, opened her mouth, and sang the most stunning rendition of "I Dreamed a Dream" from *Les Misérables* that the world had ever heard. There wasn't a dry eye in the audience as everyone rose to honor Susan with a standing ovation. She was fantastic.

For Christmas one year, I was lucky enough to get a copy of her CD, *I Dreamed a Dream*. On it was a song called "I Am Who I Was Born to Be." I cried the first time I heard it. First, because Susan sang it with the passion of truth: it was her story. Finally, at age forty-eight, she began living the life she was born to live. I cried tears of gratitude for myself as well—so very grateful to have gotten to wake up to Lifetime Two and be doing the thing I was born to do, psychotherapy and teaching love. That's what I want for you too—for you to live the life you were born to live, to feel comfortable and confident in your own skin.

To do this, you have to become an emotional grown-up.

What I'm saying is your *purpose* on this planet—my purpose, everyone's purpose—is to emotionally grow up and move from being driven by fear into being driven by love. That is, I don't think love is a big deal; I think love is *the* deal.

Love is *the* deal on this planet.
That is our purpose: to get to love.
Everything else is just details.
Everything else is just details.

Think about that: love is *the* deal on the planet; everything else is just details. As Shunryn Suzuki said, "That is more true than I can say, and more true than you can hear." It is the most important sentence in this book.

So, we need to grow up. We need to become emotional adults.

Identifying Fear

There are really only two emotions: fear and love. Furthermore, if it's not love, it's fear.

I am using that definition when I say our purpose on the planet is to grow up emotionally, to evolve from fear to love. Because fear can look like anger or rage. Fear can look like depression or anxiety. Fear can look like shame or embarrassment. Fear can look like rudeness and exclusion. Fear can look like addiction. Fear can look like bragging. Fear can look like lying and cheating. Fear can look like pride or self-righteousness. Fear can look like apathy. Fear can look like greed or hoarding. Fear can look like laziness. Fear can look like controlling behavior. Fear can look like hurt. In other words, all emotions can be boiled down to either fear or love. For simplicity, fear means the yucky stuff; love means the good stuff.

Now, a confession. When I was in graduate school training to be a psychotherapist, I was taught over and over and over again never to have an agenda when working with a client. I was told that the proper way to do therapy was to let the client set the agenda and for me to just sort of follow along.

Well, I don't do that. My apologies to all of my professors. I *always* have an agenda for my clients: to move them from fear to love, to lovingly push them along the scary path so they can get to the other side, to move them from Lifetime One to Lifetime Two, to get them to claim their powerful, authentic adult self. Why? Because it's so much better in Lifetime Two. There is no depression, there is no addiction, there is no anxiety, there is no anger, there is no fear.

My clients say to me, "So I'm going to be able to get rid of my fear? Yeah, right!"

Yeah. Right.

Think about it. If everyone's life purpose is the same—to get rid of fear and get to love—and all of us, Christians, Muslims, Jews, Hindus, atheists, pagans, agnostics, and everyone else, worked toward that end, we could heal the world. I believe that's the goal.

But a Word of Caution

The word *love* is a confusing one that is often overused and misused. For example, many religions today use the word casually, without, it seems, really understanding the meaning of it. More death and pain and suffering have occurred in the name of Jesus and in the name of Allah than are countable. So often, those who are trying to convert others are unloving, exclusionary, hateful, angry, controlling, judgmental, reactionary, and ruled by fear. They are clearly still in Lifetime One.

We can only counter this by first moving ourselves to the love vibration and then being kind and loving to all people we meet.

However, if the "love" you are giving or receiving doesn't feel good to the other person, then it's not really love. If it's violating another in any way, it's not really love. If it says, "I am better than you because I have these beliefs and you don't," it's not really love.

Nor am I talking about the feeling of being *in love*, which is actually a chemically altered state that is short-lived. I am talking about a deeper, life-sustaining, life-giving love.

I am talking about the love that means my heart is open to you, I accept you as you are, I honor you as you are, and I will do you no harm.

Our Own Boat

On our mission to shift from fear to love, we get a boat. That's right. When we are born, we get our own little boat to float in down the river of life. Nobody else is in the boat with us. We are the only one there twenty-four seven. Yes, our boats hook up with other boats throughout the day; we talk to someone on the phone, we meet someone for lunch, we have a meeting with several someones in the afternoon, we eat dinner with our family after work. But after our connection with them, we untie our boats and keep on floating down our own river.

This is important. There is *no one* else in your boat with you. The exception is when a woman is pregnant. She has another person with her in the boat, but as soon as that baby is born, they get their own boat. You are, therefore, the only person you are guaranteed to live with your whole life. That's why you have to really like the person you are floating down the river of life with: you. That's why *you* have to take claim of your life; there is no one else in the boat to do it for you. That's why it's up to only *you* to face your fear while moving from Lifetime One to Lifetime Two. It's an individual journey and, I believe, our individual responsibility.

Now I remember when I was first introduced to this concept. I was sitting in an Adult Children of Alcoholics meeting when the speaker said, "*You* are responsible for your life—all of it! *You* are responsible for your happiness—or unhappiness. There's only *you* to run your life and create it to be what you want it to be!"

On hearing this, I thought to myself, *You're kidding! I don't know how to do that!* Now, I don't know who I thought was responsible for it—for my life and making me happy. A husband perhaps? A job? A baby? I hadn't really thought that part through, nor had I really thought about my role in my life. All I know is it was quite a shock to be hearing that *I* was responsible for my life. Quite frankly, I hadn't planned on working that hard. I thought someone else was going to somehow run my life, take care of me, and make me happy.

Nope, I'm here to tell you *you* have to make it all happen. *You* have to do the work to get beyond your fear. *You* have to confront your own dragon. There is no one else in your boat to do it for you. You are the one who has to emotionally grow up. It's like exercising to lose weight. Nobody can do that for you. No matter how many sit-ups your friend does on your behalf, you will not lose weight until you do the sit-ups. No shortcuts, remember?

Life Is an Adventure

Life is an adventure. A marvelous adventure. Einstein said you can look at life as if nothing is a miracle, or you can look at life as if everything is a miracle. To me, everything is a miracle—and an adventure. We really don't know what's going to happen next as we float down the river. So whether we are afraid or not afraid, we are still in our boat floating down the river of life, not knowing what will happen next. Fear doesn't make it any less so.

For example, on March 16, 2011, I thought I was floating down the river the same direction I'd been going. I thought I was in Holland, going to enjoy a nice spring break vacation with some family and dear friends. Nope. My little boat got flung to the left, down a tributary I didn't even know existed. It was the "You Have

Cancer" tributary. I tell you, that news will throw a wrench in a vacation.

For the next eight months, I was on the cancer treatment adventure. I tied my boat up throughout my days with all kinds of people who were wonderful and had things to teach me. I tied my boat up sometimes with people who hurt my body in their effort to help me—and as soon as I could, I would untie my boat from them and keep on floating. Challenging, yes, but sacred nonetheless. I learned a *lot* from it. It was part of *my* journey down the river called life. I believe it came to help me get braver so I could continue to conquer fear at higher and higher levels.

You have a sacred journey too. You are in your boat on your own adventure. Part of the story that I make up is that we each come to this planet on purpose with a piece of the truth to contribute and lessons to learn while we are here. Each of us, including you. There has never been a person here just like you before nor will there ever be a person just like you again. Only *you* came to this planet at this point in time with these parents, in this country, with your body, with your gender, with your skin color, with your brain, with your interests, with your talents, with your parents and siblings. *You* are unique in all that has ever been and all that will ever be. It's time to claim that you and your adventure are meant to be. You are valuable. You are here on the planet on purpose. Claim your space.

Now I truly believe this adventure is better if you are awake. Floating down the river of life asleep means you miss your life. The week before I got my cancer diagnosis, I was in Seattle, where I saw a piece of artwork that said, "Some people don't know that there are angels that come to wake you up so you don't miss your life." I bought it immediately. Little did I know the cancer angel would come the very next week to wake me up to an even higher amount of love, peace, and joy.

So, think about this: you are the only one in your boat. How do you want to live your one precious life? In Chernobyl or Glacier National Park? I think each of us gets to choose. Do you want to get out of fear—or not? Be run by your wounded child self or your emotionally mature adult self? That is, do you want to spend all of your life in fear or move beyond that? It's up to you.

Yet here's the truth of the matter: you cannot get to love without walking through fear—and that's scary. Many, many, many people would rather stay angry and fearful, depressed and anxious, or even addicted and miserable than step through the door of courage that says, "I will do whatever it takes to get from where I am to where I want to be." Don't let that be you.

I had a talk with a friend back home not too long ago. Both of her parents were alcoholics, and after my friend's divorce, she turned to the bottle for comfort. After listening to all she was saying—including "I don't want to live"—it became clear to me that she had to get sober. She had indeed been kidnapped by alcohol. She also had just moved into a new house, and coincidently (or perhaps Divinely), her next-door neighbor was a recovering alcoholic and went to AA meetings regularly. I said that was great. All she had to do was ask to go along to one.

She couldn't. She wouldn't. Now how crazy is that? Here is a person who is truly, absolutely miserable—so much so that she had been thinking of taking her own life—who says, "Yes, I want to be happy," who isn't willing/able to take a step in that direction by asking her neighbor if she could go to a meeting with her. That step just terrified her.

I told her she had to get braver and more willing than that, more courageous than that in order to get to Lifetime Two and the good stuff. She had to get willing enough to say, "I am terrified of doing this, but I will pick up the phone and make that phone call anyway. I can do it. It won't kill me—and alcohol will."

Research shows us that if we are willing to feel fear for approximately two minutes, we can do just about anything. Feel the fear but do it anyway. Time it. In 120 seconds, the phone call will be over. Remember, "Life begins at the end of your comfort zone." So, feel the fear but do it anyway: begin your real life.

One of my clients said it to me this way, "So if I feel uncomfortable, I'm on the right path, right?" to which I enthusiastically exclaimed, "Right!" Remember, walking through your fear is the only way to diffuse its power over you.

I'm thinking of the woman in Las Vegas who came to a concert to listen to some of her favorite bands, and suddenly there were gunshots from a window in a nearby hotel. People were running, people were screaming, people were getting hit, people were falling from fear and injury. She found a safe place to hide but could see people out there on the concert field who weren't running and weren't safe. So she risked it, trip after trip, to pull others to safety. She told reporters afterward, "I was afraid, but I couldn't just watch people being shot at on the concert field without doing something."

Do you remember those moments in your life? "I was afraid, but ..." moments. It's okay to be afraid. It's normal. Just remember to add the *comma, but*—and do it anyway. I was afraid, but I still did it.

Lifetime One: I was too afraid to do anything. I stood idly by.

Lifetime Two: I was afraid, but ... but I did it anyway.

The Power of Me

I want to emphasize that getting to Lifetime Two is a personal decision. It is your decision and only your decision. It has nothing to do with your spouse, your parents, your friends, or your children. That is, it doesn't matter what your partner does, if he/she decides on Lifetime One or Lifetime Two. It doesn't matter what your parents choose, fear or love. Or anybody else in your life. It only matters what *you* want because it is *your* life. In other words, if your spouse decides to remain asleep, you can still choose to wake up. It's like getting sober. If both you and your partner are alcoholics, your partner doesn't need to choose sobriety for you to get sober. He or she can continue drinking. Only *you* have to choose sobriety for you to actually get sober. It's like running a marathon. It doesn't really matter if your partner, parents, and children are running the marathon or not. The only way *you* can run a marathon is for you to decide to run, train, and then get out there and put one foot in front of the other.

One of my clients said to me, "But I'm too scared to get rid of my fear!" This made me smile. We somehow believe that if we cling to our fear, we will be safe, but in reality, the opposite is true. If we cling to our fear, it will only keep us from being fully alive. Being too afraid to risk, we risk so much more: love, fulfillment, passion, creativity, and joy.

You are so worth doing what it takes to get rid of your fear. Walk toward your fear, feel the fear, but do it anyway.

CHAPTER 7

Conscious Choice

If you want to move from being asleep to awake, you can consciously choose to do so.

The operative words in that sentence are *consciously choose*, for there are other ways to get from Lifetime One to Lifetime Two. Trauma is one of those ways: the death of a child, cancer, a divorce, getting fired from a job, going to jail, having your house burn down, a severe car accident, having a heart attack, and so on. Anything that brings us deep, dark nights of the soul can shift us from Lifetime One to Lifetime Two. That is, anything that brings us to the depths of despair can wake us up and move us from our sleepwalking life into another dimension where we experience feeling fully awake.

But in this chapter, I'm talking about actively deciding or choosing to move from Lifetime One to Lifetime Two. Making the shift without having to have a trauma to get there. Remember, in the story I make up, we are all being pulled to wake up. If we don't do the work on our own, the Universe will sometimes hit us with a sledgehammer for us to get it.

I think there's an easier way: conscious choice. We can consciously choose, on purpose, to wake up without having to be run over by a train to do so.

By definition, a conscious choice implies that we are conscious—not unconscious—when we make a decision. We are fully present and not distracted. It is a decision we make on purpose after considerable thought. We have looked at the options and picked the one that resonates the most with us. We are aware of the consequences that may come with this choice. This is in contrast to doing things without much thought or doing things in an impulsive, reactionary way. A conscious choice is a slower process. We slow the roll and *think*. Then decide.

I've been told the most frequent phrase in the Qur'an is "ponder this." That's what conscious choice involves: pondering, considering, brainstorming possible options (including the one that says, "I don't have to do this. I can if I choose to, but I don't have to"), telling yourself the truth about those options, and then, on purpose, picking the one that fits best for you. This way, you are responsible for your choice and invested in it. You are able to *own* it, instead of blaming someone or something else for why you are doing a certain behavior. With conscious choice, you are doing the behavior you are doing because you have determined that is what you want to do.

I believe it's possible for you to do this in regard to living in Lifetime One and moving on over to the good stuff in Lifetime Two. In other words, you can *choose* if you want to live in fear or not. A conscious, on-purpose decision: taking ownership of your life, understanding that your life belongs to you and that you have a choice as to how you want to live it. Also, most importantly, taking ownership of this truth: you are capable of making good choices.

But isn't this crazy? Even after people *know* about Point B / Lifetime Two, many stay stuck in the lower-energy vibrations. Why? Because, quite frankly, they don't know that living in the higher-energy vibrations is a choice for them. Maybe for others but not them. Many are too afraid to believe, *I could have the good stuff.*

I am here to tell you this choice is available for every single human being on the planet. Including you. That is, the higher vibrations are available for you to live in. We quite often have experienced the higher vibrations, but what we are looking for is an ability to live there.

We can have this high-energy experience—have a taste of it—in many ways. Here are some examples: holding a newborn, experiencing a brilliant piece of music, viewing a masterpiece of art, watching an inspiring movie, sitting on the beach, listening to a moving sermon, or swaying with a group of dynamic gospel singers. All can bring us to that feeling of love or the higher energy vibration. Sometimes when I listen to my son passionately play one of his new compositions on the piano, I am moved to tears. It feels sacred. I call it the feeling of "looking at the face of God" or "stealing fire from the sun." It's being surrounded by higher-energy vibration.

It's those moments when we feel very, very alive and that all is right with the world. We might even feel wrapped in love or light. It's where we feel rich—and it has nothing to do with money.

That is stepping into Lifetime Two for a moment. Now, living in Lifetime Two, a person gets to feel that way almost all of the time. In fact, the more a person shifts away from fear, the more they are able to live in Lifetime Two. Jesus, Gandhi, Mother Teresa, Nelson Mandela, Muhammad, Buddha, Thich Nhat Hanh, the Dali Lama—these are examples of people who were/are able to live in Lifetime Two and stay at that high-energy vibration almost always. They are/were able to greet the world and everyone in it with welcoming, loving arms.

I believe we can too. But we have to keep our eyes on the prize. We have to be clear of what we are after: getting rid of our fear by becoming an emotional adult and taking charge of our life. Remember, what we are after will just feel like a theory at first. It is only by *doing* the actual emotional work, actually walking down the dark, scary, and uncharted path, that you will experience Lifetime Two in reality.

Let's use a simple number line to visualize this:

Fear ——————————————Love
1-3   4-6   7-10
low energy vibration//medium energy vibration//high energy vibration

or we can say it this way:
fear / the dark and scary, uncharted path / love

or this way:
the yucky stuff / transition / the good stuff

or:
Lifetime One / transition / Lifetime Two

or, I believe it can even be said this way:
experiencing hell on earth / transition / experiencing heaven on earth

Let's say my belief that heaven and hell are on earth sounds too far out for you. Or maybe even makes you angry. Let's use it, then, as an illustration of how one can shift out of fear/anger into love.

First, take a deep breath and calm yourself down. Slow the roll. Tell yourself the truth: it's only a belief. *My* belief. You can think it's the most ridiculous thing you've ever heard. You don't have to believe it *at all*. Remember, if my belief is different from your belief, and you feel afraid or angry or outraged, that's Lifetime One behavior. That's your scared child self showing up. I want you to get to Lifetime Two where you can hold onto your beliefs and it doesn't push your buttons when someone else has different ones. Remember the goal: to live in the higher-energy vibration of love. So, once you realize that my believing something different from you doesn't threaten you at all and doesn't diminish you at all, then you may be able to see that I am just a person, just like you are just a person, both of us trying to figure out the world the best we can. Then the goal would be for you to be able to open your heart and love me—even though I have different beliefs than yours. I am talking about the love that means my heart is open to you, I accept you as you are, I honor you as you are, and I will do you no harm.

I had a friend from a very conservative religious group who told me one day that her pastor said she needed to ask me if I believed babies were born good. When I said yes, she then said, "Well, there you have it." I asked bewilderedly, "Have what?" to which she replied, "Well, you are wrong. Babies are born in sin and must be washed in the blood of Jesus in order to be good. Well, it's been real!" And she got up to leave, telling me she could no longer be my friend.

Really?

I was stunned and said, "Wait a minute! I can still be *your* friend even though you have different beliefs than I do. Can you still be my friend even though I have different beliefs than you?" She said no, she could not be, but that she would pray for me. She got up and left.

Clearly, this is a case of fear blocking love. We cannot heal the world this way. We have to outgrow our fear of people being different from us and learn to love them in spite of the differences.

And that's a challenge but definitely the goal. Again, this can only be done by making conscious choices.

The Number Line

Fear —————————————Love
1-3   4-6   7-10
low energy vibration//medium energy vibration//high energy vibration

Take a look at the number line again. As you can see, moving from Lifetime One to Lifetime Two is a process. That is, for most people, there is not an event that moves them from one to the other. It does happen, like when people have reported flat-lining or dying and then coming back to life, but not very often. So we can't count on that.

For the majority of us, the shift is slower than just an event: it can take years to grow up. We have to keep facing fear and walking through it over and over again.

An important step in shifting from the yuck to the good stuff is giving yourself permission to have a learning curve. Be gentle with yourself. Anything worth doing is worth doing badly at first. That is, we didn't learn to walk without falling down many, many times. Be gentle with yourself in the whole process, and, as Dorie says in the Disney movie *Finding Nemo*, we must "Just keep swimming, just keep swimming!" Bit by bit, inch by inch, sometimes with an occasional leap, you will get there.

Every time you slow the roll, identify your options, try them on, and choose the one that fits best for you, it counts. Every time you choose responding over reacting, it counts. Every time you choose love over fear, it counts. You are making progress toward a happier, more fulfilling life with each and every conscious choice you make.

CHAPTER 8

A Twist to the Story

But here's the twist: I really do believe babies are born good. In the story I make up to make sense of the world, I believe they are born at the higher-energy vibration of love. You were. I was. We all were.

So, humor me and let's start with the premise that babies are born at the high-energy level of love.

> fear — transition — love
> low — medium — high
> Babies are born here.

They are love, love, love. That's one of the reasons we keep having babies—they are so wonderful! If you pick up a sleeping newborn and put it on your chest, you can feel the calm wash over you.

You were born this way. You came to this world as love, love, love. Pure, beautiful, wonderful, high-energy love vibration—just like every other baby. It's the concept of the Christ-child. Every baby is born the Christ-child: beautiful, perfect, and pure love. Hmmm …

Now hang with me. Remember this is my story that I make up to explain what we are supposed to be doing while we're here on earth.

My story says you were born perfect—amazing, magnificent, full of love. But the world doesn't support this high level of love yet. Most people still live in fear.

So, this baby is born—you, me, everyone—innocent and emotionally open, fully alive.

One of my favorite Christmas carols is "Bring a Torch, Jeanette Isabella," which begins with these words:

Bring a torch, Jeannette Isabella! Bring a torch and quickly run!
Christ is born, good folk of the village!
Ah, ah, beautiful is the mother,
Ah, ah, beautiful is her son.

And I tell you the same thing happened when you were born. People said, "Hurry up! The baby's here! Let's go see the baby! It's so exciting!"

I don't know who came when you were born—your dad, an aunt, the nurses, a midwife, grandparents, siblings, friends, the neighbors—but I know they came. *You* were celebrated when you came into this world with your tiny fingers and toes. You came to earth as that high-energy vibration of love just like every other child who comes.

Children are such teachers for us. In fact, there's a Japanese saying that goes like this: every baby is a little Buddha who comes to teach us how to grow up—and love. They understand love. They *are* love. When my eight-year-old son had the flu, his two-year-old brother ran to the bathroom and got a Band-Aid and put it on his older brother's tummy to "fix his boo-boo." They get it. Kids get it. They get that love is not a big deal; love is *the* deal.

But then what? Well, since that baby is born into an imperfect world with imperfect parents, teachers, relatives, coaches, and friends, it gets wounded. That is, the baby gets parented by imperfect parents—most of whom are still living in Lifetime One, wounded and ruled by fear. Then the baby goes to school and is taught by teachers, administrators, and coaches, most of whom are still living in Lifetime One, wounded and ruled by fear. And the baby is surrounded by other kids who are in the same predicament: being raised by people who are still living in Lifetime One, wounded and ruled by fear. Our world today, in other words, does not yet support that pure love vibration of children. It gets squashed.

Bob Hoffman, the founder of the Hoffman Institute, says it this way:

> We are raised in Negative Love. Negative Love tells us that we are not lovable.
>
> It is the intergenerational wound passed on to us by our parents, which was passed on to them by their parents, and so on. In other words, if our parents didn't feel lovable, how could they teach us that we were?

Again, that baby—who is each of us—experiences people who are hurtful, both physically and emotionally. We get yelled at, laughed at, sometimes hit, sometimes shunned. We get made fun of. We get left out. We get criticized. We get wounded. We get scared. We get abandoned. We get plunged, full force, into the Lifetime One experience on this planet. And we walk away with a lot of fear.

Our pure, beautiful self gets wounded, covered up with junk, and plunged into a lower-energy vibration. Eventually, by the time childhood is over, most everyone has shifted into the fear vibration.

fear—transition—love
low—medium—high
Eighteen-year-olds are here.

Why is it this way? I don't know. Lots of people have thrown out ideas over the years:

1. We are on the planet to learn lessons.
2. We are on the planet to entertain God / the gods.
3. We have chosen to come to earth to grow emotionally and spiritually.
4. There is no meaning—it's just random.

To me, it doesn't matter why it is this way. It just seems like it IS this way. For everyone. Whenever I notice something that is true for everyone, that it is universal all over the world, I personally label that as Divine. And good. I call it Divine order and reconcile it by saying we don't have to understand the why; we need only to understand the IS. This IS the way it is.

Embracing the IS is a Buddhist concept. Other examples of the IS of life follow:

1. Lifetimes are different lengths. I've noticed this. Not everyone gets ninety-two years on the planet. It's this way all over the world. Why is it this way? I don't know. I make up a story to explain it to myself: it's to help wake us up to the limits of our time on the planet so we don't waste it. Is that true? Who knows?

2. Siblings argue. Again, all over the world. Why? I don't know. My story about it: it is this way because it lets each child practice being top dog and underdog—life skills they will need as adults. Again, is it true? My point is we have no idea why siblings all over the planet argue with one another—but they do.

3. No one lives forever. Our bodies only last so long. and then they quit working. Sort of like appliances. Some refrigerators last ten years, others twenty, and rarely thirty. None last 250. It's the same with our bodies. We can dislike this about our bodies, we can fight it, we can eat healthily and exercise like maniacs, but it won't stop the IS that no one lives forever.

So, why is it that babies are born that loving, sweet, innocence that they bring to the planet and then get flipped into Lifetime One and get wounded? I don't know. What I make up is: it's all good. It seems we have to go through the wounding to be able to transform it into what is needed to heal the world. According to E. E. Cummings, it takes courage to grow and become who we really are. Without the challenges in life, we can't fully form. It seems to be necessary for the evolution and transformation of the world. Again, that's the story I make up to make sense of the world. You can have a different story. This is mine: We are born, we are plunged into Lifetime One, and for many people, that's the end of the story. They live their entire life in Lifetime One. They stay an emotional child and a victim. They don't even know a Second Lifetime exists. In fact, most people do this.

But what about the others? The ones who can see the ball players and have stepped into another dimension that exists on earth? Here's their path: they are born, are plunged into Lifetime One, go through some sort of an awakening process by choice or by chance, transform what happened to them as a child, and end up fully empowered in Lifetime Two—stunned at how much better life is there than in Lifetime One.

I want that for you.

Here's an example from my own life. My father was an alcoholic and a sociopath. When I was a child, he abused me every day I spent with him. When he died, my brother called me, wondering what on earth we could write in his obituary. He asked, "Should we just say he was a mean son of a bitch who hurt every single person he ever encountered?" I chuckled and said I didn't think we could put that in the newspaper. So, he worked on it and came up with this wonderful, insightful, right on the point kind of obituary. He said, "For those of us who knew him well, we were forced to bring out a better self than we would have had we not known him."

Yes. Maybe that's why each one of us is flung into Lifetime One: to bring forth a better self into Lifetime Two so we can actually be helpful in healing the world. For me, my wounding from my father made me more compassionate. It made me have deeper levels of understanding of others' pain. It helped me feel deeply. It helped me become the therapist I am today: dedicated to helping to heal my clients and helping to heal the world. I label what happened to me in Lifetime One as good, not the atrocities themselves but the transformation because of the atrocities. Certainly it didn't feel good when I was going through it, but ultimately, in the bigger picture, I have been able to transform it and use it for the good of the world. That is, my Lifetime One experiences were essential for me to become the person I am today.

Remember, though, that almost everyone you meet is still asleep and being ruled by their wounded child and fear. They need extra love, extra kindness.

When my firstborn child was about a week old, I crept up to his crib and just stared at this miracle baby who had come to live with us for the next eighteen years. He was so tiny! So vulnerable! So perfect! I immediately said a prayer, "Please, God, don't let any harm come to him!" But then, after a moment of reflection, I amended my prayer: "Well, what I mean is, please let just enough harm, struggle, and pain come to him that he will need to become a loving, caring, compassionate person—but not one ounce more!"

Maybe this is what Jesus meant when he said we must become as children to enter the kingdom of God—which is right here, surrounding us, by the way. We must return to that pure state of love that we used to be when we were very young children. Jesus said in Matthew 5:14, "You are the light of the world." I believe that. You are the light of the world. Each one of us is a light. Our light gets covered up in Lifetime One—by wounding and fear. The good news is the light is still there. Underneath all the gunk, your light is still shining.

All you have to do, then, is get rid of the gunk to get to your light. This is the work that lies between lifetime one and lifetime two.

LT1   →   transition   →   LT2
(meet the dragon)

The Transition

Let's talk about that transition area a minute—the space between the two lifetimes. Just like I believe every single person's purpose on the planet is the same—to evolve from fear to love and to become part of the healing force in the world—so I believe every single person's obstacle standing in the space between Lifetime One and Lifetime Two is the same. That obstacle is the fear dragon that is hissing, "You're not good enough! You're not good enough!" It's chanting at you, "You're not worthy!" So, we each get our very own personal fear dragon to conquer. Further, there is *no way* to get to Lifetime Two without confronting it. Not just once but every time it shows up. We have to practice, "I was afraid, but ... but I did it anyway."

The fear dragon, however you look at it, keeps us stuck. Because of the emotional wounding we encountered in Lifetime One, our brains *believe* what it's saying to be true—and it's not. *It's a lie.* You have to rise up bigger than your dragon with the *truth* that you are indeed good enough and worthy, as well as wonderful, powerful, capable, and amazing. To do this, you have to walk *toward* your personal fear dragon and tell it to leave you alone—that you don't believe that *lie* anymore.

But a puzzle. We get this wounded child in Lifetime One. That wounded child is scared. That wounded child doesn't believe they are capable of confronting *any* dragon—let alone the one called Fear. And that wounded child is running your life! I say it this way: would you let a five-year-old drive your car? No? Then why are you letting a five-year-old drive your life?

Your life will get *so* much better when your wounded five-year-old is not driving your life. You are allowed to spend the rest of your life happy. Just happy. You can do it. Your fear dragon is not stronger than your courage.

Don't worry. The Universe will help you. As PT Barnum said, "Fortune always favors the brave." It's true: the Universe listens to brave.

Be brave.

CHAPTER 9

We Are One

Albert Einstein said we are all interconnected. We are all one. Hmmm …

My stepfather was an air traffic controller for Cleveland Hopkins Airport. He worked for the FAA, the Federal Aviation Association. At the age of fifty-nine, he retired and moved to California. Fourteen years after his retirement, his old job was privatized. All of his friends who had not retired, whom he had worked with for a lifetime, lost their jobs. While this was happening, my dad started to have nightmares about the FAA. He suffered and felt angst when he awoke in the mornings. As synchronicity would have it, he had a luncheon planned to meet with his old coworkers while he was back in Ohio on vacation. When the conversation turned to what had happened with their old jobs, my dad admitted he was even having nightmares about it. The others exclaimed, "So am I!" "So am I!" "So am I!" Turns out they were all having the *same* nightmare.

And what about recycling bins? For most of my life, there were no such things as recycling bins. Then there was a moment when all of my family, spread out across the United States, had recycling bins within two weeks of each other. Ohio. Florida. Texas. California. Pennsylvania. We all got recycling bins at, essentially, the same time.

I am sure you have stories of interconnectedness too. For instance, have you ever been thinking of someone and two seconds

50

later the phone rings and it's them? Or have you ever been trying to figure out a problem and the stranger you are sitting next to on the plane says something that gives you the clarity you need? I think Einstein was right: we are all interconnected. We are all one.

After being a psychotherapist for the last thirty-two years, all I know for sure is that we are not so different from one another. In fact, I believe we are all seeking the same thing at our core: Lifetime Two. I think we all want love and the good stuff.

We all want to be happy and fully alive. We all want to live the life we were born to live. We all want to feel successful and important. We all want to contribute and feel like what we are doing matters. We all want to be seen and taken seriously. We all want to feel included / part of. We all want to feel safe and not afraid. We all want financial stability. We all want to feel empowered and joyful. We all want things to flow easily—in our relationships, in our work, in our life. We all want the good stuff for our children—and for them to be safe and happy. We all want to feel loved, be loved, and be able to give love. Right?

Christians, Muslims, Jews, Hindus, Buddhists, pagans, agnostics, atheists, everyone. We all want the same thing.

President John F. Kennedy said it this way: "For in the final analysis, our most basic common link, is that we all inhabit this small planet, we all breathe the same air, we all cherish our children's futures, and we are all mortal."

We are not so different after all.

When I speak at a church or a synagogue, I say it this way: "How many people came here today in a Ford? Honda? Chevy? Toyota? How many came in a car? A van? A truck? And yet we all got here. To the same place. Driving different vehicles."

Religions are just different vehicles. Bigger than religion and no matter what vehicle you use, the goal is to live in the high-energy vibration of love. To act toward others out of love, even those—especially those—who have different beliefs, religions, nationalities, dress, skin color, gender, and sexual orientation than we do.

What would Jesus do?

What would Muhammed do?

What would Buddha do?

What would Krishna do?

What would Gandhi do?

What would Nelson Mandela do?

What would Martin Luther King Jr. do?

What would Mother Teresa do?

What would the Dali Lama do?

What would Thich Nhat Hanh do?

Love.

I'm telling you, love is *the* deal. It is *the* purpose of this life. It is *the* purpose of your life: to get to love.

We catch glimpses of love in Lifetime One—and then chase after it in a million different ways.

It's a little like cocaine addiction. Any addict will tell you that the first time they took cocaine was absolutely indescribably amazing—and that they have spent the rest of their lives trying to have that experience again and never succeeding. They can never get back to what it felt like the first time. In fact, they have to take more and more to get less and less results.

That's how Lifetime One is: we are desperately seeking some way to get to the good stuff. We spend years desperately trying to prove we are good enough. We think we can get to the good stuff by having a lot of money or buying a lot of things or having sex with a lot of partners, or, or, or—a million different attempts that feel good for a moment but eventually feel empty, hollow.

That's because the good stuff is in Lifetime Two. And the only way to get there is to emotionally grow up. We are one, we are the same: we all want the good stuff.

CHAPTER 10

The Bigger Picture: The Fifty-First Percentile

There seems to be a bigger picture going on as well.

Everywhere I look, there are people who are starving for love and ruled by fear. I think our purpose on the planet, our mission, is to fix that. First individually and then collectively. And it seems to be happening.

That is, I believe our purpose on the planet is to individually move from Lifetime One to Lifetime Two so that we can then become part of the healing force in the world and that, collectively, it is our purpose to heal the world. To bring about peace on earth. To bring about justice and equality. To move the whole world from Lifetime One to Lifetime Two. To move the whole world from being asleep to being awake. Another way of saying this is to move ourselves from living in fear to living in love, and, when enough of us do this, then peace can come to the world. That's the endgame.

To recap, really there are just two steps involved in our purpose on the planet:

1. Individually move from fear to love.
2. Transform what happened to us in Lifetime One and use this to add to the loving, healing force in the world. That is,

once we heal ourselves, we can get out of being part of the problem and become part of the solution.

In the movie *I AM*, there is an amazing research study on red deer. The researchers were trying to understand how this large herd of deer decided when to go to a watering hole. Furthermore, there were three watering holes close by, so how did they decide which one to go to? Because when they did decide, in an instant, they all took off together to go get water at a particular hole. Now this was a big decision, because if they went too early or to the wrong watering hole, they wouldn't get enough nutrients from grazing. Conversely, if they went too late, some of the deer would become weak and dehydrated, making them susceptible to predators.

The researchers hung cameras high up in the trees of the grazing grounds of these deer. They hypothesized that the strong alpha adult male stags would be the ones who made these decisions and led the herd. But that's not what happened. What happened is the deer voted. That's right. One deer would turn its head toward a certain watering hole. Then others would turn their heads toward a watering hole. The moment the fifty-first percentile deer turned its head toward a particular watering hole, the whole herd immediately took off and ran to that watering hole to drink. That is, there was a tipping point in their interactions. They were all voting. When the 51 percent vote came in, they all cooperated and moved in that direction. This happened day after day after day.

I believe this is possible with human beings as well. There will come a 51 percent moment when there will be more people living in the love vibration than the fear vibration. The tipping point. All you have to do is move yourself from asleep to awake and then use your transformed self to become part of the collective healing energy of the whole world.

How we become part of this larger healing force in the world, then, is by taking what happened to us as a child and transforming it into something useful.

Let me give you an example of how this works. This is the story of a client I worked with. Actually, it is a compilation of clients' names and stories to protect their anonymity.

A man, I will call Thomas, came into my office one day, severely depressed. In fact, his brother had to drive him there and wait for him in the waiting room because he just couldn't drive. He was unemployed and living on disability. He was almost nonverbal, almost catatonic. His third wife had just divorced him for being a slug and failing over and over again to follow through on things he had promised.

And yet he was gorgeous. Handsome, handsome, handsome at 6'4" with a professional football quarterback's build—broad shoulders, thin waist. He was forty-five but could easily have passed for thirty-five. He was bright. He was born and raised in America. He was college educated. It looked as though he had been handed some pretty powerful cards before he came to the planet. He could have gotten the cards poverty, black, female, and Eastern Congo where rape is a strategy to keep women down. Instead, he got bright, handsome, white, male, America. Why was he so severely depressed and nonfunctional? What happened?

We started looking at step one: what wounding did he get as a child? We looked at his family of origin. Both his parents were alcoholic. His mother was the pathetic victim type who would stay in bed all day and ask the kids to bring her beer. When they begged her to get up because she was supposed to take care of them, she would sob and moan, "Oh, I know, I'm a terrible mother! I'm so sorry. I am just a bad person," and so on. This only made things worse for the five children. Now, on top of not getting their needs met, they felt guilty for even asking!

My client's father, on the other hand, was a mean alcoholic. He yelled at the kids, hit them, and punished them harshly, all while giving them a good daily dose of criticism and putdowns, and beatings if they cried.

I had my client write down all the hurts, all the hurtful memories.

Then I had him read the list out loud to me. In doing this exercise, I didn't have to prompt him to cry; he sobbed.

After a grieving period of several weeks, I wanted to help my client begin the shift from Lifetime One into Lifetime Two, which requires emotionally growing up. That is, he needed to shift from having a reactionary life based on his childhood into a proactive one where he was able to claim his life and start creating what he wanted.

I asked him what his talent was. "I don't have one." I assured him that every single person who comes to this planet gets a talent or two and that we needed to figure out his. Again, he insisted he didn't have any.

But we all have at least one. Including you. So I asked Thomas if he could do *any* job in the world, what would it be? He said he might go on the senior bowling circuit, as his average was 265. Or he might become a golf pro because he liked that most of all. I asked him if he was good at golf. Yes. Was he good at teaching golf? Yes. Did he like teaching golf? Oh, yes, it was quite a charge helping people correct their golf swings.

Then I said, "I just have to ask you—ever play football?"

Well, as a matter of fact, he did. He was the star quarterback in high school. Then he quietly said, "But my dad never came to my games." Moments passed in silence until he looked up at me with tears in his eyes and said, "Except once."

He then told me of the last game of the season when his dad showed up—drunk, yelling criticisms from the stands. Thomas was so nervous that he fumbled the ball, threw three interceptions, was sacked, and lost the game, in his words, "single-handedly." Then when he got home, he got beaten by his enraged father for embarrassing him.

He cried. I cried with him.

The next day, he quit school and joined the army. I asked if he had played ball in the army. Why, yes, he had. I asked him if he had played any other sports in high school. He had run track—and was the fastest kid in his school. I said, "Well, I think I figured out your talent."

Still clueless that he had a talent, he said, "What?"

"Athleticism."

After many denials of that as a talent and many reassurances that it was, he told me the story of an old army buddy of his who had just come to town that past weekend. He assured me that *this* guy had an athletic talent. They played a round of golf together when, to my client's surprise, his buddy asked him for help on his swing.

Me: Were you able to help him?

Him: Oh, yeah. It took a while, but we got it. And then he said the funniest thing to me.

Me: What's that?

Him: He said, "I could never have done what you just did, Tom. You were so patient and encouraging, and you never put me down but just stuck with me. Thanks." Isn't that weird?

Me: No! That's not weird—that's your talent! And that's using your talent in a loving way. You were so kind!

Him: Well, yeah—I know what it feels like to be criticized!

Bingo. That's the goal: to use your talent and to use your history to become a healing force in the world. Transform what happened to you as a child and *use it* along with your talent to send love out into the universe.

Him: You think I should be a golf pro?

Me: Yes! And love every single person who comes to you to learn.

Him: Well, that's not important work. I want to make a difference in the world. It's not as important as what you do, for instance.

Me: It's the *same thing* that I do! I am using *my* talent to love every person I work with, and you need to use *your* talent to love every person you work with. And together we heal the world.

Happy ending: Thomas is an amazing golf pro.

I am thinking of the lyrics to John Lennon's "Imagine":

I hope someday you'll join us
And the world can live as one.

Hmmmm ...

Often I ponder: are we going to be able to shift the whole world into Lifetime Two in my lifetime? Immediately, *No way!* pops into my head. But then I think, *But maybe in my children's lifetime ... or my grandchildren's ...*

Power vs. Force by Dr. David Hawkins was published in 1985. At that time, Dr. Hawkins estimated only 15 percent of the population lived beyond the negative energy vibrations or what I call Lifetime One. How far have we come since then? I don't know. Are we at 20 percent awake? Thirty-seven percent? Forty-one percent? I wish I knew. All I know for sure is there seems to be a major shift going on: more and more people are waking up. The shifting appears to be accelerating too.

I think the acceleration began in Hiroshima on August 6, 1945, when the destruction wrought by the atomic bomb happened. Where people's skin *evaporated*. When suddenly we had a weapon that was strong enough to kill every human being on the planet. With this, we started our path toward awakening. With this began the awakening to the belief that we have to learn how to cooperate with one another—with people different from ourselves—with everyone—to survive as a species.

The Japanese, by the way, dissolved their military after August 9, 1945, when a second bomb was dropped on Nagasaki killing between sixty and eighty thousand people in a flash of destruction. They said they would not participate in the violence of war anymore. They put down their arms and said, "Enough. There must be a better way."

Then the Beatles came along, civil rights, and the women's movement. All about waking up and believing there is a better way.

And then the biggest agent of change in the world happened—even more impactful than the atom bomb—the internet. We are *all* getting connected. This connection is helping us to realize we are not so different from one another.

Abu Ghraib

For example, there used to be a train of thought that went like this: we are the good guys, they are the bad guys. In fact, it is okay for us to kill people because we are the good guys, they are the bad guys. And then Abu Ghraib happened. Iraqi soldiers were being held captive by American soldiers. We are the good guys trying to keep the world safe, right? And then: click. One phone took one picture. That picture, of an American soldier holding the end of a dog leash with the dog collar around the neck of a naked Iraqi prisoner on the other end, went around the world in a matter of seconds. Suddenly, things changed in the old theory that we are the good guys and they are the bad guys. Suddenly, we looked like the bad guys too, torturing and humiliating prisoners for fun and entertainment.

Are we the bad guys? Are they the good guys? Are we both the bad guys? Are we both the good guys? This is what the internet is doing—making us question, making us think.

Personally, I think we are the good/bad guys, and they are the good/bad guys too. That is, we are beginning to realize that people are people are people. We are *all* afraid, *all* flawed, *all* the walking wounded, seeking the same thing: peace. Happiness.

Everywhere on the planet, people are seeking the same thing, including in Iran.

Ronny Edry

I am thinking of Ronny Edry, the graphic artist in Israel who started a healing movement by posting on Facebook a poster of himself holding his young daughter who was holding an Israeli flag. Under their picture in bold letters he wrote: Iranians, We Will Never Bomb Your Country, We Love You. To his surprise, he got hundreds of hits on the posting. He even got comments from Iranians! Soon his wife said, "I want a poster." He made one of her holding their young son with the same message: Iranians, We Will Never Bomb Your Country, We Love You. More hits. More comments. More connections with Iranians.

Edry then asked all his friends and neighbors to send him pictures and told them that he would make them a poster to post on their Facebook accounts. He got back more and more loving comments from Iranians. Then he posted this:

message from Iran
ISRAELIS
In the end we are all
Brothers and Sisters

Miraculously, the day after that, Iranians started responding with their own posters saying things like: "My Israeli friends, I don't hate you, I don't want war." For days, weeks, months, this conversation between Israelis and Iranians exploded into a massive love story. A revolution of peace.

It's Happening

I believe we are on the journey toward that fifty-first percentile vote. The tipping point of the revolution of peace. All you have to do to join the world's awakening movement is heal yourself: move from your wounded child running your life to your authentic, empowered adult self being in charge.

Sometimes I think about December 21, 2012. This is the day the Mayan calendar ran out. I heard so much fear from people about this date: surely it will be the end of the world! The movie *2012* was terrifying. Again, the message was: the world is coming to an end. Be afraid!

What if it was a beginning? What if December 21, 2012, was the beginning of the tipping point—when just over 50 percent of the world's population was awake? Where more people than not moved from Lifetime One to Lifetime Two: where we no longer are afraid.

The world-renowned scientist and aerodynamic physicist Daniel Bloxsom Jr. studied the original writings of the Mayans and explained the end date of their calendar thusly: there will be a newness of the people. December 21, 2012, marks the beginning of a transformation of the people.

Hmmm …

So, how do we get there? By doing the Work.

The Work is divided into three sections: the Prework, the Main Work, and the Postwork. The Prework is just laying the foundation, learning how to make it safe for you to do the actual work. Then comes the Main Work—the hard part. Finally the Postwork is filled with thoughts to support you in your empowered adult self.

Let's start with the Prework: beginning to heal the self.

PART II

The Work

The Prework

CHAPTER 11

Garbage in, Garbage Out

There is no doubt in my mind that the media impacts how much fear we feel. So the first thing that might be helpful in getting rid of your fear is getting rid of listening to and/or watching the news. I stopped listening to the news on a regular basis in 1979. It was depressing and seemed to pretty much say the same thing every day: another murder, another robbery, atrocities somewhere in the world, and a local or national scandal thrown in. I stopped listening because I came to believe that feeding my mind a daily dosage of this was not good for me. I also felt that if there was any big news, I would surely hear about it somehow.

In fact, in 1981, it was several days after President Reagan was shot before I learned about this. I remember saying, "Oh, the president was shot?" Two things happened then. First, the woman I asked stared at me in disbelief for a couple of seconds before answering, and second, I realized that it didn't even matter that I didn't know that news any earlier. It hadn't impacted my life in any way the past few days; there was nothing I would have been able to do about it; and I had missed the drama and trauma of it all, which was fine by me.

Nowadays, I still listen to the news very intermittently. I turn it on occasionally and am shocked to find how fear based the reporting has become and how hateful many of the talk show hosts are.

So, my thought for you is this: turn off the news and stop listening to the radio talk shows. They are packed with creating fear at every corner: fear of robbers, rapists, and murderers, fear of the economy tanking and losing all your money, fear of the government spying on us, fear of the terrorists, fear of war and weapons of mass destruction / chemical weapons, fear of the government running out of money, fear of guns, fear of no guns, fear of poor education, fear of the pandemic never ending, fear of losing all of our human rights, fear of pollution, fear of corporations, fear of mass shootings, fear of the president, fear of obesity, fear of powerful women, fear of Ebola, fear of the right wing, fear of the left wing. Fear, fear, fear. Fear being pumped out to us day after day after day. There is a motto in journalism that goes like this: if it bleeds, it leads. This is not good for us.

Radio talk shows are particularly adept at pumping out fear. For example, Rush Limbaugh calls his work entertainment, but to me, it is more like waging a war against people. He, like many others, impresses me as a person filling the airwaves with hatred, controversy, and fear. This is a negative impact, not even neutral. Listening to someone rage is not good for us.

So, if our purpose on the planet is to outgrow our fear, how are we going to do that by listening, sometimes for hours a day, to what the media is pumping out? It is a negative brainwashing that I believe is not good for the world. To get to our adult selves, we cannot buy into all of that. Instead, we must reframe things that allow us to get to this: there are solutions; there are answers; humans are amazing, and if we work together, we can heal the world.

Because most of the world is wonderful and amazing. Most people are wonderful and amazing. You are wonderful and amazing. Yet the media seems committed to focusing on and exaggerating the negatives. We are taught to believe that there is a murderer on every corner and a rapist right next door as well. The average child nowadays, according to the A.C. Nielsen Co., through watching television alone—not even factoring in video games and movies—sees two hundred thousand violent acts by the time they are eighteen years old. Two hundred thousand! My mind explodes with that statistic. What? This is not good for us or our children or, for that matter, the world.

In an article in the medical journal *JAMA*, dated June 10, 1992, Dr. Brandon S. Centerwall talks about the connection between television and violence. He writes:

> In 1973, a small Canadian town (called "Notel" by the investigators) acquired television for the first time. The acquisition of television at such a late date was due to problems with signal reception rather than any hostility toward television. Joy et al[2] investigated the impact of television on this virgin community, using as control groups two similar communities that already had television. In a double-blind research design, a cohort of 45 first- and second-grade students were observed prospectively over a period of 2 years for rates of objectively measured noxious physical aggression (e.g., hitting, shoving, and biting). Rates of physical aggression did not change significantly among children in the two control communities. Two years after the introduction of television, however, rates of physical aggression among children in Notel had increased by 160%.

Who are we kidding when we tell ourselves the media is not increasing violence—and thus fear—in the world? So, turn off the television as much as possible, and turn off the talk show radio stations as well.

Luckily, there are many, many, many people who are fighting against all this negativity. I love the TED talks that can be seen on YouTube. Each one focuses on ordinary people doing remarkable things. Then there's the new show *Some Good News*, the *Intelligent Optimist* magazine, *Yes!* magazine, upworthy.com, and the Daily Om—all committed to writing and reporting about things that are going right in the world. They believe, as I do, that what we put out into the Universe matters. What we send out multiples. It comes back a hundredfold.

You can fight the negativity too. Do all you can to put energy toward the solutions and not be part of the complaining, whining, scared, angry, victim thinking that so much of the media encourages.

Really honestly look at what you are putting into your brain. Is it fear? Anger? What are you exposing yourself to? I believe it matters.

Self-Talk

Garbage in, garbage out also refers to what you tell yourself. I have a new client who spends most of her session telling me things like "I'm worthless. I'm a loser. Who would want to be with me? I don't have any friends. I've never had a good relationship, and I never will. I'm stupid. I am *not* capable. I have had an awful life, and I will continue to have an awful life. There's no hope for me. Don't you understand? I have *no* value."

Really, what good is going to come out of that? If you said those things to a child, they would not be able to blossom and grow. They would get depressed and withdrawn. Well, guess what? If you say those things to yourself, that's what happens too.

I believe the number one difference between people who are happy and people who are not happy is self-talk. It is vital to get on your side when you are speaking to yourself. Think about it: whose side are you on anyway? Are you for you or against you? Against you is, of course, your wounded child driving your life: victim, I have no power, there's nothing I can do to change my life. To get your authentic adult self to begin driving your life, you must hush those messages from your wounded child. Just confront that self-criticism by saying to yourself, "I don't believe that anymore!"

Remember, you are the only person with you twenty-four hours a day, day after day after day. You have a huge influence on yourself. If you are constantly feeding yourself garbage, it matters. What you say to yourself will either keep you in victim mode—or help you get out of it. It truly is 100 percent up to you what you say to yourself. Nobody can change your internal dialogue but you. What you say to yourself *matters*. Be careful what you are feeding your brain. Remember the words of Henry Ford:

> Whether you think you can, or you think you can't—you're right.

Furthermore, think about this: *not* changing your internal dialogue to support yourself is really just a way of avoiding growing up. It's a way of avoiding doing the hard work of taking responsibility for your life. If you continue to say, "I don't know what to do. I'm not worthy. I'm too afraid," you are really just clinging tightly to "I'm a scared little child. Someone else, please take care of me so I don't have to." It's an avoidance technique that keeps you stuck in Lifetime One. This would be okay but for one thing: the good stuff is in Lifetime Two. Empowerment, peace, love, joy, happiness. We can't get those things by staying an emotional child.

So, the question becomes, do you want to grow up?

CHAPTER 12

Resistances

It is amazing and amusing to me the extent to which we will go to avoid growing up. We resist taking charge of our lives.

For example, when I was in my twenties, no matter what I tried, I couldn't seem to get birthday cards sent on time. Not to my family, not to my friends. I mean, there were all these steps involved: remember the birthday far enough in advance to actually send a card, go to the store and get a card, fill out the card, find the address for the envelope, get a stamp, and then remember to put it into the mailbox several days earlier than the actual date.

I couldn't do it. I might get everything done only to find I was out of stamps. Or I couldn't find the right address. Or I had a whole stack of cards that needed to be sent out, and I just didn't want to bother with them. I didn't want to. (I can almost see my four-year-old self stamping her foot and saying, "No! I don't want to!")

When the day had passed when the card could actually arrive on time, I would then beat myself up for being late *again*. Every time, I couldn't believe that I had messed it up *again*. Finally, I just admitted to myself that, for whatever reason, I didn't have what it took to get birthday cards sent on time. I resigned myself to only buying belated cards for about two years—and felt like a loser.

Then one day it occurred to me: adults mail birthday cards on time. I looked down at my full-grown body and thought, *Hey! I'm an adult!* And then, *When are you going to start acting like one?*

You see, my inability to send birthday cards on time was a resistance to growing up. I didn't want to grow up! I didn't want all that responsibility. I wanted someone else to take care of me—someone besides me.

Yet, when I realized adults send cards on time, I realized I could too. I set about figuring out how adults do that. This was before we had computers, so I got myself a birthday book where I wrote down the dates of everyone's birthday. I got myself an address book where I organized all my addresses. Then I went to the store and bought ten birthday cards. At the beginning of each month, I got the cards ready for the birthdays that month. If I was running short on cards, I'd go buy ten more.

Amazingly, by deciding to take responsibility to get my cards off on time, I was able to do just that. The responsibility was not a burden; it was a freedom. I no longer went through the long, agonizing cycle of trying, failing, and feeling like a loser. I, instead, every month felt good about staying connected to all the people in my life who are important to me. I, for the first time in my life, felt like a grown-up.

When I told this story to some of my friends at church, they asked, "What else do adults do? Do they pay their bills on time? Because I never pay my bills on time, and I'm thirty-four years old! I always pay late fees!"

I said, "Yes, adults pay their bills on time."

Another friend chimed in, "Do they unpack their suitcases when they get home from a trip?" Yes, they do. Pretty soon, there was a group of twenty-somethings and thirty-somethings joining in, asking rhetorical questions one after the other:

Do adults do their laundry before they are completely out of clothes?

Do they mow the grass before it's knee high?

Do adults manage their money so they don't get bank charges and bounce checks?

Do you suppose they change their air filters for their air-conditioners before they turn black?

Do they file their taxes on time?

Do they file their taxes at all?

How about doing their dishes right after dinner and not waiting until the next morning or three days later?

We were all laughing by then—at ourselves. Each of us seemed to have our own way of resisting growing up and taking responsibility.

It is something we have to be ever vigilant of, however. It's easy to give ourselves grace when our behavior is young and we are young. But this behavior of resisting taking responsibility is exactly what this book is about: growing up emotionally by taking responsibility at every opportunity, at every age, in every situation. It will, I promise, lead you to freedom and empowerment.

Yet know this: resistances are sneaky.

Our subconscious is powerful and wants to be in charge. In December a few years ago, I decided to go to seminary. My last child would be graduating high school the following May, so I decided I needed to get started on the next chapter of my life. So I did all the work to start a graduate degree in divinity: deciding on a school, filling out the application, getting all of my school transcripts, getting the letters of recommendations, writing the essays, and doing the interviews. When my acceptance letter arrived, I was quite pleased.

I decided to take one course that started in January and went through May. Having not been in graduate school for decades, when I downloaded the course syllabus, I was a bit stunned at the course load. There were four textbooks to buy, read, and evaluate, plus two major research projects, each requiring a fifteen-page paper and a thirty-minute PowerPoint presentation, not to mention the class time of three hours a week. I said to my good friend, "I don't want to do any of this!"

She said, "Well, go and see if it energizes you."

So I went. And it did. Energize me. I loved it. I loved the students in the class, I loved the professor, I loved the topic, I loved the research and even doing the projects, but as the semester dragged on, I realized *all* of my spare time was being used up with this one class.

Including *all* of my writing time. This book was about half-written—and that's how it remained for the whole semester. I didn't write one word on this manuscript. It took me until about March to realize what I was really doing in seminary was avoiding finishing my book. Since writing does not come easily to me, I was trying to get out of doing it.

Ah. I then had to call on my adult self. I had to first tell myself the truth about it, allow myself to laugh at tricking myself, and then get more honest: acknowledging in order to finish my book, I had to knock off the distractions. When the course finished, my professor asked me if I'd be interested in taking a new course he was designing for the fall. Politely, I declined. The dean of the school asked me what course I would be taking in the summer. Again, I declined and started to write again.

Adults are willing to call themselves on their own stuff, their own resistances. So, look for yours. Then be gentle with yourself when you find them.

More Resistances

The most common type of resistance I have seen in my thirty-two years of practice, however, is remaining oblivious—just denying there is a problem. Pretending. Keeping the eyes tightly shut despite the evidence. Having magical thinking the same as a six-year-old who believes in Santa Claus. Magical thinking says, "If I don't look at the problem, there is no problem."

We all do this to one extent or another, but it's important to become aware of it as much as possible. Listen to what your partner is telling you. Listen to what your friends are telling you. If you are hearing the same message over and over again, there is a growth lesson for you. You are probably running full force into a resistance of facing a fear.

For example, I have a client who gained seventy-five pounds during her pregnancy—and kept fifty of it after the baby was born. Prior to that, she had always been slim and fit. Then she had another baby and packed on thirty-five more pounds. Her husband begged her to get back in shape, her friends were shocked to see her, and even her doctor was telling her she needed to exercise and lose weight. Yet she remained oblivious to the problem and continued to eat. Of course, there was a lot more going on psychologically than just her weight, but her willingness to take responsibility to deal with the issues and then deal with her weight was zero. She held fast to "There is no problem." Unfortunately, she woke up to the problem only after her husband began an emotional affair with someone at his office. In a session following this revelation, she said, "I looked in the mirror, and it was the first time I could actually see myself. I was aghast."

Fortunately, at that point, she did the emotional work to get out of her wounded child (her mother insisted she enter beauty contests as a child, rewarded her for not eating, and gave her the message that she was only lovable if she was thin). Consequently, when her husband started urging her to exercise and lose weight, she subconsciously rebelled and let her wounded child be in charge of her behavior. Fortunately, she was able to call on her empowered adult self and take charge of what she was eating, her relationship, and her life. She was able to do so only after she decided what *she* wanted—not doing it because her mother or husband wanted it. She decided that if she was honest with herself, *she* wanted to lose the extra weight she had gained during her pregnancies. And so she did.

Avoidance

Another resistance to growing up shows up in the form of avoidance. Often when a child is raised in a house with a raging parent or a power parent or violence in the home, they learn to hide and to avoid conflict. This pattern continues into adulthood, of course. I had one client with a raging father who told me, "I just run away when my wife gets upset. I can't get hurt that way. I guess I'm a conflict avoider." Yes, and a growing up avoider too. To get to Lifetime Two, he will have to move his five-year-old self out of the driver's seat and make room for his adult self to show up.

It's the difference between short-term gratification and long-term gratification. The child self opts for short-term gratification to avoid an uncomfortable, painful, or fearful feeling. The irony is this only makes their world smaller and more self-restrained. They are, in a way, being blackmailed by their feelings. The problem is never really handled and thus festers, becoming bigger and scarier the next time around.

The adult self, on the other hand, is striving for the long-term gratification where they don't have to run away from an uncomfortable situation. Instead, they are able to feel their feelings, then handle whatever challenge life hands them, and thus expand the size of their world and their comfort zone.

Another resistance to growing up is just not making decisions. Here people stand quietly and let everyone else make the decisions. They defer by saying, "Oh, it doesn't matter to me." Then they feel like a victim because the decision isn't what they would have decided. In other words, not making a decision is an avoidance technique, a way of avoiding growing up emotionally. People who don't make decisions feel they are protecting themselves in case something goes wrong or someone gets upset with the decision. Then they can claim, "Well, it's not my fault! I didn't decide this!" However, not making a decision is making a decision: a decision to stay in the powerless child self.

What about you? Can you identify when you are resisting growing up and taking responsibility for all the behaviors that you are doing or not doing? What are you avoiding? Are you ready to face your resistances and decide to do what it takes to make room for your adult self to show up?

CHAPTER 13

Deciding

You have to decide: Are you in? With both feet? Because, basically, to grow up and become your empowered authentic adult self will require both feet in.

Doing so means taking over the reins of your life. Taking over your life. You have to stop letting your five-year-old wounded self run you. That is, you have to become aware of the subconscious programming you got as a child, confront it, and define yourself separate from it. By confronting it, I mean really looking it in the eye—clearly seeing the baggage you carry around, taking ownership of it, and saying to it, "Hey! You! You don't own me anymore!"

Be aware, emotionally growing up is the most difficult thing you will ever do. Not even childbirth without drugs, which I can attest to is no easy task, comes close to the courage needed to grow up. But the reward of having your authentic power and adult self is worth it. It's going to feel like your five-year-old self has to confront your raging father. It's going to feel scary. Just know: you can do it.

Now, a lot of people will tell me rather testily, "I am a grown up! I have had to be responsible since I was eight years old (or twelve or fifteen or whenever)!" I know these people: the ones who had to take on an adult role as a child are more than ever stuck in their child self, in Lifetime One. They just can't see it since they have been "responsible" all of their lives. I am talking about being responsible to self. The programming these people got was this: take on responsibility that isn't even yours, have no boundaries, don't have needs, don't take care of yourself, disconnect from your authentic feelings, be serious because life is serious, be a workaholic. Or, because we tend to react to childhood wounding by either joining it or rebelling against it, someone who had to be overly responsible at age eight might just chuck the whole responsibility part and become homeless and sleep on the beach. Either way, the wounded child is still running the show.

I will admit to you, though, that sometimes it is hard to believe that a person is not an emotional grown-up when so many areas of his or her life are working. I worked with a client who was, literally, a multimillionaire, a Nobel Prize winner, and extremely successful in many areas of his life. Yet he was in his fourth failing marriage, unable to voice his opinions to his fourth domineering wife. Further, he had no boundaries in this relationship and, quite frankly, acted like a little boy. He was stunned when he said to me at age sixty-four, "I've been a child my whole life!"

I had another client, a heart surgeon, who said to me, "My wife won't even let me roll down the window in the car!" Confused, I asked him to explain, to which he said, "When she's driving, she puts on the child window lock! Even when I ask her to take it off, she won't. So, I have to sit there with the window up!"

This is a heart surgeon. He's very accomplished. Yet when it came to his marriage, he felt like a victim, acted like a victim, believed he was, indeed, a victim with no power in the situation. Almost always, our emotional child shows up in our primary relationship.

So, here is a test to see if you are an emotional grown-up: How is your marriage/primary relationship going? Are you reactionary? Is your partner? Are you fully present? Do you avoid dealing with things with your partner? Do you feel safe? Do you trust your partner? Does your partner trust you? Do you have trustworthy behavior? Do you have a secret life? Do you avoid conflict with your partner? Does your partner remind you of one of your parents in any way? Do you even have a primary relationship? If you don't have a primary romantic relationship, what is your primary relationship? Is it with work? With alcohol? With another addiction? This is important because it is usually in our primary relationship that our unresolved stuff shows up the most. Therefore, this relationship can serve as a barometer to let you know where you are in the shift from Lifetime One to Lifetime Two. It will tell you where you are as far as being ruled by fear/anger/pride versus being ruled by love/peace/joy.

So, the important question is: do you want to do the work? Because you've got to have a want to. Without that, you are going nowhere. Are you serious about changing your life? Even though it will mean doing things that are scary, that are outside of your comfort zone? Remember: if you are uncomfortable, you are on the right track.

Are you in for that? Or do you want to just give it lip service?

Are you in for facing your fears and feeling uncomfortable for a while?

This decision is a lot like deciding to lose weight. If you are two hundred pounds overweight and the most you have lost "trying" to lose weight in the last year is five pounds, you are not serious about changing. You can say you are, but your body reveals the truth.

It's the same in a relationship. When I work with a couple whose marriage is in deep trouble, one that is on life support barely, barely surviving, a code blue, I tell them they must immediately start spending fifteen hours a week alone with each other doing positive things. I tell them they have to wipe their schedules clean this week and pump in oxygen to their relationship by getting reconnected. I tell them to go away together for the weekend by themselves. I tell them not to talk about the relationship during these fifteen hours but to do fun things together: go bike riding, go bowling, go to the boat show that's in town, go test drive the new BMW at the dealer, watch a comedy together, go for a walk every day together, cook dinner together, or whatever other thing that might be fun to do. When they come back the next week and tell me they were only able to spend one hour together all week because of their schedules or their kids' schedules, I know they are either unaware of how urgent things are or they are not serious about healing their marriage. They want their marriage healed—but without having to do the work.

Part of getting to our adult self is telling ourselves the truth: if you want your life to be different, you have to do what it takes to get there. Part of what it takes is rigorous self-honesty. I have found the more honest you can get with yourself, the faster you can get to Lifetime Two. Honesty is the key. So, do you want to?

That is, if you believe you have the opportunity to live two lifetimes on the planet, one in Chernobyl and one in Glacier National Park, then all I'm talking about here is deciding that you want to move. Often what stops people from moving is the fear of not feeling worthy, good enough, or deserving, or the fear of not being capable of crossing over to the good stuff. Remember, the universal wound is "I'm not good enough." Everybody gets it—some more, some less. And the shocking part is it's not even true!

Actually, you have what it takes. You are worthy, good enough, and deserving. You are capable of crossing over to the good stuff. You don't have to know *how* to get there; you just have to know you are ready to move.

My experience is that by the time people come to my office for psychotherapy, they usually come with a "want to" change. They are sick and tired of being sick and tired. They are depressed or full of anxiety. They are in dreadful relationships. They are unhappy, tearful, lonely, lost, or all of the above.

Pain does motivate us to change. So, as I said before, if you are in some kind of emotional pain, that is a good thing. Of course it doesn't feel like it's a good thing, but in psychological terms, it's a good thing. It can give you the *want to* you need to make the shift from Lifetime One to Lifetime Two. It can give you the push to move out of fear into doing the things you are afraid of, thus being able to own your life.

Want It Like Air

So, how strong is your desire to get rid of your fear, anger, depression? There's an old story about Socrates. He is sitting on the beach meditating when a young lad approaches him and says, "Teach me. I want to learn." Socrates glances toward him and then returns to his meditation. The boy feels irritated and says, "Teach me! I want to learn!" Socrates slowly looks him over and then returns to his meditation. At this point, the boy practically screams in frustration, "Why won't you teach me? I want to learn!" Socrates rises and suddenly picks up the boy. He walks into the water with him. Deeper and deeper. Finally, Socrates pushes his head under the water. The boy kicks and thrashes and tries to free himself. Finally Socrates releases him.

The boy gasps frantically for air and asks incredulously, "Why did you do that?" to which Socrates replies, "When you want to learn as much as you wanted air, then I will teach you."

Want it like air. A warning though: sometimes the fears we have to face feel like life and death. They are *not* actually life or death or anywhere near life or death, but they sometimes, in the beginning, feel that way.

Why? Because our emotional wounds happened when we were so little, and it *was* a matter of life and death. As a small child, if we didn't have adults to take care of us, we really would die.

It's a matter, then, of realizing you are not that small child anymore. I know this sounds ridiculous, but sometimes just looking down at your body or looking in the mirror at the size you are, and then saying to yourself, "I'm a grown-up," can help you come back to the present moment and realize you are not a child anymore—and that it is not a matter of life and death. It's a matter of getting over being afraid of being afraid. Again, you do this by realizing you are not a small child anymore and you are not facing life or death—fear is only a feeling, and it will pass. Tell yourself the truth.

Think about it like making a phone call you don't want to make:

the scariest phone call, the hardest phone call, the most awkward one, the one you've put off and put off and put off. If you can take a deep breath and make the phone call, within just a couple of minutes, you are either into the conversation, have left a message, or no one answered and the whole call is over. In any case, the terror has subsided.

Are you brave enough to do that? Are you brave enough to feel afraid for two minutes / 120 seconds? Because here's the good news: it doesn't get any harder than that. Really. Two minutes of confronting your fear at each little step will get you to Lifetime Two.

A common definition of insanity is doing the same things over and over again, expecting different results.

You've done that long enough. Sometimes I have a couple who comes into my office declaring they want to fix their marriage—that they really want things to change. Yet, within five minutes, they are back into their old arguing patterns. I just stop them and tell them they can do that at home for free, and that here, in my office, we are going to be doing some new behaviors.

In other words, doing things the way you have always done them will not move you from where you are to where you want to be. Honest. So, you've got to decide to do things differently.

Habits

Habits sure are hard to break though. That's why I am emphasizing the power of deciding. Consciously, on purpose setting a goal for yourself: *I am committed to myself and changing my life so that I am happy and not driven by fear.*

I have an amazing alcoholic client who got sober twenty years ago and became about 250 pounds overweight. She was addressing lots of issues in her life but not her weight. Finally I brought it up. I said, "You are an amazing person. You got sober twenty years ago. That's amazing. You quit smoking fifteen years ago—one of the hardest addictions in the world to break. That's amazing. You went to medical school in your thirties! That's amazing. So, I'm just curious. What keeps you from addressing your weight? Because, really, you have what it takes to lose your weight."

She said, "This I know is true: I can do anything I decide to do. I just haven't decided."

Yeah, you've got to decide *I am serious about change this time.*

Since that conversation with my client about a year ago, she decided. She has lost more than one hundred pounds and is going strong. She intends to lose the whole 250 pounds, and I have no doubt she will. That's the power of deciding.

Encouragement

Next, I want to remind you to be your best friend along the way, deciding to give yourself credit and encouragement. This is the opposite of garbage in, garbage out. Start putting positives in, and you will get positives out. Remember, you are the only one in your boat. You are the only one in your boat floating down your river on your journey called life. Say nice things to yourself!

It doesn't matter if someone else doesn't approve. It only matters that you approve. Rosita Perez, in her book *The Music Is You*, says it this way: "We dilute our dreams when we share them with others prematurely." Doing your emotional work is nothing you have to tell people about—just do it.

Remember, too, the work I'm talking about is *individual* work. Individual evolving. It is the mission *each one of us* must do, and nobody can do it for us. It is your fear dragon to confront—and you can do it. Stay on your own side and use your energy to face the hard stuff and to encourage yourself. If you have a child or children, think of what lengths you are willing to go to in order to encourage them. Go that far with yourself. Be on your side.

Telling Yourself the Truth

Part of the hard stuff in making the shift from Lifetime One to Lifetime Two is learning how to tell yourself a deeper truth. For example, if you are spending your time and energy trying to get someone else to "get it," and you are reactionary and acting out of your wounded child, you need to get more honest with yourself. It doesn't matter if they don't get it and are stuck in their emotional child behavior. It matters that *you* get it and get out of *your* emotional child behavior. In fact, you can stop trying to get them to get it. That is just a waste of your energy and actually an avoidance technique that allows you to avoid walking through your own fear and emotionally growing up. It's a way to use up all your time and energy—working to get them to get it—when, really, you are the one who has to get it. There is work to be done. Stop wasting your time, energy, and life trying to get someone else to get it. Instead, use your time, energy, and life doing things that are terrifying to you and are keeping you stuck.

For example, this letting go of trying to get someone else to get it can be your first behavioral change stepping toward your emotional adult. Every time you want to explain or defend yourself, take a big breath of *air*—and close your mouth. Every time you want to tell the other person what they should or should not be doing, take a big breath of *air*—and close your mouth. Then walk away. They may try to hook you into battling about it. You can take the bait—or not. Which would get you closest to living the life you want to live?

Focus on what needs to change in your life. Focus on what you are avoiding and do *that*. Tell yourself the truth about it.

For example, I have a colleague who wants to write a book. She has been talking about writing this book for many years. One day she called me and asked me to talk to her about whether or not she should use an agent, and also how I found my publisher. I asked her if her manuscript was done, and guess what? She hadn't even started it! I told her to call me back when her first draft was in hand and *then* we would talk about the next steps because, the truth is, having an agent and a publisher is not the same as having a book. She will have to make a deep-level decision to actually write the book before she will have a book.

In my own life, when I was in my twenties, I bought a piano because I had always wanted to play the piano. It was beautiful, and I sat and tinkered at it occasionally. I took a few lessons, but the reality is I very rarely practiced. The end result? I never learned how to play it, of course. At that point in my life, I was still acting from my child self: I had magical thinking that said, *If I buy a piano, I will be able to play the piano.* Now my adult self can look back with a chuckle and say, "Not so." My adult self knows, since I have no innate musical talent, if I want to play the piano, I have to learn how to play it by taking lessons for years and practicing hours and hours and then more hours.

Zero Days

To help you change from where you are—being run by fear—to where you want to be—being run by your powerful adult self—it is a good idea not only to be on your side but to adopt the concept of no more zero days. What's a zero day? It's a day where you do absolutely nothing toward achieving the goals you want to achieve. A zero day is where avoidance and procrastination reign. They are in charge, and you are not.

For example, when I was working on my first book, I set aside every morning to write. That was a good plan, but it was amazing how many things were shouting for my attention just then: My garage was saying, "Hey! Look at how messy I am! Come and clean me out!" My gardens were saying, "Wow, have you seen how many weeds are out here? Get on it!" My kids were saying, "You really aren't feeding us healthy enough. You really should take some raw food cooking lessons or something!" All of these inner voices were working hard at keeping me from facing my fear: *Can I really write a book? Do I have anything worthwhile to say? Does everyone already know everything I'm writing about? Is this a waste of time? Will it be good enough?* All of these inner voices were doing their best to get me off track. No more zero days kept me on. No more zero days allowed me to face my fear bit by bit in manageable pieces. One page at a time, sometimes only one sentence in a day, the book got written.

It will be the same for you too. Every day you have to show up and stare down that fear dragon of *Am I good enough?*

Listen to me—if you were right here with me, I'd stare in your eyes and say this—let me make it clear to you: you *are* good enough. You are capable enough to face down your own fear dragon. If I can do it, you can do it. I promise you.

Let's review a minute. So far, the prework involves three things:

1. Turning off the garbage in—both with the media and with self-talk.
2. Identifying your resistances and calling yourself on them. Be brutally honest with yourself about this.
3. *Deciding* to do the work to get you moved out of Chernobyl and into Glacier National Park.

The next part of the prework is learning to think differently.

CHAPTER 14

Thinking Differently

Rich people think differently about money than poor people do. Thin people think differently about food than fat people do. Athletic people think differently about exercise than couch potatoes do. To shift from Lifetime One to Lifetime Two, you are going to have to learn to think differently about yourself and about life. Happy, joyful, empowered people think differently about themselves and about life than unhappy, depressed, victim, stuck-in-the-muck people. Below are some steps to get your process started.

There isn't a particular order to these steps. They all need to be done simultaneously in a way. Of course, I can only write about them one at a time, and you can only read about them one at a time, so it's important to just keep glopping them together.

The last chapter was about deciding to do what it takes to get to empowerment. Now, **Step One** in thinking differently is: you must make that same decision—to get to empowerment—over and over again. That is, throughout the whole process of moving from child to adult, you must keep deciding. Just like with losing weight where every day you must decide to eat well, so it is with getting rid of your fear: every day you must decide you are worth it.

Step Two: Don't be willing to settle for anything less than fully alive where you feel abundantly happy, empowered, and free. Don't be willing to settle for anything less than feeling fully congruent: that you are living the life you were born to live, and it feels wonderful. Don't be willing to settle for anything less than being powered by love and not ruled by fear. You are worth it. You are allowed to have an amazingly fulfilling life: don't settle.

Again, you must decide this over and over again. It's very much like an alcoholic getting sober: they must decide on sobriety at a deep level and, at the same time, not be willing to settle for anything less. It's a determination, I suppose. A determination to commit to walking down the dark and scary path by stepping one step further in, then one more step. It's a decision over and over again not to run back when you feel scared.

Step Three: Be brave.

So:

Step One: Decide. Over and over again.

Step Two: Don't settle. Over and over again.

Step Three: Be brave. Take a deep breath as you step *into* the scariness. Do not run away from it—step *toward* it. Over and over again. This is like the story of a man being chased by a ferocious dog. Instead of running away from the dog, he turned and ran full force toward the dog yelling at the top of his lungs. This startled the dog so much that he started running away from the man! Use your courage to go toward what scares you. Walk right up to the problem and look it in the eye.

Remember, this is a process and not an event. Give yourself grace through it. I have found that people in general are much harder on themselves than anyone else is. They absolutely would think nothing of someone misstepping as they were trying something new but are unwilling to give themselves that same latitude. So:

Step Four is this: Say only nice things to yourself.

That's right. If you criticize yourself and beat yourself up in this process, it will take longer. Remember, whose side are you on anyway? The sooner you get on your side, the sooner you will walk out of your fear and start living the empowered life you were born to live. This step is about stopping the negatives you say to yourself so there is room for the positives.

Voice Dialogue

When we were growing up, our brains got programmed. For example, if you were told you talked too much when you were little—even *one* time at the right time—you have that message running in your head at some level. It's surely morphed a bit over the years as well, sounding now something like this, "Shut up—no one wants to hear you go on and on. You talk too much." That is, we tend to take the original message we were given, give it a little negative twist, and believe it as *truth*.

I, therefore, often ask my clients to do a voice dialogue. That is, I ask them to say out loud two distinct voices that run through their heads: the critical voice and the affirming voice. Almost without exception, the critical voice is stronger and more powerful than the affirming voice. All too often, I have clients tell me, "I don't really have an affirming voice. I can't think of *anything* positive that I say to myself."

Try this exercise yourself. What are the negative messages you tell yourself (i.e., "I'm too fat, old, stupid, ugly. You can't do that! Shut up! You're such a jerk, a wimp, a wuss, too needy, pathetic, nobody likes you. You're not good enough.")? It helps if you write them down. Then, what positive messages do you tell yourself ("I'm wonderful, amazing, intelligent, capable, Divinely made, beautiful.")? Again, write these down. Which voice did you find was in charge? If you are like most people, the critical voice wins hands down.

Not to state the obvious, but this critical, putdown voice is not good for you. Think about it. How can you feed your brain all that negativity about yourself and get out of fear? How do you change your internal dialogue? It's time for a computer overhaul. You'll need to delete the negative messages. When a critical, negative internal voice shows up, tell it, "I don't believe that anymore! That's a lie!" and replace those messages, of course, with encouraging and supportive messages that are gentle with yourself. You need to start giving yourself a break even when you mess up, which you will. You absolutely will stumble and fall and make lots of mistakes along the way. To these, you must learn to say, "And that's okay."

Step Five: Use the tagline "And that's okay" when you get it wrong or less than the level you had wished for. If I had the power to give everyone on the planet a gift, it would be these three words. We get wisdom by not having wisdom, so it really is okay when we get it wrong, miscalculate, mess up. It helps us learn and grow.

Step Six: Stop apologizing for yourself.

When I was younger I was in a ballet Master Class where the instructor was a professional Broadway actor. He came into our class of about twenty-five dancers and had us all stand in a circle and introduce ourselves. When we finished, the instructor pointed out that every one of us—without exception—had introduced ourselves with an apology. We did these apologies, of course, because we felt insecure and wanted people to like us. Some had said their name and then looked down at the floor or up at the ceiling, avoiding eye contact. Some had said their name almost in a whisper, while others introduced themselves with a hand wave or a big, gushy smile. Still others giggled. One rolled her eyes. But none of us—*not one*—was able to stand straight and tall, and with energy that commanded attention and respect, introduce ourselves.

So, in moving from our child self who doesn't feel good enough into our adult self who does, we must learn to stop apologizing for ourselves. By this I mean stop saying things like, "Oh, I'm sorry—I'm so stupid!" "Sorry, I can never get it right." "I'm really sorry—I'm such a screw up." "OMG, I'm so slow at this! I should have it by now!" "I'm so bad at this!" Become aware of how many times you apologize for yourself throughout the day. It might surprise you.

I'm not saying that you shouldn't apologize when you hurt

someone's feelings. I'm not saying don't take ownership of mistakes you make. I am saying stop apologizing for being *you*.

You have done nothing wrong by being an imperfect human. In fact, you, like the rest of us, are doing it quite well.

Step Seven: Let go of the lie that you are supposed to be perfect.

All human beings are imperfect. In fact, the only way to be a perfect human being is to be imperfect. It is an amusing circular argument actually: that if we were somehow able to become perfect, we would have failed at being a human being, since all human beings are imperfect. Anyway …

When we come to terms with our humanness, life gets a lot better. More importantly, I believe if we do not accept and embrace our humanness, we can't get to Lifetime Two. It's that important.

The reality is we are not having a god experience on this planet, we are having a human experience. We came to the planet, got a body, and are bumbling along trying to make the best of the craziness we found here. Or as C. S. Lewis said, "You don't have a soul. You are a soul. You have a body." So we are having a human experience on earth where no one is perfect and no one is supposed to be.

The trick is having the courage to love ourselves as imperfect. That's a very important sentence: we must come to love ourselves as imperfect. We must come to love ourselves when we make mistakes, have judgment errors, even when we really, really, really screw up. We must come to love ourselves as beings that have shadows— dark parts of ourselves that we are not proud of. We must come to love ourselves even when we are not nice, we think bad thoughts about others, we react like a two-year-old. We must come to love ourselves when our courage fails, when we are not thoughtful, when we are lazy—and crazy. We must come to love ourselves when our impulsive self shows up and bumbles up the whole situation. We must come to love ourselves.

You have to come to understand that your imperfection—my

imperfection—everyone else on the planet's imperfection is just perfect. It is the way the world is meant to be—and *is*.

Consider you are just right exactly the way you are. I had a twenty-four-year-old client who abruptly stopped me one time when we were talking. After a pause, she said, "Are you trying to tell me that I am all right already?" I almost shouted, "Yes!" She was blown away. And cried. She was overwhelmed with the idea that she just might be lovable after all, and that her incessant preoccupation with trying to be perfect was unnecessary.

You are all right already. You see, you don't need to be perfect to be lovable. You are already lovable. Sometimes your behavior isn't lovable, but *you* are lovable. Always. You are more than your behavior at any point in time. You are more than your worst decisions. Nothing—no behavior, no decision—makes you unlovable.

You are all right already. You are lovable. Period. Nothing can take that away.

Yes, there are still areas where you can grow, but even as you learn more, you will remain imperfect. Just remember, we do better when we know better—but we can never get it all right. Life is messy—for everyone. We're not supposed to get it all right.

One of my friends is a world-renowned scientist who is quite brilliant. I remember her telling one of my sons when he was younger, "I have worked with some of the very brightest people on the planet. I have worked with people who are so smart you can't even believe it. But I have never—never—met someone who knows everything. So keep learning. You can always learn something new because *every* person you meet in your entire life will know something you don't know. But *you* will know something they don't know!"

That's how it feels to come to terms with our humanness. It's coming to know that you will never—never—meet someone on this planet who is perfect. Including you.

In fact, it seems to me that we each get an Achilles' heel when we come here: something that will drive us crazy trying to figure it out, and just when we think we have it figured out, it pops back up. That is, we all get a "stuck" to figure out while we are here on earth. A puzzle. For example, Oprah got her weight issue, Robin Williams got genius—and depression, Michael Jackson struggled with his looks, Beethoven went deaf. Many people get an addiction issue, some people can never figure out money, dyslexics never learn to spell, some people go from one codependent relationship to the next. My point is it seems we each get something to keep us humble.

In fact, embracing the idea of being "ordinary" helps us let go of the drive for perfection. When we let go of the "I have to be 'better than' to be good enough," and claim, instead, "I am just like everyone else, bumbling along doing the best I can," we can relax into our authentic selves. Everyone has challenges, everyone has a nemesis or two, everyone—*everyone*—spends time feeling lost and alone sometimes. You, like every single other person on earth, are good at some things and not good at other things. There are no exceptions to this rule. None. In the play *Pippin'*, the lead character keeps trying to prove that he is special. He believes his specialness keeps him from having to follow the rules of the world. He sings a song where he cries out, "No! Don't you understand? I'm special!" It's only when he claims his ordinariness that he is healed and finds happiness. His ordinariness allows him to be part of and feel connected to the rest of the world.

Embracing our ordinariness helps us relax. This, in turn, helps us become the person we were born to be. It actually allows space for us to develop our talents—without the pressure of having to get it all right.

So, you can let go of trying to be perfect. It takes so much time and energy. Instead, begin today by giving yourself grace. Begin today when you mess up on something saying to yourself, "That's okay. You are still a good person. You are still a light in this world. You'll do better next time." Grace. Love. Tenderness—toward yourself.

I remember in my early twenties I had a job with a very critical manager. One time when she was dressing me down in her office, I said to her, "Yes, I didn't get that done, but I'm still a good person." She stopped dead in her tracks, looked up at me, and slowly said, "Yes, you are. That's a given." Needless to say, she was nicer to me from that point forward.

So, *claim* that you are a good person no matter what errors you have made. Own it.

It's time to lighten up on yourself. Stop saying the "I'm not good enough" lie to yourself, because, in reality, you are good enough to be an imperfect human being. We all are. Welcome to the planet and the human condition.

In other words, you can stop lying to yourself. The goal is not, and never has been, perfection. That was a goal you made up. Growing from emotional child to emotional adult requires deeper and deeper levels of self-honesty. The big lie that many, many people believe is this: I have to be perfect or I am a "less than." This is not true. Every human being is acceptable, is enough, is lovable—and is wildly imperfect. There are no less thans on earth. There are only those asleep, those awake, and all those on the path in between.

In the book *Wild*, author Cheryl Strayed chronicles her story of hiking the Pacific Crest Trail as a single woman. She starts her journey with a backpack she can't even lift. It is crammed packed with everything she might need. As she puts miles behind her, however, she slowly but surely lightens her load by leaving behind things for other hikers that she feels she no longer needs: her foldable saw, one half of her guidebook, her old hiking shoes, a T-shirt here and there, extra packets of food. That is, the more she grows into herself on the trail and sees herself as capable and competent, the less she needs to carry along.

That's how the lie that says, "I have to be perfect to be lovable," is. It's baggage. It's something you *must* leave behind in order to get to Lifetime Two. You must come to know deep in your being that you *are* loveable just the way you are.

Step Eight: Embrace your imperfect, befriend it, enjoy it.

It really is such an astounding relief to come to know that

you are lovable and good enough even though you are a flawed human being. You are enough even though you get things wrong— sometimes in little ways, sometimes in big ways. It's a freedom to know that you are not God, and you don't need to be. We must come to accept our experience here on planet Earth as one of imperfection, blunders, screwups, mistakes, and lessons. We only get wisdom by not having wisdom. That is, nobody becomes a wise old soul without having been a dumb young soul who learned from their mistakes along the way. It's so nice to understand, then, that making mistakes is part of how we learn. The mistakes are not something awful— they are something valuable.

I had a new mother who came to me for therapy to learn how to parent in such a way that she didn't make any mistakes. I thought she was joking. I laughed out loud. Seeing her confusion, I then had to tell her the truth: there is no way to parent without making mistakes because there is no life on this planet where there are no mistakes. You have to, instead, get comfortable with making mistakes—since you will be making lots of them.

We can, in fact, come to be entertained by our mistakes. Envision being able to laugh at yourself when you make a mistake, giving yourself grace as you say, "Well, *that* didn't work!" If you can come to see the humor in your humanness, life gets a lot easier.

Recently, I heard a young chap interviewing a 101-year-old man on the radio. The man had spent his lifetime as an expert on China. At one point, he said something like, "I thought it would take China one hundred years to move from communism to capitalism, and yet it seems like it happened overnight!" The interviewer came back with, "You mean you're surprised you were wrong?" To which the man with the wisdom of age started to laugh and said, "Are you kidding? I'm 101 years old! I'm used to being wrong!"

We have to get used to being wrong. We have to get used to making mistakes. We have to get comfortable with our screwups. Why? Because life is full of mistakes! You are allowed to make them too. Not only are you allowed, you are going to become really good at making mistakes because you will make so many of them. We all do. You are not a space alien; you are a human being bungling along trying to do the best you can. Just like the rest of us. Give yourself a break. Tell yourself the truth: imperfect is part of the human experience. And that's okay.

Not only is it okay, it can also be funny. For example, I think of my stepfather as a computer guru. One day he told me a computer "tip." He was amazed that most people did not realize that they could reset their computers simply by pushing F-11. I asked why anybody would do that, and he said, "Well, if you get a virus in your computer, it will usually get rid of it."

Oh! Wow! *What a valuable piece of information*, I thought.

So one day, before there was the Cloud, when my computer was running very slowly, I thought, *It must have a virus!* So, guess what? I pushed F-11. The screen said: "Are you sure you want to do this?" Yes! The next screen came up: "Are you sure you want to do this?" Yes! I kept pushing yes until the computer stopped asking me questions.

And then it stopped working. Well, it was still working, but my email wasn't. Do you know why? It's because F-11 takes your computer back to the first day you turned it on. It wipes out *all* the programs you have added, *all* your emails, *all* your photographs, and *all* your files.

My husband was aghast when he got home. I could hear him screaming in exasperation from the office, "Why did you do this? You're a smart person! Didn't it tell you it was going to wipe out files? Didn't it give you a warning screen and ask you if you really wanted to do this? Why did you do this? What were you thinking?!"

Oops. I had to laugh at myself. I am not technologically savvy, and I guess it shows … Somehow the computer "geeks" at the store were able to recover most of what I'd done, and the sun came up the next morning, and it really wasn't a major disaster after all. Now, fifteen years later, it's part of our family lore.

You see, our imperfections make great stories. A friend of mine who is a wedding photographer always tells her brides, "Things will go wrong on your wedding day. Someone will forget to pick up Aunt Martha at the airport, the audio won't work at the church, the ring bearer will drop the rings, or your brother will get lost and be late. Don't worry—these are your stories."

So, the sooner you let go of your goal to be perfect, the sooner you will get to happy. The sooner you can learn to laugh at your foibles, the sooner you'll get to happy as well.

If you hold onto "I have to be perfect to be lovable," it will take you longer.

Step Nine: You are going to have to fall in love with yourself.

For most of my clients, at least, their response to that is usually something like, "Yeah, that's going to be hard," because most people don't love themselves. As stated earlier, it's intertwined with that "I have to be perfect" lie.

This coming to love ourselves, or falling in love with ourselves, requires intention. We have to—on purpose—put in time to look at and acknowledge to ourselves what we are doing right.

Just like, when working with little children, we must become "good finders," so we must do the same with ourselves. Write three things down today that you did *well*. I don't care if it's just brushing your teeth; that counts.

To me, falling in love with yourself means claiming, really claiming, how amazing you are. Marianne Williamson says, "We ask ourselves, 'Who am I to be brilliant, gorgeous, talented, fabulous?' Actually, who are you not to be?" This is how you were Divinely made. Not claiming with gratitude the amazingness of *you* is a bit like snubbing your nose at God / the Universe. Remember, *nobody* has ever been exactly like you, and *nobody* ever will be. You are a one of a kind—beautiful, amazing, capable, and unique in all of the world.

I tell my clients who have attention deficit disorder (ADD) or Asperger's or dyslexia or bipolar or some other of what society calls a handicap that actually their brains are *exactly* the way they are supposed to be. One of my sons skipped second grade. When he was in fourth grade, he said to me, "Really, Mom, I'm just supposed to be in the third grade." I said back to him, "No, honey. If you were supposed to be in the third grade—that's where you'd be. You are *supposed* to be in the fourth grade—because that is, in fact, where you are."

I believe your path is leading you to your spiritual mission on the planet. You have exactly what you need to do your mission—your brain is *exactly* the way it needs to be. There are many ways to be on this planet; there is not just one way and that is the right way. No. That's what the child self says. The adult self knows there are many right ways. There are many right answers. Think of it like going to the movie with a friend. As you leave the theatre, your friend says, "That was a great movie!" and you say back, "Really? I hated it!" *Both* of these things are true. Both are right answers. You are amazing just the way you are.

Think of the great cards you were dealt. If you are reading this, you were dealt an education. That's big. You were also dealt a male or a female card or maybe a trans card. Embrace it. You were dealt a marvelous brain. I know this because you are capable of doing introspection. You were dealt the country you were born into. That's big too. You were dealt electricity and clean water. Most likely, you were dealt vision and hearing too. You were dealt this point in history, with the invention of the internet and the interconnectedness we now experience through it. I believe this is the most exciting time to be alive. Be grateful for it. Be grateful that you got invited to the party—coming to planet Earth at this point in time. All of these are *great* cards. The humility piece? You didn't do anything to get them. You were just given them.

And what about your talent card? You were dealt one or two of those as well. So many people say to me, "I don't have a talent," which again is one of those lies we have to shed to get to Lifetime Two. Everyone who comes to this planet gets something they are good at. I have a client whose talent is taste. It has made him millions of dollars with his ability to create flavorings. So, like my client, you might not have an obvious talent, but you've definitely got one.

Sometimes we don't recognize our talents because they are so second nature to us. We don't think they are any big deal because they come easily to us. But they are a big deal. They are part of what you are supposed to be doing on the planet. Look closely at what comes easily to you. Being organized? Appreciating light and shadows? Putting colors together? Talking to people? Telling jokes? Lassoing ropes? Leading? Making origami? Working with animals? Coming up with ideas out of the box? Exercising? Putting together the office parties? Composing songs? Poems? Shooting guns? Making bread? Making movies? Statistics?

One of my sons, for instance, is a statistics genius. He can tell you the stats of all the players on all the teams for all the sports. It's unbelievable to me, as I can tell you none of them! That is a talent *he* has.

My other son is brilliant at Socratic discussions. He is a deep thinker who comes up with ideas that he loves to bat around with a group of friends. Will he be a statesman someday? A college professor? An inventor? A television interviewer? I don't know, of course, but the fact remains that he has a talent in probing and discussing.

There are a zillion different talents—and you've got one or more of them. Sometimes connecting to your talent is a surprise encounter. For example, I now know I have a talent in math. I discovered this when I was in the ninth grade doing algebra homework. One of my close friends said that she didn't understand the math homework. I was stunned by this, thinking, *What is there not to understand? It's so easy. Straightforward.* Yet it was anything but easy for her. I explained it to her with example after example. The teacher explained it to her with example after example. She struggled and struggled with it, but eventually it clicked, and she got it.

That was the first time in my life I realized not everyone's brains think alike. Up until that point, I truly believed all of our brains processed information just the same. Wrong. Nothing could be more inaccurate. We each have our own way of learning; some of us are good at learning academically while others don't learn academically *at all*. Some of us are visual learners, some auditory. Some learn with hands on, others with a computer screen. All are valuable.

So, start telling yourself the truth that you got a talent card when you came to earth, and set about being open to discovering it. Then fully embrace it as amazing.

You are amazing. Remember, you are a light in the world. We come to this planet as a light in the world. Yes, our light gets covered up with gunk in Lifetime One, but it's still there. It never goes away. Underneath the gunk, your light is still shining.

Take a moment to say thank you to God / the Universe for the light that you are, for your unique journey, and for all the cards you were dealt. It's all good.

Step Ten: Use the tag "It's all good."

I personally use the tag "It's all good / it's all God" because I believe there is a spark of the Divine in everyone and in everything.

It reminds me of the words from Representative John Lewis on the fiftieth anniversary of Martin Luther King's March on Washington. Lewis, remembering that day, August 28, 1963, stated, "We truly believed that in every human being—even in those who were violent toward us—was a spark of the Divine."

I believe that too. Even with suffering, there is a spark of the Divine. It has a very important purpose—so why run from it? It, too, is sacred. That's part of the story I make up that works for me. Remember, you don't have to believe my story—you have to write your own.

Believing "It's all good" seems to be part of the journey from Lifetime One to Lifetime Two, however. It is transforming the notion of things happening *to* you into one that says things happen *for* you. It is shifting from thinking, *I am a victim*, into thinking, *I am never a victim*. Instead, I am willing to embrace the obstacle tossed in my direction so I can figure it out, grow, and practice loving even more. It's changing the angle from which to look at a challenge.

Which brings us to **Step Eleven**: Learn to ABC your thoughts.

Let me start by saying beliefs are not facts. Beliefs are thoughts we have about facts. We assign beliefs to facts and label them as true. But, in fact, they are not true; they are only true for us in a particular circumstance.

For example, I have a bookshelf full of wonderful, thought-provoking books. To me, they are wisdom. However, what are they to people in a poor village in Ethiopia? Wisdom? No, of course not. They don't speak English, and they don't read. But they are valuable to them, nonetheless—as firewood.

So, this is important. It means the meaning we assign to things is variable. That is, we can see the same thing—in this case, my books—in two completely different lights. Both are true.

Actually, this is true about our beliefs about everything. Our beliefs are variable. That's very good news because that means we can *change* our beliefs to work better for us.

Jiddu Krishnamurti, an Indian author and philosopher from the early 1900s, said, "Thought is crooked because it can invent anything and see things that are not there." That statement is indeed more true than we can truly comprehend. It is profound really. Our thought can invent anything! Wow. We can—and do—invent anything and everything to make sense out of facts.

The problem, of course, is that our thoughts can be crooked—they can be dead wrong—and we still believe them as true because we think them. That tells me we'd better get clear of what beliefs we are assigning to the facts and make sure those beliefs are working in our favor.

This concept is beautifully outlined in Albert Ellis's 1975 book, *A Guide to Rational Living*. There, he says it in ABC terms:

A: an action happens
B: we assign beliefs to that action
C: our beliefs will determine our consequence—or how we get to feel

A → B → C

Let's look more deeply at the ABC technique.

At A, an action happens. We have no control over it. It just happens. We get hit by another car while we are stopped at a red light, we have a miscarriage, we get fired, our electricity goes off, there's a plane crash, and so on. We did nothing to cause what happened at A—it just happened. It's a neutral fact that occurred.

At B, then, we assign our beliefs to the action, making it not neutral anymore. We can make what happened into a big deal or a small deal, we can beat ourselves up about it, we can be gentle with ourselves about it, we can laugh about it, we can cry about it—it's all up to us and what beliefs we assign to the action that just happened.

It's here at B, then, that we determine C, our consequence, or how we get to feel about what just happened at A. *We* determine our feelings! In other words, the power is at B where we assign beliefs about what happened at A. The only place we have any control in this equation is at point B. Belief. Belief is not fact. It is a belief. *If* we change our belief about what happened at point A, we will change our outcome at point C. Let me say that again: *if* we change our belief about what happened at point A, we will change our outcome. For example, if we want to feel happy, we can assign beliefs that work in our favor—and not against us. That is very powerful because it means that in our nonreactionary, authentic adult self, we can choose to look at a situation from a different angle and decide to be happy.

Remember, beliefs are variable. They are just a story that we make up—that we assign—to the action that just happened. We make up a story about it! Most people react to the action at point A and awfulize it at point B where they assign beliefs to it. Then they get to be unhappy. I say, if you are going to make up a story—which we all do at point B—make up one in your favor. That is, at point B we have *choice*. What we choose will determine whether or not we get to be happy or at least at peace with what happened at point A. In other words, our power is at point B where we assign beliefs.

So here's my confession: I, Patti Henry, *always* make up a story at B in my favor. Why not? Life is short, and I want to be happy.

I don't use the word *always* casually here either. I feel there are very few uses of the words "always" and "never" that are valid. But there are some—like we never have sex with children.

So, for me at least, this is one of the rare occasions where *always* makes sense: I always think of beliefs about the action that happened at A that will lead to my feeling happy or peaceful.

Let me give you an example of this ABC thinking.

Let's say someone cuts you off in traffic. That's the A—the action that happened. Road ragers immediately assign these beliefs:

1.   That guy's an idiot! (or a long line of curse words)
2.   That guy thinks he owns the road!
3.   That guy thinks he can push me around!
4.   That guy needs to be taught a lesson!

The result? The C or consequence? The road rager feels *rage*, anger, and hatred and is motivated to do behaviors that may well not work out very well for him.

I, on the other hand, assign different beliefs:

1.   That guy's wife must be having a baby, and he is trying to get to the hospital, and he is out of his mind right now because of it. Or:
2.   That guy has no power in his life. He has a minimum-wage job where he has to punch a time clock, and he's late for work. He's already been late twice, and if he's late today, a third time, he'll get fired.

The result? My C or consequence? I get to feel compassion for him. I get to feel forgiveness. I get to feel happy and joyfully invite him to cut in front of me.

Do you see how what we tell ourselves about the action that happens determines how we get to feel? Okay, admittedly, that was an easy example. But remember, you *always* have choice about what beliefs you assign to the action. You *always* have influence over your beliefs—no matter what the circumstances are at point A.

Here's a harder example—with the facts and names altered to protect anonymity.

Our old house was in a neighborhood next to neighbors where a twenty-two-year-old lived with his dad. I will call the twenty-two-year-old Mike. Unfortunately, Mike's mother died when he was seventeen, and his dad traveled three hundred days a year with his work. This left Mike, an only child, a lot of time to get into a lot of trouble—which he did. By the time we moved in, Mike was already addicted to hard drugs and alcohol. Seeing this out-of-control behavior and being a therapist, I decided to talk to his dad about possible treatment facilities. To put it mildly, he was not interested in any of my suggestions.

So, time went by. Mike got a DUI, driving under the influence. In Texas, your first DUI is a misdemeanor. His dad hired an attorney, and Mike got a little slap on the hand. I decided to talk to his dad again. Again, not interested. So, I decided I'd better go directly to Mike.

We started chatting. Anytime he was outside working on his car when I was home, I'd walk over and talk to him. We talked about just about everything under the sun: cars, motorcycles, his mom, girls, gout, cooking, roses—and sobriety.

Time went by. Mike got a second DUI. In Texas, your second DUI is a misdemeanor. Again, his dad hired an attorney, and again, Mike got a little slap on the hand. I was desperate to convince him that he was worth sobriety.

So he went to AA a bit. He cut back. He only did heroin and

crack and coke on the weekends. We kept talking: about treatment centers, about options.

One day, Mike said to me, "Miss Patti, your gardens look *bad*. Do you mind if I replant them for you?" Who could refuse that offer? He had a ton of rocks brought in. He ripped out all of what I had and made my front gardens into a showcase of gorgeous flowers and shrubs. I'd be cooking and happen to look out my front window, and there Mike would be: spraying for white fly, adding a new rose bush, or pulling weeds.

Time passed, and then he got a third DUI. Well, in Texas, your third DUI is a felony. You go to jail. He went to jail. I missed him. He was gone six months. When he got home, he swore to me that he was going straight, getting off of everything because he was not *ever* going back to jail. He told me stories of it, and they were not pretty. We cried together.

He worked hard to turn his life around. He found a really nice girl, he went back to school, and he said no to his "friends" who wanted him to use with them. All except one. This friend gave him some pure heroin one night. It was quite a trip. The only problem was he beat up his really nice girlfriend during it. She called the cops, and sweet, wonderful, amazing Mike was arrested again.

Three DUIs and a domestic violence assault charge. This time, his dad hired a very powerful and expensive attorney; the stakes were high. This time, Mike wasn't so lucky: he was assigned a very punitive judge who would surely throw the book at him. His attorney said, "Realistically, you'll get twenty-five years—out on good behavior after maybe twelve to fifteen."

The night before his court sentencing, Mike kept his word: he was never going back to jail. He committed suicide.

It was four in the morning when I awoke to the police lights outside my bedroom window. I went out to ask what happened as I watched the police string out the crime tape. The officer would only tell me that there was a deceased body in the house. I said, holding my breath, "Well, is it an old body or a young one?" The answer, of course, was a young one.

I went into my house and sat on the couch and sobbed. My husband came out, and I said, "I am *so mad* at his dad! Why didn't he get him into treatment?"

My husband helped me by saying, "Why be mad at his dad? He didn't have good fathering skills around addiction because nobody taught him."

That clicked me into remembering, "Oh, yeah! ABC! ABC it, Patti!"

So, I started the process:

A: Mike committed suicide. He's dead. He's no longer here.

B: Beliefs:

My first belief is always this: it's all good / it's all God.

My immediate thought was, *What the heck is good about this?*

My second belief: I don't know what's good about this, but I believe it will be revealed to me.

Third belief: Lifetimes are different lengths. I've noticed this. We don't all get ninety-two years.

Fourth belief: We live everyday of our lives. No life is cut short; it is exactly that length.

Fifth belief: Mike lived every day of his life.

Sixth belief: every lifetime matters.

Seventh belief: Mike's lifetime mattered.

Eighth belief: the time I spent with him was sacred, and I am glad I had it.

Ninth belief: every lifetime has a spiritual mission, including Mike's.

Tenth belief: no one gets out of grieving.

Eleventh belief: You are allowed to grieve, Patti. Let yourself cry.

Twelfth belief: Your crying is honoring him. He knows you loved him.

C: Consequence:

I was starting to calm down.

Now, I didn't get out of grieving—grieving is essential for emotional health—but I did get out of reactionary so I could consciously *choose* how I wanted to respond to Mike's leaving the planet.

The next day, his dad asked if I would speak at Mike's funeral since I knew him "better than anyone." I said yes, of course.

At the funeral, the first two rows were full of Mike's pall bearers: his drinking and drugging buddies. Suddenly I realized what Mike's spiritual mission on the planet was: to contribute to their sobrieties and therefore change generations. I spoke right to those eight young men. I told them Mike wanted to be sober—and he wanted each of them to be sober. I told them if any one of them got sober, Mike would not have died in vain.

Three of them, so far, have gotten sober. Though I miss him terribly, I know Mike's life—and death—helped to heal generations.

It's all good / it's all God.

The point is you can use ABC no matter what the circumstance.

Step Twelve: Remember fear is just a feeling. In the twelve-step programs, they say fear is False Evidence Appearing Real. So there's no need to be afraid of false evidence. As Franklin Roosevelt said in his inaugural address in 1933, "The only thing we need to fear is fear itself." The only thing we need to fear is reacting to false evidence appearing real. That can certainly get us into trouble—leading us down paths that are completely off course and wasting our time. We have to slow the roll when we feel fear and *think*.

Fear is just a feeling; it won't kill you. To grow up emotionally, to get out of fear running you, remember, it will be scary—at first. When you learn to ABC your fear, the fear will go away. You will have conquered it. Rewrite the story you are telling yourself.

For example, let's say you are afraid to face your financial situation. Your finances are a mess. You don't even know how much you have on credit cards. You don't want to know because you know it's going to be ugly. You haven't filed taxes for years. You feel shame and embarrassment just thinking about it all. So, first of all, ask yourself who is in charge at this point: your child self or your adult self?

Clearly child: pretending if I don't look at the problem, it will magically somehow go away. Child fears the feelings of shame. Child wants to run away from it all.

So, you call forth your response-able adult self who decides, "I can do this." Yet even gathering together the credit card bills creates so much anxiety you are tempted to get up and do something else. *Anything* else. The laundry, mow the grass, take a nap, surf the internet, watch your hair grow, whatever. You are tempted to run away and, as Rumi says, "go back to sleep." But going back to sleep will only keep you stuck in your financial mess. So, ABC it.

The A is: getting out the paperwork makes you almost explode with anxiety.

The B, your beliefs, where you have power, can be:

1. Wait a minute—I am capable.
2. This is going to be a challenge, but challenges make me grow.
3. I've done hard things before. I can do this hard thing too.
4. I usually run away, but this time I can breathe deeply and face the problem.
5. If I avoid the problem, it won't go away. It will get worse.
6. Okay, so I feel uncomfortable! So what? It will pass as I walk through this.
7. I don't have to figure it all out at once.
8. I am not a victim. I can get up and walk around the room right this minute and then sit back down calmer. I don't *have* to do this—I am choosing to.
9. It's all good. As I figure it out, I will learn a lot and eventually resolve the problem.
10. This is going to be a victory for me.
11. I am bright. I can do this.

12. I am not alone either. If I can't figure it out, there are people who can help me.
13. I can ask for help just like I would give that grace to others.
14. All I have to do is start. I've collected all the papers together, and that counts. This is already a nonzero day.
15. I can do step two now or I can do step two in an hour. I'll do one more step now and then quit.
16. I am already in the process of fixing things. I am amazing.

The C, then, would be that you get to calm down and experience being on your own side rather than suffering through shame and embarrassment. You also give yourself credit for what you've done right—collected the bills—and encourage yourself to get one more step done, perhaps adding together all of the amounts due. You have given yourself a stopping point for the day. You can feel good about your progress.

Review

The twelve steps in this chapter are ways to begin to think differently as you step into doing the deeper levels of work. Again, it all happens simultaneously, rather like Einstein's description of the time spectrum.

My son was explaining the fourth dimension to me one day and Einstein's understanding of the time spectrum. I must have looked a bit lost because, after a couple of hours of explanation, my son sighed at my puzzled look and asked, "Is this making sense to you?" When I admitted some of it did and some of it didn't, he said, "Okay, I'll make it easy for you. Think of yourself standing at this wall. Then run as fast as you can away from the wall. Then, at the same moment, you will be at the wall. Does that make sense?"

I said, "Of course not! How can I be at the wall and be away from the wall at the same moment?"

"Because all points in time exist at the same moment, Mom."

Oh. Really?

This shifting from Lifetime One into Lifetime Two is like that: you are actually working toward doing all of these things at the same moment, which will lead you to thinking differently.

So, here are the Thinking Differently steps again:

1. Decide you want to be an emotional grown-up and be powered by love and not fear—over and over again.
2. Decide you won't settle for anything less—over and over again.
3. Be brave—step *toward* your fear.
4. Say only nice things to yourself.
5. Use the tagline "And that's okay" when things don't go as planned.
6. Stop apologizing for yourself.
7. Let go of the lie that you are supposed to be perfect.
8. Embrace and enjoy your imperfections.
9. Fall in love with yourself by claiming all you have been given.
10. Use the tagline "It's all good."
11. Master the ABC technique: action, belief, consequence.
12. Remember fear is just a feeling: don't be afraid of false evidence appearing real.

CHAPTER 15

The IS of Life

Emotionally growing up means not only learning to think differently but also coming to terms with life. It's learning not to be afraid to accept life on life's terms. Growing up means telling yourself the truth: you do not have the power to change life's terms. You are not God.

As I talked about earlier in this book, there are ISs in life—things that just are the way they are whether we like it or not. Like, as humans, we have to have oxygen to survive. You can argue the point, but it doesn't make it less true.

There are other ISs in life that, once you personally come to peace with them, you will be able to outgrow much of your fear. It is actually a Buddhist concept to learn how to flow with life, even suffering, instead of resisting it. The sooner you let go of the resistance to how life IS, the sooner you can get rid of your fears. I don't believe the goal in life is happy. I believe the goal in life is peace and serenity, which you will find in Lifetime Two. Coming to terms with the ISs will help you get there.

As I see it, there are four challenging ISs that we need to absorb into our awareness and label as human, normal, and good:

1. Trauma is a part of this adventure called life.
2. Challenge is a part of it.

3. Loss is a part of it (grieving); deep, gut-wrenching pain is a part of it.
4. Surprise is a part of it.

What I've noticed is that often people cling to Lifetime One because they don't want trauma, hard/challenging lessons, loss, unexpected surprises, or messiness. They live in fear of those things.

Which is silly—because they are going to happen to them anyway. Fear does not keep the ISs of life from happening. Fear only keeps you from being fully alive and fully present in your life. It keeps you from peace and serenity.

So the goal is to be able to be one with the ISs when they come to you. That is, the goal is to be able to joyfully float down the river of life in your little boat when the waters are smooth or choppy, or even when you crash over a waterfall. Because those things will happen. That is part of the human experience on earth. If you live long enough, nobody—and I mean *nobody*—gets out of these experiences.

Why is it designed this way? I don't know. The story I make up is that there is a Divine order that is unfolding that will lead to world peace. The story I make up is that it is all good—because it is moving the whole planet toward spiritual awakening. The story I make up is sometimes bad things must happen in the world to help us wake up. Now, is that true? It's true for me. It puts order in my world. Beyond that? Who knows?

Regardless, let's look at the four ISs listed above.

Trauma

First, trauma is part of this adventure called life. Again, if you live long enough, trauma will come to you. I remember when my older son graduated college at twenty-one, thinking to myself, *I hope he got what he needed*. I hoped he got what he needed to face head-on the trauma that would come to him, because he had a pretty easy, trauma-free life up until that point. His grandfather died when he was in middle school, but his grandfather was old and sick, and so, though it was sad for my son, the trauma was minimal to him.

But it's coming. I don't know if one of his best friends will get killed in a car accident or murdered, or he'll have a child who is born blind, or he'll find out his wife cheated on him, or his house will burn down, or he'll develop an addiction, or he'll get a debilitating disease at a young age, or lose all his money, or get fired from a dream job, or what, but trauma will come to him. It's part of being on this planet. The story I make up is that the trauma comes to wake us up, mostly to wake our heart up. The trauma comes as a way to help us move from Lifetime One to Lifetime Two. Or not.

Some people miss the messages of trauma, clinging to fear, being a victim, and suffering, and miss the opportunity to evolve. Don't let that be you. For example, there were many Holocaust survivors after WWII who had been through unbelievable and indescribable, horrific trauma. Research shows us, though, that there were two types of survivors: those whose heart continued to beat but were stuck in the trauma, and those who came back to life and used the trauma to educate and change the world. Another way of saying this is some stayed stuck in Lifetime One, in fear and the belief that the world would never be safe, while others were able to transform the trauma and move into the love energy vibration of Lifetime Two and work to make the world safe. That is, they were able to use what happened to them to help awaken others in the world.

All this is to say be aware that trauma will come to you sometime. Maybe more than once. But here's the good news: you will have an opportunity to be transformed by these traumas. You can be awakened by them. In the story I make up, traumas come to help us wake up. That is, things don't happen *to* you, they happen *for* you. Once you accept this as part of life—that trauma will come, and it will be hard, but you will learn and grow from it—then there is no need to fear it. Even trauma is part of the small stuff on the planet:

the only big stuff is evolving from fear to love. In the story I make up, trauma comes to help us get there.

I suggest you label that as good/God, listen for the lessons, and do the best you can while you are in it. Give it time too. Trauma can take years to heal.

Now I'm not saying trauma is easy. It's not. Often when we are in trauma, our brain seems to zap its circuitry. We are in a fog for days, weeks, months, even years. We can't think straight. Here's the good news: when you are going through trauma, you don't have to think straight. Just do the best you can. I tell my clients that if you get up in the morning and you brush your teeth, that's great. Give yourself credit—you've done a good job. That could be all that you get done for the day, and that's okay. That is, lower your expectations of yourself when you are going through trauma. Be extra, extra gentle with yourself. It will all make sense later. You will not be able to figure it out as you go through it, so you can stop trying. Just be kind to yourself and acknowledge it is your turn to be in trauma. Try to be very present with the trauma. Acknowledge it, respect it, and give yourself permission to not be on top of your game. No one is on top of their game when they are going through trauma; you can let go of that expectation of yourself. It will make sense later. As Steve Jobs said, "We can only connect the dots backwards."

I was once asked to confer on a case where a woman had been thrown from her car in an accident. With several broken bones, including her skull, she lay on the road and watched in horror as the car suddenly caught fire and trapped her three children in the back seats. They burned to death in front of her eyes. Four months after the accident, she was still in the hospital, staring into space, not talking, spending most of her days in the fetal position. The psychiatric team asked me my thoughts on how to proceed. I felt she was doing the best she could to get through the trauma: curling into a ball, sometimes rocking herself, rethinking the trauma over and over again, processing it. Among other recommendations on treating the PTSD, I told the staff to lower their expectations for her progress and to honor her process. That's what you need to do when you are going through trauma: lower your expectations of yourself and honor your process. Do the best you can to get through it, and that will be good enough.

I have two examples to think about concerning this.

First, having lived through one of the worst droughts in the history of Texas with one-hundred-year-old trees dying, crops dying, and people's fears escalating into panic, I know many prayed for rain. Others, on the other hand, prayed for strength to be in the drought, to embrace it, to understand it, to look for meaning at a higher level. Not to change it—but to flow with it. That's the difference between Lifetime One and Lifetime Two thinking.

Being one with the drought leads to action. When we are in fear, we can't think straight. When we are flowing with the problem, unafraid of it, we can see solutions. We need a water plan. We need to figure out how to move water around the state—how to capture flooded areas' water and transport it to the dry areas. We need to call our congressman/woman to talk to him/her about this. We need to stop watering our lawns. We need to only water the trees. We need to get a rain barrel to capture water when the rains come.

A second example can be taken from the Easter story / the resurrection story in the Bible. There are four Gospels in the Bible: Matthew, Mark, Luke, and John. If you read the crucifixion/resurrection story in each, you will find that the details vary. Some talk about an earthquake; others don't mention this. Some talk about an angel; others don't mention this. Some said Jesus was in a cave; others say a tomb. One says after he left the cave/tomb, he went to Mary Magdalene's, and she did not recognize him. Another said he ran into the disciples, who did not recognize him. I say the details don't matter.

Here's the story I make up using the consistent "facts": Jesus died, he was placed somewhere and stayed there three days, then he was not in there, and he ran into folks who did not recognize him. Metaphorically, perhaps he was role modeling to us how to go through trauma. First, the trauma happens, and it feels like a piece of us dies. Second, we must retreat from the world to heal from the trauma as well as process it. Third, when we come out of this retreat, we will have changed so much that we will not be recognizable. We will have been transformed.

Again, with trauma, the message is this: there is no need for fear. For whether you fear it or not, trauma will still come to you. There is only a need to accept it will happen, you will go through it, and when you are done with being in the cave, you will be different. In a good way.

We get in trouble—get to feel pain and suffering—when we resist the trauma. When we say it shouldn't be happening. When we say, "*Why* is this happening to *me*?" When we try to control the trauma. Instead, we can learn to flow with trauma if we realize it is a *normal*, predictable part of life and that each of us takes a turn or two with it. Why is it happening to you? Because you're human, and it is as much a part of the human experience as birth and death. It is happening to you because it is your turn to go through it.

It's like getting a traffic ticket. I get a traffic ticket maybe once every ten years. When I get pulled over, I tell the police officer I don't mind getting the ticket at all because it's my turn to pay. It's my turn to put a little extra money into maintaining the police department or the fire department, or into building the roads and schools. It's my turn because usually it's not my turn. I often go over the speed limit if I'm in a rush. I often go through red lights when I'm out at midnight and there is no traffic at all on the road. Sometimes I even make a U-turn where it says, "No U-Turn," and I don't get a ticket—because it's not my turn.

With trauma, it's usually not our turn. Most of our lives, we are not in trauma. But sometimes we are. Sometimes it's our turn to go through trauma because nobody gets out of it. So, just accept it when it arrives, recognize it as part of life, tell yourself, "Oh, boy. Here it is. It's my turn," and do the best you can through it. Cry, cry, cry, deep-belly sobs cry. Remember trauma is temporary and absolutely part of the process of waking up to a higher understanding of the importance of love—though it often doesn't feel like that when we are going through it. It feels like the pain will last forever and that we will never get on the other side of it. In my experience, that is not the case. The world will keep turning and, eventually, though it may take years depending on the magnitude of the trauma, you will come to peace with it—and you will be transformed.

Let me remind you, when you are having your turn in trauma, you will not be your best self. That's okay. Give yourself permission to not be as sharp as you normally are. Be gentle with yourself, saying, "I'm in trauma now. Of course I'm not thinking straight! I feel like a zombie who is just surviving—and that is enough."

When I have a client who is in trauma—their four-year-old was killed by a drunk driver, their eighteen-year-old just died of alcohol poisoning at a graduation party, their mother was murdered, their mother and father died within a week of each other, they were fired from a job they loved, they just found out their spouse is cheating, they were raped, their baby was just diagnosed with autism—again, I tell them, "Wash your face, brush your teeth. Don't expect anything else from yourself right now." That is, let yourself *be* in the trauma. Walk with yourself as you are going through it. Be gentle with yourself and know, in time, you will get on the other side of it.

When I think of trauma, I think of Christmases. If we are lucky, we get about ninety Christmases in a lifetime. Of those ninety, some will be the best moments of our lives: the dream dollhouse, the new bicycle, the sled, the keys to a car, the moment we got engaged, the first one when our child knows what's going on and is so excited, and so on. Some will be the worst: the first one after the baby, parent, partner died, the one where I felt completely alone and friendless, the one where I was broke, the one where my partner left me, and so on. And the rest will be somewhere in between.

When trauma hits, it's the time when it's the worst Christmas ever. And yet Christmas will come again, and it won't be so bad as last year's. Eventually, there will even be a joyful one again. That is, life goes on even though trauma is a part of it.

The second IS:

Challenge

Sometimes when I ask clients to stretch outside of their comfort zones, they will say to me, "But that's hard!" Yep. It is. But what I tell my children is this: don't ever be afraid of hard. All hard is is a bunch of smaller easies glopped together. Just figure out the smallest first step and do that. Remember, too, adults do hard things. They do things that are really hard. They do things they don't want to do—but they do them. Why? Because it's a means to an end. We have to do hard things to reinforce that we are capable, and vice versa is true too: we are able to do hard things because our adult self is capable. The challenges, then, are here to help us grow up. Claiming that *you* are capable is a step toward Lifetime Two, the good stuff. It is a step toward living in no fear.

After all, you've made it this far in your life—having done hard and amazing things. Really, look back at your life. You have done some really hard things. *Really* hard things. You are amazing. You have handled every single thing that has been handed to you in your life, and you will handle this too. You will make it through to the other side of the hard stuff.

When I was in college, we were on a ten-week quarter system. At the beginning of each quarter, the professors would hand out the syllabus for each of their classes. It would list all the projects, all the tests, all the reading that was expected in that ten weeks. Every time—I mean, *every* time, I would think to myself, *How on earth am I ever going to get all of this done? It's impossible.* Yet, every quarter, it all got done. Not perfect—because there is no perfect—but done. Good enough.

I often had to remember my mother's words, "If all else fails, lower your standards." One quarter, I took three courses that each required reading a book a week. That is, I had to read thirty books in ten weeks. I am not a fast reader, so I cut corners. I chose to because time kept ticking. I bought the CliffsNotes for most of the books and read those. The ones that didn't have CliffsNotes, I read every other chapter. Not perfect but done.

So, if something is hard—which it will be—you need to do it. Do the best you can, and that will be good enough. Even stuff you don't want to do: confronting someone, changing jobs, paying the bills, taxes, reports, taking that defensive driving course to get out of a ticket, finishing a college class you are failing, standing up to your boss, separating from your unfaithful spouse, going back to school, setting boundaries, cleaning out that stuffed closet, redoing your résumé, daring to step toward your dream job, getting organized, leaving a bad relationship, asking for help, making that phone call to someone you've been avoiding. No one gets out of this stuff. Even if you procrastinate it or don't do it this time, the challenge will come back around. That's because challenge and the hard stuff is just part of living here on earth. The sooner you come to terms with this, the better your life gets. Another way of saying this is the sooner you get your strong, capable adult self in charge of your life—and have your young, wounded child that is egocentric step aside—the better your life gets, the closer you get to living in Lifetime Two and becoming your authentic, empowered self.

So, challenges *are* going to come—why be afraid of them? Just recognize them when they show up. "Oh, it's my turn to be challenged. Okay. Bring it on." Then knuckle down and break it down into small, easy steps. If it's hard, step toward it. Do the first step.

Remember, your adult, authentic self is capable, capable, capable. The Universe will keep handing you problems. Our child self says, "I can't do this!" or "I can't figure it out! I don't know what to do!" or "I don't want to do that!"

Our adult self says, "Well, here's a problem. I don't know what to do about it, but I am smart, I am capable—and I can figure it out. I don't want to do it, but I will do it because it needs to get done. I am not afraid to figure things out." Then the adult self simply brainstorms: looks for possible solutions, asks others for their thoughts, accepts help, seeks expertise where needed, delegates where possible, looks at as many options as they can think of, is nonreactionary—and then consciously, on purpose, picks a course of action. The adult self takes full responsibility for this course of action.

Also, when hard stuff comes, remember, you *always* have choices. Brainstorm. You can choose not to do it. You can put it off. You can even choose to become the champion of procrastination. However, what I've noticed is that when a person avoids hard, their life actually just gets harder. That is, procrastinating seems to just delay getting to your powerful adult self. The story I make up, again, is that these things don't happen *to* you—they happen *for* you. The Universe is trying to give you opportunities to practice being a grown-up. Metaphorically, I envision the Universe handing you a challenge knowing that this challenge will help you wake up / grow up. If you table it, refuse to look at it, and procrastinate it, the Universe says, "Okay, I know that didn't get your attention, so I'll try again. I'll ramp it up a little bit so you don't miss the lesson this time." Again, the sooner you can accept and get one with this IS, that life is full of challenges, the sooner you can move to the good stuff. The sooner you can take responsibility and move toward challenging instead of away from it, the sooner you can move on down the path between the two worlds.

I will tell you the story of when my oldest son was eighteen, and I was trapped on a beautiful tropical island with him for five days. I say trapped because, as everyone knows who has teenagers or who has raised teenagers, they are hard! They are definitely an exercise in challenging.

I was invited to speak at a church down in the Virgin Islands, and part of the compensation was getting to stay in a furnished apartment with a car provided. The director of the church said, "Why don't you bring along your family and make it a vacation?"

That sounded like a good idea. Since it was over Mother's Day,

I invited my mother along, plus brought my two sons, aged twelve and eighteen. I was to be on the island for ten days, speaking at two church services and leading a workshop as well. Since it was May, my little one was still in school, so he couldn't stay the whole time, but my oldest had just finished his first year of college and was free for the full ten days. My husband was not able to join us, so we developed a plan so my mother would bring my younger son home after five days, and my oldest son and I would stay on for the additional time. It sounded like a great plan.

Until it came to the day my mother and younger son were leaving. That morning, we drove them down to the ferry that they had to catch to another island to get to the airport. I opened the trunk of the car where there were two suitcases. My older son took out the one closest to him.

Me: Aren't you going to take out Grandma's suitcase?

Son: No. You're standing right there!

Me: Yes, and you are big and buff, and I am not. Take out Grandma's suitcase, for goodness sakes!

Well, he huffed and he puffed and angrily took out her suitcase and slammed the trunk shut. I thought, *Oh, what was I thinking? I am trapped on an island with a teenager for five days!* With trepidation, I waved goodbye to my mom and little guy as I watched the ferry pull away, and then I turned to my very angry eighteen-year-old.

We went in search of breakfast as he stomped his way along. I wondered what on earth was going on in his teenage brain. Finally, I had had enough, but as an adult, I remained calm and nonreactionary. As an adult, I knew his behavior wasn't about me and that I needed to really listen to try to figure out how to help him, how to be a healing force.

Me: Okay, we are going to have this out right here and now. *What* are you so angry about?

Son: Nothing!

Me: Clearly not. Please tell me why you are so angry. Did I do something to offend you?

Son: I *hate* when you tell me what to do!

Me: [*Ah! that's it!*] Well, you are eighteen years old, and I shouldn't have to tell you to take Grandma's suitcase out of the car.

Son: I'm doing everything!

Me: [*Hmmm … what could he be talking about? The luggage? Does he want to be thanked?*] Well, it's true you have carried all the luggage—from the plane to the taxi to the ferry to the car to the apartment—and I very much appreciate that—but you have to realize that while you were doing all that, I was getting the taxi, the ferry tickets, calling to make sure the car was waiting for us, and getting the apartment keys. Your grandmother, in the meantime, was watching your younger brother and making sure he wasn't running off with pirates. We are a *family*, and we all contribute.

Son: Whatever!

Me: (very softly) Okay, what is *really* going on?

Son: (after a long pause) I am going to say something very mean to you.

Me: That's okay. I am strong. I can handle whatever it is you need to tell me.

Son: I don't even want to live with you this summer!

Me: [*Ah!*] Ah, that makes sense. You've been on your own for the past nine months with no rules, no curfews, no dishwasher to empty, nobody telling you what to do. I get that.

Son: Yeah! And, whether you like it or not, Mom, you're an *authority figure* in my life, and I *don't* want you to tell me what to do!

Me: Yes, of course. That makes sense. So let me explain something to you. When you turned eighteen, your father and I turned over the authority of your life to *you*. We don't want to be the authority of your life. I don't want to be. From now on, if you get in trouble with the law, they won't be calling mommy and daddy. Oh, no—*you* are in charge of your life. How you act, how you treat people, what you say, what you don't say, what kind of person you are going to be in this world. You are the authority of your life. You are responsible for all your thoughts, feelings, and actions—not me!

Son: But, Mom, the problem is you know yourself really well. You are strong. You know your opinions clearly. You are not afraid to say what you think out loud. And, me, well, I'm just beginning to figure out all of that stuff about myself. I can't be around you and hold on to me. The only way I know to be around you is to have a shield of anger—to keep you out and me in.

Me: [*Beautifully spoken, son!*] I completely understand. Let's do it this way. No rules this summer (now I already knew he had a great internship for the summer and would be getting up each morning to go to work). You will have to use the rules that are inside of you. And if you don't want to be around me or talk to me, I am strong, and I can handle that. I support *you* in becoming who *you* are.

My son smiled, we hugged, and we had a great five days together.

He tested the waters though. That night, he ordered an alcoholic drink with dinner—to which I said nothing. At the end of the meal, having drunk maybe half of the drink, he said to me, "Wow, Mom, you did great! I thought you'd freak out if I ordered a drink!" I reiterated that *he* was the authority of his decisions—not me. The outcome? We had a very pleasant summer together.

Don't be afraid of hard. Remember, challenges will come to you. They happen for you to practice nonreactionary so you can grow. You are capable, you are strong, you can do it.

The third IS:

Loss

Loss is a part of this adventure called life. Along with loss comes grieving. Part of grieving is deep, gut-wrenching pain.

It reminds me of the opening words my oncologist said to me when I met with him early on in my cancer treatment, "Your cancer is so aggressive that we will take you to the brink of death—but we won't kill you." I thought to myself, *Oh, sign me up for* that.

However, that's how the reality of loss is in this lifetime: it's going to hurt—but it won't kill you.

Again, no one gets out of losses. No one. In fact, life is rather a series of losses and also a constant loss. The day we are born, we are moving toward death. The day our children are born, they are moving toward leaving us. The river of life *moves*. It isn't stagnant. We can't go back to the good ol' days. We can only learn to enjoy *this* day.

I think part of how we get to Lifetime Two where we can enjoy *this* day is giving ourselves permission to grieve. That is, those who grieve well live well. You can postpone it and carry it around with you for years, but you don't get out of it. Not dealing with your losses will keep you stuck in Lifetime One, blackmailed by the feelings you are too afraid to feel.

I had a client whose son was accidentally killed when he was thirteen. He was over at a friend's house whose parents had a gun. His friend whispered to him, "I know where the bullets are." So, they got the gun, they got the bullets, they put the two together, and they played around—until the gun discharged and killed one of the boys. My client's son.

When she got the news, she did the strangest things. First, stone-faced and rigid, she identified the body. Then she went home and emptied her son's room. I mean *emptied* it. She threw all of his things away. She threw his furniture out in the backyard. She packed up all of his clothes and took them to the Goodwill store. She threw all of his trophies, toys, pictures, and mementos away in big black trash bags. She told all of her friends and family that his name was never to be uttered again. She never cried. She vacuumed the carpet in his room. She moved living room furniture in. She was driven.

Then she skipped the funeral.

She was, of course, pretending that her son had never existed. The loss and the pain were too big to face.

I met her eight years later. Her opening words to me were, "I've had a major loss in my life, and I'm ready to deal with it." So we did. Slowly but surely, I helped her move into her grief. I helped her move into those deep, gut-wrenching belly sobs.

I had another client whose mother killed her eight-year-old son and herself on my client's twenty-first birthday. I met her fourteen years later. She said to me, "Help me have more to my life than that one day. I've been numb since that day. That's all I've lived for the past fourteen years." Again, slowly but surely, I helped her move through her grief. Because I knew if she didn't grieve, she couldn't get to the joy that life has to offer.

Part of grieving is making sense of the losses. It's making up a story to make sense out of what seems to have no sense at all. It's giving meaning to it at a larger level—at the awakening of the planet level. At the healing of the world level.

You see, we live on two levels, the micro level and the macro level. The micro level is all the things we do on the human level. We eat, pay our electric bills, put gas in our cars, and so on. The macro level is the higher, spiritual level. It is the level where we come to understand our purpose on the planet: to individually and collectively move from the lower-energy vibration of fear into the higher-energy vibration of love. I believe we come to earth with some kind of spiritual mission to help the collective heal. That is, we each come to contribute to the spiritual awakening of the world—in one way or another. It could be through positive means or negative ones.

For example, let's look at Princess Diana's death. Her dying, particularly in such a sudden and dramatic way, brought forth an opening of the world's heart, especially in Great Britain. The British are known for having a lockdown on their emotions. Princess Diana's death unlocked that door. It gave people permission to feel deeply, to cry, to grieve. Her death helped opened the hearts of the British people—an important step in healing the collective, healing the world.

Now let's look at Hitler. Hitler was a sociopath. A very good one. In fact, he was one of the most effective sociopaths the world has ever known. I believe his spiritual mission on the planet was to teach—in an extreme way—what happens when we separate people into us and them. I think he role-modeled what *not* to do to heal the world. I think he was sent as a warning. He role-modeled what the world can look like if we don't see *all* people as part of the *one*. I think his spiritual mission was to wake up the world to how necessary it is to love and accept all people: every religion, every race, every gender, every sexual orientation.

Again, this is just my story that makes sense to me. I humbly offer it to you. Take what you like and leave the rest.

Others transform their losses by becoming teachers and/or motivational speakers. Some write books; others start organizations. Think of MADD, Mothers Against Drunk Drivers. This organization was started by mothers who had lost their children to drunk drivers. The National Center for Missing and Exploited Children was created after its founder's son, Adam, was kidnapped and murdered. Lizzie Velasquez was born with a rare disorder called neonatal progeroid syndrome, which makes it almost impossible to gain weight. She has never weighed more than sixty-two pounds. Her life changed at the age of seventeen when she saw herself on a YouTube video titled "The World's Ugliest Woman." She took that and ran with it. She is now a national speaker teaching people to think about bullying and "What defines you?"

There are thousands of examples of people who took their loss and transformed it into being part of the healing force of the world. Some do TED talks or put up their experience on YouTube. Some privately use it to help the people who come into their six feet of influence. So, try to do your best at making sense of your losses. Look at them through a higher spiritual lens.

Remember, certainly loss is never fun, but it is part of our human experience. So, there is no need to fear loss; it won't protect you from it. It will happen anyway. There is only a need for acceptance of it as part of our human experience and allowing yourself to feel the feelings associated with it. It is, really, a sacred part of life.

The last IS: life is full of surprises.

Surprises

The next IS we need to reconcile in order to get rid of our fear is that life is full of surprises. Some of them are fantastic surprises, some are good surprises, some not so good, while still others are horrible. That is, life is unpredictable and incredibly messy. Things don't fall into place just in the order we think they should. Remember, the only constant in life is change. If we can become one with the fact that life is like a river, ever flowing, ever moving, then we can relax and enjoy life on life's terms. So many times, people are so afraid of what might happen that they miss what IS happening.

When I was in the throes of chemotherapy, too weak to even raise my head off of the pillow, I remember thinking to myself, *I can't wait to get my life back.* Then it occurred to me, *Hey, wait a minute! This* is *my life! This* day has been given to me to live. What can I do to enjoy *this* day? I decided what I could do was tell myself the truth about the situation: for the first week of every cycle, I slept about twenty hours a day; that left me with four hours every day to think. What a gift! When did I ever have four hours a day, day after day, to think? That realization turned out to be a delightful surprise.

Here's an example of a negative surprise.

A few years ago, I was asked by the Chicago center director of the Mankind Project, Glenn Barker, if I would go with him to a taping of the *Oprah Show* and help promote the Mankind Project. The Mankind Project hosts the New Warrior Training Adventure for men, which is a weekend for men by men that promotes emotional healing of men. I have literally sent hundreds of men through this program because it is so effective. So, I said, yes, of course! It was a nice surprise.

He then told me to call the audience coordinator and tell her what I could contribute to the show. He even gave me her cell phone number to call her directly. *Wow,* I'm thinking, *they must be friends—this is great!* So I called the coordinator and told her I was the author of *The Emotionally Unavailable Man: A Blueprint for*

Healing, was a psychotherapist, had sent hundreds of men through the Mankind Project programs, and had worked for the past twenty-five years in private practice healing men. She was so excited and said something like, "Great! We'd love to have you on the show as an expert in the audience!" Oh! Another surprise! Another nice surprise.

So I flew to Chicago and got to meet the Chicago center director, who I call Mr. Chicago, and also the international Mankind Project marketing director. By this time, I am understanding a little more of the logistics. Oprah's people had contacted Mr. Chicago and asked him for help in creating an audience of men who were raised without fathers. He sent out the call to all Mankind Project graduates and rounded up a good hundred-plus men from all over the country. In return, he was to get a chance to promote the Mankind Project on air. He asked me along as an expert who could testify to the remarkable results of their program. So far, so good.

The next morning, we arrive early at the Harpo Studios. I am the fifth to be ushered in. However, soon the news shakes down to the audience coordinator that she is only to have fatherless men in the front section. Also, they will not be taking any questions or comments from women, or men who were raised with fathers. Well, there was a surprise—and a not so good one. Mr. Chicago gets bumped, Mr. International gets bumped—because they were both raised with fathers—and I, as a woman, get bumped. The three of us were then seated in the front row of the back section. It felt a little like getting four out of six of the lottery numbers right—having *almost* won but then not winning at all. Not even getting the runner-up prize.

I was definitely a little stunned and crestfallen, but I looked over at Mr. Chicago and thought, *Oh my gosh. Are you kidding? He's the one who put this whole show together!*

So, what do we do when we get bad surprises? How do we act from Lifetime Two behavior of nonreactionary? Because, remember, getting surprises, sometimes good, sometimes bad, *will* happen because it is part of this human experience we are all having.

At the *Oprah* taping, there was some attitude adjustment that had to happen at that point for us to get our bearings again. Mr. Chicago says out loud, "It's okay. It's not about me." And I say out loud, "Yes, it's okay. It's not about me." But inside, my little girl part is thinking, *It's not about me at all?* I mean, I *knew* it wasn't about me, but I thought it would be about me just a *little*.

Nope. Not at all. In fact, my publisher had promised that she would send a case of books to the hotel where I was staying so I could hand them out to the *Oprah* people. They never came. Another surprise. The person in charge of this at the publishing company was rushed to the hospital with an acute kidney infection and forgot to tell someone else to mail them out.

Not to worry—I had brought three books along with me. Thinking I would have forty books waiting for me, I gave one of my three books to the man sitting next to me on the plane—because he needed it. I gave one to Mr. Chicago so he could have an autographed copy, and then I had one left. *One.*

This was not how it was supposed to turn out.

This happens to us, right? We think things are going to go *this* way, and they don't *go* this way. We think they *should* go this way—and they *don't* go this way.

We have these moments when we are reminded that we are not in charge of the universe, that we are not in control. That we don't get to dictate how it's all going to be. Whether it's in a marriage or in a work situation or something financial or whatever—we get these wake-up reminders that we are not in charge. We get a surprise.

And there is no way to get out of the surprises; they are here by design. They seem universal; they happen to everyone in every country, in every religion. Again, I call that Divine. We can resist it, or be afraid of it, but it still IS.

For example, one of my dear friends died from a brain tumor last year. It wasn't supposed to be that way. He was supposed to get better. But he didn't.

So, what do we do when we are so *sure* of the *right* answer—and it doesn't exactly turn out that way? We have to learn to let go and flow. That is, we can stop trying to control the outcome. Do the best you can, but then if it's not going the way you thought it would or it "should," it's time to let go and watch. If it feels like you are trying to get a square peg to fit into a round hole, it's time to let go. This is where the serenity prayer comes in:

God grant me the serenity to accept the things I cannot change,
the courage to change the things I can,
and the wisdom to know the difference.

Like I was in Chicago in January, freezing—it was twenty-nine degrees and windy—and thinking, *Why am I here? Why did I come all the way to Chicago? I don't get it.*

So what I decided to do was ABC it. Rewrite my belief about what was going on. I'm reeling a bit inside, and I want to get back to happy. I could have let my child self write my beliefs this way: This is ridiculous! This is awful! This isn't fair! I feel duped! I cancelled a day of clients for this? Why did Mr. Chicago ask me up here if he didn't need me? Why did the audience coordinator tell me how happy she was to have me as an expert in the audience? Why did they bump Mr. Chicago's front-row seat after he was the one who brought more than a hundred fatherless men with him? This isn't right!

What would my C—my consequence—be if that's what I held onto about the situation? I would be mad. I would be upset. I would get to be unhappy. Why would I want to be stuck in all of that? Life is short. I want to get to happy.

To do so, I have to rewrite my beliefs, right? So I did:

1. One, it's all good; I'm not sure how this is good, but I am smart, and I will figure it out.
2. Next, I don't believe in accidents, so I'm on a course that needs to run.

3. Third, there must be a reason I am here, and it will be revealed to me.
4. Fourth, I am a silly willy to think I am in charge of the universe!
5. Fifth, this is an opportunity for me to practice flowing with how it unfolds.
6. Sixth, maybe she said, "Happy to have you *at* the show" and not "*on* the show." I am human, after all, and could have heard that wrong.
7. Seventh, life is an unpredictable adventure.
8. And finally, I concluded, the audience is important too.

My C or my consequence? I relaxed, enjoyed the tapings, and was happy to be there having an adventure.

As it turns out, it was sacred to be there. There were 125–150 men all raised without a father—telling their stories. And on the *Oprah Show*! I was thrilled. Oprah has been incredible at empowering women—but she's seemed to have some men issues. Now, finally, she was hearing how desperately men needed healing too. She had a whole show about men!

Men stood up, one after another, and told their stories. A disabled man who had cerebral palsy said his father had left him because of his handicap and that the Mankind Project was the first place where he got the emotional healing he needed. Another man who had no father growing up decided to go through the Boys to Men program at the Mankind Project and mentor a teen at risk. His teen had grown into a twenty-one-year-old man successfully attending the Chicago Art Institute. Another man stood and cried as he told the story of the day his father left him.

Oprah said, "Well, men, this is probably the first time for many of you that you have even talked about this topic."

Then one man, one beautiful man, stood up and said, "Oprah, you don't understand. That is what the Mankind Project is all about.

We make a safe space for men to *talk*—to talk about the holes in their souls." And then it seemed a lightbulb went off for Oprah.

She said, "My word, I think *every* man on the planet should go to the Mankind Project! Put it on our website! What is your website address? Put it on the screen! Put it everywhere!" By then, the audience was standing and cheering. Yes, let's put it everywhere! Men need healing—and there is a program that can help.

I was so moved I cried. I was there to support the Mankind Project (MKP), and they got a home run. They didn't need me. The men said it better than I ever could have. It unfolded in a perfect way—without me. It was a nice surprise.

I knew once again that Divine, the order of the universe, is bigger and better than me. I am not in charge, and I don't need to try to be. As I said earlier, sometimes we just need to let go and flow with how things are unfolding.

After the tapings, I gave my last copy of my book to the woman who sat next to us in the front row in the back. It turns out she was the guest's best friend. So, who knows? Maybe it will make its way back to Oprah. But maybe she'll just give it away to a man who needs it. Either way, it's okay. It counts.

After the cameras stopped rolling, Mr. Chicago invited the whole audience back to the Chicago Mankind Project Center for lunch. Probably 150 men came. Some women. It was nice. Then we were asked to take a seat in an area where we could share and learn a little more about MKP. We were asked to pick a partner—someone we didn't know—to do an exercise with.

There was a man about fifty next to me, and so I asked if we could be partners, and he said sure. I asked him if he had gone through the Mankind Project program, and he said no but that he was thinking he would. I gave him my strong endorsement and encouragement. He said maybe he could do it next fall. I said, "Wow, it's January. That's a long ways away. Why not do it sooner?"

He said, "Well, I just got this seventeen-year-old boy dropped off on my doorstep to raise." It was his nephew.

I said rather casually, "Well I suppose there's a story behind that! How did that happen?" He said his brother had just died, and this was *his* son. The boy's mother was a drug addict and had left the scene when he was young, so this man took him in.

Oh, wow. I grew serious and said gently, "I'm so sorry. It must be really hard to lose a sibling." He hesitated, then looked me in the eye, and choked up as he told me in the last two years he had lost all three of his brothers, his mother, and his girlfriend. I said, "Oh my! You're kidding! How are you even standing?"

By this time, I had totally blocked out the speaker. It was just me and this broken, broken man. I asked if he had any kids and—this is the truth—he said he had only had one son—who was murdered when he was a teen. I looked into his eyes for a long moment and then said, "I am so, so sorry." I asked if I could give him a hug. He said yes, and he sobbed in my arms.

And that's when I knew—that's when I knew why I was in Chicago freezing. *This* man was why I needed to come—and be right there—in that moment—sitting right next to him. Surprise: it didn't have anything to do with Oprah.

Sometimes we think we *know*—but we don't know. We have to be open to the truth being revealed to us. We have to learn to be open to being used—in any way—to be part of the healing of the world.

My Oprah adventure taught me we don't have to be a star to make a difference in the world. We just have to show up. Mother Teresa said it this way, "If you can't feed a hundred people, then feed just one."

So even though I never got to meet Oprah or even say a word on her show, it all worked out. Even though it was a surprise—a bad surprise at first—it all unfolded just right.

Surprises are part of this human experience we are having. Let's embrace them. Henry David Thoreau wrote this:

If we will be quiet and ready enough,
we shall find compensation in every disappointment.

So while floating down the river of life, if we can be open to whatever happens to be around the corner—the good and bad surprises—then we can let go of our fear and just be amazed by it all. Even the hard stuff.

Albert Einstein put it this way: "The most beautiful thing we can experience is the mysterious. It is the source of all true art and all science. He to whom this emotion is a stranger, who can no longer pause to wonder and stand rapt in awe, is as good as dead: his eyes are closed." May we keep our eyes open, pause to wonder, and stand rapt in awe at this mysterious adventure called life. May we learn to flow, and not resist, life on life's terms.

The Main Work

CHAPTER 16

Your Own Personal Dragon

Now starts the deeper-level work.

Remember the goal: getting rid of fear or at least learning how to harness it. Each of us gets our own personal fear dragon to confront and stare down. Nobody can do this for us. We have to do it ourselves. In taming it, we are then free from the power it holds over us. We are able to break the spell of being asleep and completely wake up to our true, authentic, powerful self.

What Are We Afraid of Anyway?

It's usually the fear of the unknown. So often, people stay stuck in the yuck because at least they know the yuck. They know the pain, they know the predictable cycles, they know how to feel what they are used to feeling. So, even if what they are feeling feels bad, it is, in a strange way, comfortable—because it's a known entity.

Another fear is of being alone. People have this fear when they have had an abandonment in their childhood. I have worked with countless clients who are in *horrible* relationships, but they stay because they fear being without a partner. Even people in physically abusive relationships often stay because the fear of being alone outweighs the pain of being hit. Wow.

And then there's the fear of death, the fear of getting it wrong, the fear of getting it right, the fear of being powerful and not knowing how to handle that, the fear of getting hurt, the fear of being out of control, the fear of not knowing what to do. Fear, fear, fear.

Only One Real Fear

So many fears. All these fears are much like millions of trees in a forest, however. We could look at this fear or look at that fear, or that one or that one or that one, but really, that would take a long time. What we have to do instead is see the forest. The forest is this: all those fears can be boiled down to the same fear for every person. That is, everyone has the same dragon to conquer: Am I good enough? Am I worthy of the good stuff? Am I good enough to handle whatever life hands me?

We all carry the deep-seated fear of not being good enough to be loved, not being good enough to be worthy, not being good enough to be successful, not being good enough to do our dream job, not being good enough to fit in, and so on. We fear we are not brave enough, smart enough, pretty enough, or rich enough. We fear we will be abandoned. We fear we will be judged. We fear we will be made invisible. We fear we won't be able to do it—whatever it is—because we aren't good enough.

There are lots of variations to the "I'm not good enough" theme, but they are all about fear, and they all came from what happened to us in Lifetime One. It is the universal wound; nobody escapes it in childhood.

So let's start looking at what happened to you.

Chapter 17

Ghost Drivers

This is the most important chapter in this book.

This is because what happens in our first twenty years on the planet *determines* us until we can see it clearly. That is, until we wake up to our subconscious programming, it runs our lives. It's like a computer that is programed to run a program over and over again. The program will continue to run until we stop it, delete files, and put in new ones. How we were programmed can run our lives for ten years, twenty, forty, or even sixty years. It can even run our whole life.

Carl Jung put it this way: until you make the unconscious conscious, it will direct your life, and you will call it fate.

Socrates said it this way: the unexamined life is not worth living.

So, now is the time to be a detective and figure out what you are carrying around at a subconscious level. You have to know this in order to make it to Lifetime Two. Everything that happened to you as a child got inputted into your computer, your brain, and the cells of your body. It is essential to know what got put in there. Some of the files you were given are very helpful in life: family traditions, values, how to treat a cold, and so on. Some are neutral. For example, one of my closest friends doesn't ever go to the doctor. Why? Her mom and dad never went to the doctor, and they lived into their nineties with no health issues. Okay, so, we are not worried about those files that we use without thought that don't really interfere in our lives. Instead, we are looking for the files that get in the way, cause us pain, keep us stuck.

Of course, we never know at a conscious level *all* that is in there, but we *can* become aware of some of the bigger files that are there and are in control of our thought patterns and behaviors. Once we know that, we can start deleting files we don't need anymore and replace them with updated information that will help our brain work more effectively toward peace and empowerment.

This is the part about being asleep or being awake. We are asleep to the subconscious programming we got in the first twenty years of our lives, yet that subconscious programming is in charge of our thoughts and behaviors. Isn't that amazing? That subconscious programming is driving us around without our having any control of the wheel. It is like being on a ride in Disney World where you step into a car that is moving on a track that you cannot steer some other way. I call this subconscious programming that is driving us around our Ghost Drivers. We are, in Lifetime One, generally not aware of them.

Furthermore, no one gets out of childhood without Ghost Drivers coming along. No one. Including you. Even if you had a wonderful childhood, the Ghost Drivers are in charge and are driving your life until you wake up to them.

This explains how children who were sexually abused can grow up and become sexual perpetrators. The Ghost Drivers are in charge and are just repeating the behaviors that were programmed in as a child.

This explains how people who were raised struggling financially and then win the lottery of $100 million often end up broke. The Ghost Drivers are in charge saying, "You are not allowed to have money. You are supposed to struggle financially, just like when you were a child."

This explains how people who were raised in a raging family

grow up to become either ragers themselves or people-pleasers and conflict avoiders—so much so that they often develop a secret life.

This explains how people who were raised with constant change and instability often grow up and marry people who don't have any backbone. They spent their childhood with things feeling so out of control that they gravitate toward someone they can control.

This programming we got as a child holds fast and continues to run until someone notices the programming is outdated. However, if we don't overwrite or delete the old programs, they just keep running.

Let me give you an example from Steve Jobs's life. He was adopted at birth when his twenty-three-year-old mother gave him up for adoption. The thought of his parents abandoning him was devastating to him. In fact, he felt it was the most impactful and damaging thing that ever happened to him in his life.

And yet, at age twenty-three, the same age his biological mother had been, Jobs fathered a child and abandoned her. Disowned her. Wanted nothing to do with her. Disclaimed paternity. Knowing how harmful the exact same behavior had been to him, it begs the question, why? Why would he do to his own child what was the most hurtful thing that was ever done to him? Why would he do that to his child?

Because that's how strong Ghost Drivers are.

Jobs had no awareness that his subconscious was in charge. He had no awareness of the parallel in his behavior to what happened to him. In fact, several years later when it was pointed out to him, he was stunned. He could instantly see what he was totally blind to when his child was born. He immediately set about rectifying the situation and welcomed his then eight-year-old daughter into his life and his family.

Steve Jobs, the genius and mastermind behind Apple Computer and Pixar Films, was asleep to the impact of his childhood. Just like the rest of us.

I'm telling you, there is nothing more powerful than Ghost

Drivers at a subconscious level. The only way we can stop them from driving our life is to shine a light on them, become aware of them, and make conscious choices to get rid of them. And fair warning: they *don't* want to turn over the wheel.

So, how you get to experience Lifetime Two is by shining a light on Lifetime One. What happened to you? What do your Ghost Drivers look like? You have to understand your past to get beyond it.

Furthermore, after we have found the wounding and programming that happened to us, we must feel the pain of it. Yeah, I know, sounds like fun, right?

It reminds me of the day my oncologist took me way down a very long hallway to have a spinal bone marrow aspiration. I had aggressive large B cell lymphoma. In fact, the surgeon who did the biopsy of one of my tumors described it as being the most aggressive cancer she had ever seen in her forty-plus years of practice and told me I'd be lucky to have three more months to live. My oncologist said he had to do the aspiration to see if it had spread into my bone marrow yet. I asked why we were going to the last office on a very long hallway. "Is it because it hurts and people scream?" He said, "Yep."

Again, on my cancer adventure, I thought, *Wow. Sign me up for that.* He was, by the way, telling the truth. I'm telling you the truth too. These next few chapters are a little like that. They are about having to feel the pain of what happened to you as a child.

It's not about blame though. There is no need for blame. It's about the Ghost Driver called "not good enough."

More about the Universal Wound

The wounding of our beautiful, pure love self can be summarized in just those three words: *not good enough.* This wound leaves the child with the feeling that they are defective somehow and unworthy of love.

It is intergenerational. In other words, I don't feel good enough to be lovable because my parents gave me that wound because they didn't feel good enough to be lovable because their parents gave them that wound because they didn't feel good enough to be lovable, and so on for generations. I always say, if you are going to blame someone, blame Adam and Eve, because the wound has gone on for centuries.

At a conference, I heard Louise Hay, author of the remarkable book *You Can Heal Your Life*, say, "All of the people who have ever come to me for therapy come believing they are not good enough. *All* of them."

It's the same with my thirty-two years in practice; *all* of my clients arrive with some variation of the same wound: I am not good enough, I am not worthy, I don't have what it takes, I am not lovable, I can't do it. This is the dragon we each have to face, wrestle down, and get power over.

However, my clients don't always see their wound. Just like with Steve Jobs's abandonment wound, it was very obvious to those on the outside yet totally invisible to him. Sometimes I have clients who come in and tell me that they were not impacted by their family of origin at all. I am usually able to utter something like, "Really? You believe that nothing that you were exposed to as a child impacted you?" When they say yes, I know it's going to be harder for them to shift from Lifetime One to Lifetime Two because their Ghost Drivers are 100 percent invisible to them. However, the Ghost Drivers are still there. I can see them. Usually their partner can see them too.

Sometimes people tell me they had a great childhood—two parents who loved them and are still married, no fighting, idyllic really. And yet their adult life doesn't reflect that: they are in an unhappy second or third marriage, are a workaholic, and have a rage brewing ever close to the surface. They cannot see any of their childhood Ghost Drivers. When this is the case, I start looking for emotional incest. Far more times than not, I find it.

Emotional Incest

Emotional incest is when the parenting energy gets backwards. In a healthy parent-child relationship, it is the parent's job to take care of the emotional needs of the child. In an emotionally incestuous parent-child relationship, it is the child's job to take care of the parent's needs. Adults who were the "chosen child," or their parent's "best friend" or the "surrogate spouse" while growing up most likely have emotional incest feeding their *I'm not good enough* dragon. In that case, it is very difficult for them to see that they are, indeed, being driven by their Ghost Drivers.

Now, I believe, no parent emotionally incests their child on purpose. They are unaware of the damage they are doing. I think, in general, people love their children and are doing the best job they can at raising them—given the tools and the wounding they have. That is, everyone's behavior makes sense once you know their history.

There are some circumstances, too, that lend themselves to emotional incest. If a parent is married to an emotionally unavailable partner, they will often turn to a child to get their emotional needs met. The child becomes this parent's primary relationship, instead of the partner. If a child is an only child being raised by a single parent, there is a high probability of emotional incest as well. If a child is extremely talented in sports, music, or academics, they are sometimes put on a pedestal and almost worshipped, getting benefits their siblings go without. They learn *in order to be loved, I have to perform*. They also get a guilt Ghost Driver that constantly reminds them to feel bad when they are made to "feel special." If there is addiction in the family, this increases the chances of emotional incest too.

Let me give you an example. I am working with a fourteen-year-old boy right now whose mother is an alcoholic. He is an only child. His father has, for the most part, checked out of the situation, having moved to a separate bedroom years ago and going to bed as soon as his wife has had two drinks. This leaves the son to worry. He waits up until one, two, or three in the morning when his mother passes out, takes off her shoes, brings her bed pillow to her, and covers her with a blanket. For this, he gets praise in the morning, "You are the *best* son!" This is a family who has brought him to therapy because he is not doing well in school. Of course not! He's exhausted. They are totally blind to what is going on at a deeper level.

Emotional incest is so very, very hard to see while you are in it. Sometimes the parent hovers constantly over their child, vicariously experiencing life through him/her. The parent often takes the child's side over the spouse's. They can become their child's "best friend" by insisting that the child do social activities with them. I worked with a woman whose father took her to all of his office dinners and dances because his wife "didn't want to go." This made the little girl feel very, very loved and special. Little did my client realize the *I'm not good enough* Ghost Driver could come from this—but it did. It manifested itself in raging at her husband because he was unable to make her feel loved "like her dad did." She was angry all the time because the world did not recognize her as the princess she felt she was. At the same time, she felt incapable of taking charge of her life because she should be taken care of. She felt abandoned and betrayed by her father after he divorced her mother and married a much younger woman. She hated her stepmother. All of her behaviors were actually emotional incest Ghost Drivers running her life, of course. My heart went out to her with compassion since emotional incest Ghost Drivers are so, so hard to get rid of. They're the worst. Their damage is as severe as the ones from actual incest.

Here's another version of it. One of my clients told me about her stay-at-home mom:

"My mom was severely depressed, never happy. My parents were having a hard time in their marriage, and their therapist told them to have a kid. I was the kid. I was somehow, from the day I was born, supposed to make my mom happy."

Emotional incest can also be done in a negative way: one parent will scapegoat a child, releasing all of their rage onto him/her. The child is the "chosen child," but is used as the parent's lightning rod. So damaging.

There are many, many ways that emotional incest manifests itself, but all use the child to get the parental emotional needs met. The child learns at some level not to have needs of their own and that love is not safe.

This leads to the person having a split in their self-evaluation. They embody both ends of the self-esteem spectrum at the same time: I am special (and therefore the rules don't apply to me), and I am worthless (because I know I am a fraud because I learned to hide the real me).

Emotional incest Ghost Drivers tell the person they are not safe in opening up to love. Love to them equals suffocation and disappearing, so they are only able to half commit in a relationship. This fear of commitment may manifest in having one foot in and one foot out of their marriage. It may result in affairs, a secret life, or just an emotional wall that keeps their partner at a distance. When I see these things in a relationship, I know the emotional incest Ghost Drivers are in charge.[2]

In therapy, I work hard to make it emotionally safe enough for anyone who was emotionally incested as a child to eventually be able to see, as Steve Jobs did, what is glaringly obvious to others. But it is difficult.

So, if you are aware that you are carrying around some variation of the I'm not worthy/I'm not good enough wound and you can connect it somehow, somewhere to your first twenty years of life, that's good news. Why? It makes it easier to find your subconscious Ghost Drivers. If you do not have this awareness, you may need some

---

[2] If you would like to learn more about emotional incest, please read Pat Love's book, *The Emotional Incest Syndrome*, as well as my first book, *The Emotionally Unavailable Man: A Blueprint for Healing*.

outside help to get there. Do not hesitate to seek out a therapist who is familiar with emotional incest.

You Are Not Alone

Because you, because all of us, carry *the* intergenerational/universal wound of *I am not good enough*, you can rest assured you are not alone. In fact, you are having the human experience on this planet. As stated earlier, our world, at this point, is not such that it supports the pure, wonderful love that comes with every baby. We have to change that—and you can be part of that change—but for now, for your growth work, it's important for you to realize you are just like everyone else. You have Ghost Drivers running your life. You have Ghost Drivers who are reacting, trying to escape the feeling of I'm not good enough.

Each of us somehow believes that we are the only one walking around with this deep, at-our-core feeling that we are somehow lacking. We feel everyone else is okay but not us. Everyone else has it together but not us. Everyone else's life is wonderful—but not ours. Social media has fed into this untruth.

And it is an untruth. I have a cartoon picture that has a big sign in a large hall that says: Seminar for People Raised in Perfectly Functional Families. There are five hundred seats in the hall—two are taken. And those two, I would bet, were emotionally incested and can't even see the dysfunction they were raised in.

Egocentricity

Every person on the planet gets the *I'm not good enough* wound handed to them when they are growing up to one extent or another primarily for two reasons: we have imperfect parents who are carrying their own *I'm not good enough* wound and because children are egocentric. That is, they are only able to see things from their point of view. They feel as if they are the center of the universe, causing the universe.

Think of a fourteen-year-old who wakes up to find a big pimple right on the end of his nose. His reaction? "Well, I can't go to *school*!" I mean, the school building would surely fall down, or all of the students would run out of the doors horrified to see a pimple right on the end of this guy's nose! That is, as a child, it's all about *me*.

When my youngest was about four years old and we would be having a discussion at the dinner table, after a few minutes, he would often pipe up and say, "Okay! Now it's time to talk about me! Who knows what my favorite color is? How about my favorite ice cream?" Egocentric. That's an example of the fun side of it, but the other side of the coin is where the damage comes in.

From a child's perspective, if something goes wrong, it's their fault. That is, if my parents get a divorce, it's because I didn't work hard enough to keep them together. In fact, one of my six-year-old clients told me her parents got a divorce because she didn't keep her room clean enough. Egocentric. If I get yelled at, it's because I'm bad. If a parent abandons me, it's because I'm unlovable. If there is yelling or tension in the household, it's because I, the child, caused it.

I have a client whose parents were divorced when he was five. He then lived with his mother but had regular contact with his father. One day, when he was about twelve years old, his alcoholic father was yelling and screaming at him, and this adolescent boy spouted off, "Don't yell at me!" The father said, "Fine." He then took my client home and never spoke to him again. *Never*. Do you think that boy developed an *I'm not good enough / I'm not worthy of love wound*? You bet he did. When his father wouldn't return his phone calls, never sent him another birthday gift, packed up and moved to another state, do you think that young boy was able to see there was something wrong with his *father* and not him? Of course not. He blamed himself and fully embraced "There's something wrong with *me*."

That's because that's how children's brains work. They make

it about them. Period. Consequently, my client's Ghost Drivers helped him find just the right marital partner—one who would abandon him.

In my own life, I had an alcoholic, sociopathic dad who didn't love me. It took me many years to come to the awareness that his inability to love didn't make me unlovable. In fact, I was always lovable, and because of *his* childhood wounding, he never developed an ability to love. Anyone. It had nothing to do with me, but as a child, of course, I made it all about me. Then as an adult, my Ghost Driver took over trying to prove to me that because my dad didn't love me, nobody would. I, of course, picked partners who, because of their own wounding, were not able to be there for me. It took me a long time to see that Ghost Driver—and fire him.

The War

I had a soul-opening experience with my younger son one day just after his eighteenth birthday that underlined to me how stealthy Ghost Drivers can be.

He was lying on the couch. When I sat down next to him, he pulled a pillow over his head. Asking him what was wrong, he said he was a little depressed. When I asked what was going on, he said, "I thought when I turned eighteen that I would get rid of all the baggage you gave me. And all the baggage Dad gave me."

That got my attention.

He thought turning eighteen meant you were an adult, and therefore you would feel the freedom of an emotional adult and live in Lifetime Two with no Ghost Drivers. I hated to be the barer of bad news: "No, honey, that's your baggage. That's the stuff you have to figure out and get rid of. That's your dragon to conquer. You have to find your Ghost Drivers and fire them. I'm so sorry."

In the process of our discussion, a light came on in a new room in my brain, one that I had never been in before. Suddenly, and I do mean suddenly, I saw clearly that *he* at eighteen was *me* at eighteen:

an overachiever who was highly successful at almost everything he took on but with no self-esteem to back it up. He didn't feel good enough!

I literally felt without air at that moment. *How* could this have happened? I am a psychotherapist. I am in therapy all day long every day. I consider myself a person who is awake, yet how could I not have seen it? Hello—because Ghost Drivers are *ghosts.*

I apologized. I told him that he was *absolutely* right—that I *had* given him baggage and that his dad had too. But unwittingly!

I explained to him the parenting I had received and the parenting my parents had received. I told him my grandparents had passed their wounding onto my parents, who had passed their wounding onto me, and that I had—he finished my sentence—"passed it onto me." "Yes," I said with sad resignation. "Passed it onto you."

I went on to explain to him that I wanted him to know, to really *know*, that the personal war I was fighting when he was growing up had nothing to do with him. It had to do with me—and all the messages I was given when I was growing up. In other words, I had been fighting my Ghost Drivers. Also that the war his dad was fighting had nothing to do with him as well. His dad's war had to do with fighting against all the messages he was given when he was growing up: his Ghost Drivers. Further, I said, it took me a *long* time to understand that the war I was fighting had nothing to do with his dad. And the war his dad was fighting had nothing to do with me. We were each just fighting the *I'm not good enough* war.

Further still, I told my youngest that the war his older brother was fighting had nothing to do with his girlfriend—and that the war his girlfriend was fighting had nothing to do with his older brother. That, instead, we are all fighting fear around the erroneous messages of "not good enough" that we were given when we were growing up—usually projecting that onto those closest to us. Our fear is, *What if what they told me is true?*

As the discussion progressed, I explain to my son, as I will explain to you, the way the war ends; the way you are able to put down your weapons is to fall in love with yourself. Your real self, your authentic self. And then, to fire your Ghost Drivers.

The hope for my son is that he was having this discussion with me at eighteen years old. I didn't have this discussion with my parents until I was thirty-eight—a full twenty years later. My son and I committed to working through his baggage as best we could so that, perhaps, he could be rid of it by the time he had his own children. One can hope. Confronting his *I'm not good enough* dragon, however, is a battle he will have to fight himself. He will have to work through his egocentricity, identify his Ghost Drivers, grieve, fall in love with himself, reprogram his computer, wrestle those Ghost Drivers down, and then fire them. Only then will he be able to take over driving his own emotional car and experience the freedom of being an empowered adult.

In therapy, I say it this way: Growing up has three steps. The first step is recognizing your family of origin issues and identifying your Ghost Drivers. The second is to fall in love with yourself, fire those Ghost Drivers, and step into the responsibility of driving your own life. The third is realizing that growing up is a process, not an event. That means you will likely have to repeat these three steps over and over again until those Ghost Drivers take you seriously and leave you alone at least for a while. But then, I'm sorry to say, they will show up again, and you will have to recognize them as fast as you can and fire them again, all the while continuing to love and celebrate your authentic, empowered adult self, doing hard things, walking toward things you'd like to avoid. So let's find your Ghost Drivers.

CHAPTER 18

The Need to Grieve

Let's look first for your Ghost Drivers in the family you grew up in, your family of origin, your FOO. This is where you got a lot of your childhood wounding but certainly not all of it. Still, let's start there.

It is essential to figure out what happened to you as you were growing up, feel the feelings around that, work on forgiveness, and then let it go. These next two chapters are about that. However, a word of caution: you may have already done your family of origin work—ad nauseam. In that case, it is time to focus on the letting it go part.

So many times, people are stuck in their story. They are stuck in what happened to them and what was done to them. They know quite clearly what their mom did to them, or didn't do to take care of them. They understand the absent father they had. They can tell of the silence in their house or of the screaming. They can outline beautifully what it was like in high school when they felt friendless and had an eating disorder. They can vividly recall their suicidal thoughts. They feel the feelings when they tell the stories. They cry. The problem is they have done this for years with a myriad of therapists. In other words, they are stuck in Lifetime One.

If this is you, it is time to move on. You must be honest with yourself: is it time to let go of your story?

For example, I had a client who had been sexually abused when she was twelve years old. She met a cute boy who was twenty-two years old, thought she was older, and had sex with her. This led to years of promiscuity. The deeper issue was that she had an emotionally unavailable father as well as a distant mother, so she spent so much of her lifetime looking for someone—anyone—to love her. As an adult, she was in one awful relationship after another—and at one therapist's office after another as well. By the time she got to my office, she had been in therapy addressing all these issues for more than twenty-five years. It was clear to me that she understood where she got her unlovable wound. She understood the dynamics of her FOO very, very well, as well as the sexual abuse that happened to her at age twelve. She had grieved and grieved and grieved these things but was stuck in feeling like and reenacting a victim stance. Her work with me, then, didn't include looking at her family of origin or even the sexual abuse very much. Her work was to move from reacting to the wounding, putting that behind her, emotionally growing up, and taking charge of her life.

I had another client who came to me at age seventy-two. She was still crying—literally crying—about the way she had been treated in high school. She had been left out of the popular group. Since then, she had gone to therapy for forty years, telling the same stories to different therapists. She, clearly, had done that enough, and it was time for her to actually do the work to grow up. Her story was being used to avoid taking responsibility for creating a life that was happy and full.

So, if you are a person who has worked on your FOO stuff for years, just skim through the next couple of chapters. Your work is in letting go of your story. Your story no longer serves you. It just keeps you stuck in Lifetime One. It is what you are using to avoid growing up.

However, if you have *not* done your family of origin work, pay very close attention to this chapter as well as the next one. Do the exercises in them. It is essential to know at a conscious level what you carry around unconsciously.

Off the Pedestal

So, where do we start? We have to be willing to take our parents off the pedestal and look at them honestly. We have to separate our love for them from their behavior. They are/were good people—but they had some holes in the parenting they gave you. I know this, or you would already be living in the higher love vibration all the time. Since you're not, something happened to you when you were thrown into Lifetime One that is still not resolved. What was it?

You'll have to dig deep. The Ghost Drivers are ghosts, after all, and they like to hide. Still, we have to find them.

I'm not a big fan of written exercises in books, but occasionally there is one that is just so necessary to do. This is one of them. Please do this one:

In private, write down on a piece of paper what went *wrong* in your childhood. We don't have to fix what went right, so don't bother to write those things down. Focus instead on what didn't work. Start with your parents and write down every time you were hurt by them. Then expand your writing to include every time you were hurt by anyone. Write and write and write.

The things you write on your list don't even have to be accurate. They can just be from your point of view as a child. They will be things that absolutely made you feel wrong or stupid or unlovable. They can be big; they can be small.

For example, when I was nine years old, before bed sheets were permanent press, one of my chores was to iron everyone's sheets. My mother showed me how to iron the first one and then left me in the basement with a pile to do myself. After a short time, she passed back into the room to check on me. Evidently, I didn't have the ironing thing down quite right, as my mother said very seriously, "Honey, the object is to iron the wrinkles *out*—not to iron them *in*." She took the iron out of my hand and ironed out a wrinkle I had ironed in, then handed the iron back to me. I felt humiliated. I felt less than. I felt mortified that I couldn't even iron a flat sheet correctly! I took it as criticism and grabbed hold just a little bit more to the I'm not good enough wound.

Now I think, *What the heck was a nine-year-old doing ironing by herself anyway?*

Regardless, this is an example of writing events where a child's perception wasn't even accurate. My mother wasn't saying, "You're not good enough." She was saying, "Be more careful, and let me show you again," but because I was an egocentric child, I heard it as a criticism of *me*.

So write down everything you can think of where you got the message that you weren't okay, lovable, good enough, and so on. See it from the child's eyes—not the adult's.

This exercise may take a couple of days to do, as you will take a while remembering. Add to your list each day. Try to think of yourself as that pure, innocent love—and notice what happened to you to make that go away. Think of the abandonments. Think of the discipline. Think of all the things that weren't fair. Expand beyond your family. Think of the people at school who hurt you. Think of your siblings who hurt you. Think of edicts your mother or father said about you. Think of when you were laughed at. Think about whether you were left alone a lot. Think of when you were forced to sit and listen to your mother rant and rave at you. Think of when your father sat there passively as you were treated unfairly. Think of when you were not protected and should have been.

Think of any craziness in the house. Think of how your parents treated each other. Think of when you were embarrassed. Think of any moves you had to make as a child. Think of spankings/beatings. Think of when you cried. Think of when you shut down and stopped crying. Think of harsh things your father said to you. Think of wounds that happened with your classmates, your teachers, your coaches. Think of losing a beloved pet. Think of all the times you were confused. Think of the rejections. The betrayals. Think of your losses. Think of all the hurtful things anyone said to you, and write them down. Think of when your parents gave your dog away

153

when you were at school. Think of the failures. Think of the times you lied. Think of yourself as a teen—did you feel good enough then? Think of family dinners and family holidays. Think of the disappointments. Think of when you were scared or lonely or left. Write, write, write.

Remember, every time a child is yelled at, they are changed. Were you yelled at? Write every single incident down that you can possibly think of. Write down even the ones you don't personally remember but were told to you. For example, here are a few things my clients have told me they were told:

1. We wanted a boy (girl) but got you instead.
2. You were a surprise baby. We didn't plan this pregnancy.
3. Your father wanted nothing to do with you from day one.
4. I never wanted kids.
5. You were a horrible baby—all you did was cry, cry, cry.
6. Don't worry, you're just in your ugly stage.
7. You always were wanting more and more time, and I was busy!
8. You're stupid.
9. Just leave me alone!
10. Just shut up and keep the peace. Don't say *anything*. Got it?

Here are some examples of clients' perceptions of their childhoods:

1. I was raised by a pack of wolves. No one talked.
2. At my house, there were four of us. Each night, we got our dinner from the pan on the stove and then retreated to our own rooms to watch television on our own TVs. We never ate supper together.
3. My dad never stood up for himself. He was a nonentity.
4. My parents had twelve kids. We were called by our number, not our name. I was #8.

5. In my family, we lived on a farm. The kids were a bother because there was always work to be done. We were expected to do our chores and not have any needs. We were not talked to. We were ignored—unless we didn't get our chores done. Then all hell would break loose, and we'd *all* get a beating.

6. My mother had the power—she was a hurricane, completely out of control.

7. My brother had autism. That says it all. He took up all the space.

8. I have three sisters. They are all doctors. I didn't do well in school, so I was the scapegoat.

9. My parents were done parenting by the time I came along. They were tired. So I was allowed to do anything I wanted. My friends were envious of me, but it really made me feel like I didn't matter.

10. My dad would buy me video games that my mom said I couldn't have. He told me just to lie to her if she asked about it, so I did.

Write it all down. Write down anything you were told—and remember, it could be a small thing, a big thing, something done to you on purpose, or something done to you by accident. And it could be just your perception of what was done to you.

I was recently visiting my sister as she was watching her two-year-old grandson. Suddenly he leaned on an end table that had a glass tabletop that began to tip. We all screamed, "No!" Her little pure-love grandson looked up at us confused and then, slowly, seemed to shatter before our eyes as he collapsed on the floor into sobs. I don't think he had ever been yelled at before, and he was brokenhearted by it. We felt horrible, but the damage was already done. We were not saying to him, "You did something wrong. There is something wrong with you." We were saying, "Be careful! We love you so much we want you to be safe." That, of course, is not the message he received.

Do you remember any of those moments happening to you?

If you are having a hard time remembering things, don't hesitate to ask your siblings and relatives what they remember about your childhood. They may say, "Nothing," but they may have invaluable information for you.

When I mentioned this idea to one of my clients who was about fifty-five and highly, highly successful and sought after in his field, he literally shuddered at the thought. He was the youngest of six children, a surprise child born nine years after his next older sibling. He had always felt less than since they all knew so much more than he did while he was growing up. They laughed at his innocence, they made fun of his ignorance, and they dismissed his ideas as juvenile. So, he wondered, how could he ask *them* for memories? He was terrified at the thought, thinking he would be made fun of all over again. Talking further, he discovered it never occurred to him that he could talk to his sibs as an adult and not the little brother. With this idea in mind, he was able to take his adult self along as he asked their help in figuring out what lurked at a subconscious level for him.

One thing he found out was his father had written an autobiography. He read it, and though it was written when my client was nine years old, his father talked about each of his five siblings in detail—and left him out. There was *no* mention of him in the book. This gave him information: the rejection from his father was bigger than he thought. He was beginning to understand why he felt so less than when he was among a group of men.

So, don't be afraid to use your siblings and other relatives as a resource. Add their memories to your list. I have a client who is fairly young who has no memories of his childhood—not even his teachers' names. He asked his sister to help him remember their childhood, and she said she didn't want to remember it because it was too painful. That's a clue he was given the I'm not good enough wound. In fact, when people have few, if any, memories of their childhood, it usually means there was a lot of trauma and chaos in the household. We tend to block trauma from our conscious memory as a coping mechanism to survive.

For example, another client, who was about age thirty, had very few memories as well. When he asked his older brother to tell what he remembered, he told him of the time they had a dinner party at their house and someone said something that made their dad mad. The result? Their dad flew into a rage, picked up the table, and dumped it over, food and all. The guests and the family sat there stunned. Again, a clue. This kind of behavior is not adult behavior. It is two-year-old temper tantrum behavior. Children being raised by emotional two-year-olds get wounded. This father clearly was not coming from an "I am enough" place.

And, if your parents didn't know they were lovable and good enough, they couldn't teach you that you were. Thus, the wounding got passed on.

You might write down on your list, too, what happened to you after you left home that seemed to reinforce that feeling of not being good enough or worthy. It might have shown up in relationships, maybe in jobs, maybe in friendships.

Look at your current behaviors too. That is, you can find your Ghost Drivers by doing things in reverse. Look at your behaviors and then try to connect them back to your history. Look at how your life is/isn't working. Look for any feedback you get repeatedly. Look for any "stucks" that you are currently experiencing. Look for things you say repeatedly to your partner. All of these things will help you find your Ghost Drivers.

For example, if you find yourself constantly feeling judged, that is probably a childhood wound that you are projecting out to others. People say to me, "No matter what I do, it's wrong! No matter what I do, it's not good enough!" Then they try over and over and over again to be "good enough." This is an example of the child being in charge, driving the car. The other side of the coin, of course, is doing things to prove you are not good enough: not paying the bills, showing up late for work every day, lying to your partner, and so on.

Tie it back to childhood messages. It will involve recognizing that you felt you were never good enough as a child. Perhaps it was not feeling good enough to deserve a parent's love or time or attention because your parent was gone a lot, worked a lot, or was just preoccupied with other things. I have one client whose mother would lock herself in her bedroom after he got home from school each day. He would stand at the door, begging her to please open it. She would not. This lent itself to my client feeling, "No matter what I do, it's not good enough to get my mother's love." He replicated this behavior with his wife, of course.

Remember, children either join a wound—believe it as given—or they rebel against it—do the opposite of what they were given to "prove" it isn't true. For example, if a person joins the wound "No matter what I do, it's not good enough to get my mother's love," they come to believe no matter what they do, it doesn't measure up, so they start being not good enough. They start doing behaviors to prove what the child believes. Or, if the child rebels against this message, they become superstars who are constantly seeking outside approval to prove they *are* good enough. They get three PhDs, they run ten marathons in a year, they buy a huge house. Either way, their Ghost Drivers are in charge.

Perhaps you were emotionally incested as a child and never felt loved for *you* but only for taking care of your parent's emotional needs. The result of this wound? Now you are constantly taken advantage of because you never say no. You have no boundaries. You let people walk all over you. That's a Ghost Driver. Or, you might never let anyone in too close because love means de-selfing—having to be what the other person wants you to be instead of being who you really are. That's a Ghost Driver.

Or maybe you were called a tease when you were a little girl, "boy crazy." Children, of course, live up to or down to their parents' expectations. The problem with this is the mother and father's expectations are coming from *their* woundedness! Anyway, this Ghost Driver may look like infidelity. I have a client who is married to a wonderful, beautiful, successful man, and yet she keeps finding herself picking up men to sleep with every time she is out of town, living down to the names her father had called her as a teen: a slut, a whore. Another way this wound may show up is to rebel against it by becoming sexually anorexic and having no sex drive.

So look hard for your Ghost Drivers. Some will be glaring, some will be a surprise to find. Some will be almost impossible to see.

Learned Helplessness

One such childhood wound is learned helplessness. It can look like not being bright. It can look like being lazy. It can look like disinterest. This term, coined by psychologist Martin Seligman in 1967, came from his experiments with animals as he was studying the causes of depression.

What he found was, when an animal is repeatedly hurt by an adverse stimulus, in this case an electrical shock, there comes a moment when the animal will just stop trying to escape the pain. It will no longer bark, it will no longer look for ways to escape the room, it will no longer jump from one area of the room to another. It will lie down and endure the shocks. Finally, when opportunities to escape the room are presented, this "learned helplessness" will prevent any action. The dog will stay exactly where it is, enduring the pain.

This happens to humans too. There comes a point where we just give up. We come to believe we are helpless, there is no hope of change, and so we are paralyzed and do nothing. We become passive. A very interesting part, too, is that a child can learn this by watching a parent encountering uncontrollable events. This happens when there is domestic violence in the house. This happens when a child is raised in a war zone. This happens, sometimes, when a parent has an out-of-control addiction where verbal abuse and rage is prevalent.

I work in a foundation with a man who watched his mother be beaten daily by her boyfriend. One day, as a child of twelve, he came home and found his mother had been shot to death, five times in the face. Even after dealing with the trauma, it took this man *years* to understand and believe his mother's helplessness was not his helplessness. Up until that point, he didn't try in school, eventually didn't go to school, and spent his days sitting on the couch passively watching television for hours. He had no concept that *he* could design a fulfilling life for himself. His Ghost Drivers, of course, were in full control.

Posttraumatic Stress Disorder: PTSD

I suggest to people who have had such severe trauma as watching a murder, being gang-raped, being in an active war having killed people, watching someone be tortured, or another such atrocity, seek professional help to deal with the trauma. The trauma needs to be recognized and felt before the Ghost Drivers from the trauma can be identified. Sometimes the circuitry of our brain explodes. This has to be rewired by confronting the trauma and can only be done one inch at a time. The best way is working with a therapist who is trained and has experience in EMDR, eye movement desensitization and reprocessing.

I once worked with a man who was raped in the shower by a beloved uncle when he was six years old. He was told not to turn around or he would be killed. He was told never to mention this to anyone, or his whole family would be killed. By the time I met him, he was thirty-six. He didn't let anyone touch him—ever. He worked by himself at home. He lived by himself. He very rarely left his apartment. He had no friends. He identified feeling numb. The fact that he sought therapy was a miracle to me, but something inside of him started pushing him to grow.

So, I told him his work was going to need to include massage therapy. It took him four months to agree to see a massage therapist who I knew was excellent. In their first session, he was able to enter the room where the massage table was set up, lean against it, and take off his jacket. That was it. His recovery from the trauma took another year. Then, and only then, could we start to identify how and where the Ghost Drivers were in charge.

So, if you have had this level of trauma, I am sorry. Recovery is possible, however. Just get professional help to guide you through the healing process. After that, then you can go back and do the rest of your grieving.

Time to Grieve

So, after you have written at least ten to twenty pages of hurtful incidents, I want you to go to a very private space and, if you can, look at a picture of yourself at the youngest age you can find. If you only have your senior yearbook picture when you were eighteen, then use that. But if you can find one when you were two or three, all the better. You might find a happy picture, you might find a sad one. One of my clients used a picture of himself at about eight or nine years old, holding a brand-new puppy, staring blankly at the camera with no smile or life on his face, and with distant and dead eyes. His wounding had clearly happened earlier in his life. That was a clue for him. So get your picture or pictures. Then close your eyes. Try to feel like little you—sweet and innocent. If you have a small child in your life currently, think of how loving and wonderful they are. You were like that too. Feeling like the child, breathe deeply and exhale three times. Next, read all the things that happened to little you out loud—and cry for him/her. If the real tears don't come, fake them. That's right. Lean over and pretend to cry. Make sounds as if you are crying. This often will prompt the real tears to flow. If not, don't worry. The fake tears will suffice. Rock yourself with your eyes closed. Cry for that little boy or that little girl. That sweet, precious, pure-love little boy or little girl that you once were.

This is all about grieving what happened to you. I know it sounds like a weird thing to do, but it is a very important step that has to happen in order to leave Lifetime One. That is, finish Lifetime One as much as you can. Shine a light on those Ghost Drivers.

Anger

Now, you might not be able to get vulnerable enough to get to your tears. You might just feel anger—and lots of it. That's okay too. Anger is a secondary emotion that covers up hurt. If you feel angry, start there. Eventually you will break through to the more vulnerable place of hurt.

Sit down and write a letter to each of your parents and/or caregivers telling them how mad you are. Tell them how they hurt you. Use curse words every other word if you would like, but mostly tell them all about how much pain you have been in because of their parenting or lack thereof. These letters are *not* to be sent. They are only a vehicle to help you get to the unresolved pain that you are carrying around.

After you write the letters, read them out loud. If your parents are dead, go to their gravesides and read your letters to them. Hopefully this will allow you to get to the more vulnerable place of tears. Then burn the letters.

This exercise is good to do every time you feel stuck. Write to your parents. Connect it back to the messages they gave you in childhood. Again, these letters are not to be sent.

When I first began my practice, I had a client who would call me at home, having gotten my number from the phone book, and rage at me. After the third or fourth time, it occurred to me that I needed a boundary! So, I told her she could call me only after she had written a letter to her mother. She called the next day raging. I asked her if she had written the letter to her mother, and she had not. I told her to call me back if she needed to after she had written the letter. She didn't call back. She didn't need to. She used this letter-writing technique over and over again for about three months. And then she was done. The anger was gone, the hurt was gone, the fear of the pain was gone. She was free.

Now, go back and read the list to your picture of yourself when you were young. Fake the tears and cry if you can. Big belly sobs.

Then, in closing, visualize yourself at the age you are today going through a time portal and finding yourself when you were little, little. Have the adult you take the hand of little you, saying, "You are coming with me now. From now on, I will protect you. They can't hurt you anymore." Then walk back through the portal and into the present with your child self. Take a deep breath. With your eyes closed, give yourself a big hug and whisper, "I will keep you safe."

This is an exercise you may need to do repeatedly to get rid of all your grief. For some people, one time is enough; for others, they may do this exercise over and over again for weeks.

Just a word about if you cannot come up with any incidents that were negative in your childhood: this is not good news. It means your heart is blocked. You may need to do an experiential program to get to your grief and your heart. Experiential means that your body will be involved in doing the emotional work. We hold memories in our bodies. Getting your body involved—rather than just talking—seems to be necessary when there is a lot of trauma in a person's history. I like the Hoffman Institute's one-week program, the Hoffman Process, for healing your heart. That is my number one recommendation, though I like the Mankind Project's New Warrior Training Adventure weekend as well. I like Colin Tipping's Radical Forgiveness program. The Landmark Forum is helpful too. Of course, if you have an addiction, the twelve-step programs are the best. There are many other programs available too. Look around for something that you would feel uncomfortable doing—and do that one. Read the books that are on the recommended reading list at the end of this book as well.

Denial

Just know, we are all capable of incredible denial. This is either an avoidance technique to resist taking the reins of your life, or it happens when the pain is too great to face. When a client tells me their childhood was, "Great! I had a *great* childhood! There was no negative at all—it was just great!" it makes me a little nervous. I know it won't be long before we uncover *a lot*.

In my own home, I definitely thought we had a perfect family. I just had to overlook the alcoholism, the sexual abuse, the neglect, the valium, the divorces, the suicide, the depression, the raging, and the lies. And I did—for many years. I was finally able to break through my denial system when a friend took me to an Adult Children of Alcoholics meeting when I was in my twenties. I thought he had asked me to go along to support him. Turns out he could see the pain I carried long before I could see it myself.

So we have to get to our pain in order to get rid of it. We have to feel our pain so that it can't hold us hostage anymore. Once we go through the pain, our past won't have so much power over us. That is, if we are terrified of feeling emotional pain, we have to keep everything tightly packaged up from our childhood. The problem with this strategy is we can never find our Ghost Drivers this way—and they continue running our lives.

If, on the other hand, we are willing to go deep *into* the pain, letting ourselves feel it thoroughly, we find that we are free. The fear of feeling the pain has kept us from being able to fully claim the reins of our life. And remember the goal: to outgrow our fear. Thich Nhat Hanh says it this way:

> No fear is the ultimate joy. Once you have
> mastered the insight of no fear, you are free.

I meditated on this quote for six months. Every day, I read it. Every day, I thought and thought about it.

No fear? What the heck is that? Is that even possible?

Is the ultimate joy? Really? The ultimate joy, beyond all others. I wondered, *Is that true?*

Once you have mastered—mastered? So it's not a one-time thing; it's a mastery of something, which takes time and energy. Okay, so I need to put in time and energy.

Mastered the insight—oh, now there's a word. *Insight. Webster's* defines it this way: the capacity to gain an accurate and deep understanding of something. Again, this implies time, study, effort.

The insight of no fear—the wisdom of it, the deep knowing and understanding of it, the experience of it. I realized I could not master the insight of no fear without walking it. That is, I could not learn to swim without getting in the water. I had to push myself toward things I was afraid of in order to grow into no fear. I had to let myself feel pain so as to diffuse its power over me.

You are free. Wow. *Free?* I wanted to be free. I wanted to be free of the fear and all the gunk I'd been carrying around. I wanted to be free of the fear of not being good enough. I wanted to be free of the fear of not having enough money. I wanted to be free of the fear of being part of something big and important. I wanted to be free of the fear of never finding a partner who really loved me. I wanted to be free.

What about you?

We cannot master fear by avoiding it. We must be willing to feel our emotional pain in order to realize we have been controlled by fearing it. We must face it and feel it, as stated above, to diffuse its power.

The fear is much bigger than the event. I remember at age thirty-five finally getting my ears pierced. I had been terrified of the thought of how painful it would be to have a hole pierced into my earlobe for more than twenty years. Then one day I got brave enough to be willing to go through the pain. I went to the mall—and poof! In less than one second, the earring was in my ear. I had been afraid for so long about this, yet, as it turned out, it was nothing. I was more than capable of going through the process.

You are capable too. The pain you have bottled up is manageable. People tell me, "I'm afraid if I start crying, I'll never stop." No, you will. Everyone does. And when you do stop, you will no longer be afraid of looking honestly at any situation, feeling your feelings about it, and then being able to take action to create the peace and joy that you want in your life. Feeling your pain is a way of not letting emotions blackmail you. It's a way of outgrowing your fear—which is what you want, right?

Then forgiveness and moving further down the dark and scary path is possible. In fact, the path doesn't seem as dark and scary anymore. It's only by doing what we are afraid of that we outgrow our fear.

For example, I used to be deathly afraid of needles and shots. I mean, major anxiety. I would sweat, have a racing heart, and sometimes pass out. Then I had to have a five-hour glucose tolerance test. This means that blood is drawn every thirty minutes for five hours. The first time they took my blood, they strapped me into the chair so if I passed out I wouldn't fall. Thirty minutes later, they strapped me into the chair again. Thirty minutes later, I told them I didn't think I was going to pass out, so there was no need to strap me into the chair. Thirty minutes later, I was almost calm when they drew the blood. Thirty minutes later, I was calm. By the time they were on the last drawing of the blood, I just sat in the chair 100 percent calm and put my arm up joyfully with no reservations or hesitation. Since then, more than thirty years ago, I have had absolutely no fear of needles. None.

That's how confronting our pain works. Using your courage you step up to your pain, let yourself feel it, and then in short order, you will be through it. After that, it will no longer have power over you. Your Ghost Drivers will no longer be driving you around convincing you to do crazy things to avoid the pain. You won't need to avoid it.

You'll know you are capable of facing it, feeling it, and being done with it.

Furthermore, the irony of it is that you will look back and be shocked by what you were afraid to face and feel. You will be able to see the little old man behind the curtain pushing levers and buttons pretending to be the great Wizard of Oz.

Next, let's look at forgiveness.

Chapter 19

Forgiveness

There are two areas where you have to forgive. First, you have to forgive all those who hurt you, particularly your parents or primary caregivers; and second, you must forgive yourself.

But what exactly *is* forgiveness?

Basically, forgiveness is a decision to let go of any resentment, anger, and thoughts of revenge toward someone who has hurt you in one way or another.

Forgiveness doesn't deny or minimize the wrong that was done to you. It doesn't say you are excusing the act or condoning it. It is simply the act of letting go of the hurt, anger, resentment, and desire for revenge you carry around it.

I am often asked by clients who have been wronged—especially in a big way like they were sexually abused as a child, or their sister was murdered, or their parent committed suicide, or something else big—do they have to forgive that person?

I say yes. Not now. But some day.

Why? Because I believe forgiving can heal not only marriages, families, communities, nations, and the world—but it can heal *you*. If you are carrying around hurt, anger, resentment, or the desire for revenge, it is taking up your brain space and most definitely blocking your heart. It is an energy drain, and it keeps you stuck in the yuck.

The goal is to get out of the yuck and to get on with getting to the good life. Forgiveness is definitely part of that equation.

The Mayo Clinic tells us it's even good for our health. It can heal disease.

Marianne Williamson says it this way: "The practice of forgiveness is our most important contribution to the healing of the world."

Desmond Tutu: "To choose to forgive rather than demand retribution is to know that my humanity is inextricably caught up in yours."

But, to me, Mother Teresa said it the best: "If we really want to love, we must learn how to forgive."

There is a universal longing, a hunger in every human soul for forgiveness—both to be able to give it and to receive it.

In Ernest Hemingway's short story, "The Capital of the World," he writes about a young man who wrongs his father and runs away from home to the city of Madrid. Out of great love for his son, the father takes out an ad in the Madrid newspaper, "Paco, meet me at the Hotel Montana, 12 noon Tuesday. All is forgiven. Papa." Now Paco is a rather common name in Spain, and so when the father gets to the hotel, he finds eight hundred young men waiting for their fathers.

So forgiveness is a *big deal*. Very important. So how do we get there? Let's start with your parents. We want to be able to get to the point where we can forgive our parents for being imperfect and not being the people we wanted them to be, for not being the parents we needed them to be and wished they had been.

First, it's good to take a hard look at your parents' childhoods because, remember, this process is not about blame. It's about understanding. So, what happened to them? Did they get The Lie that said "you're not good enough" handed to them? Of course they did. Because they, too, were egocentric as well as raised by imperfect parents who had gotten The Lie handed to them.

So, what happened to your parents? What kind of parenting did they have?

How did it affect your parents? Most importantly, how did it affect their parenting? How did the intergenerational wound get passed down to them? To you? You have to look at when they were little. Don't look at your parents as they are today—they may have long outgrown their wounding—but look at them when they were little. See them as little, little, crying all by themselves. Honestly assess the kind of parenting they received and see how it got passed onto you when you were little. Again, don't look at them as they are today; look at the parenting pattern that was passed on to you from them when you were little. Do this with your mom, your dad, and any other primary caretakers you had.

For example, if you met my ninety-year-old stepfather today, you would meet a very calm, kind, loving, amazing man. But if you had met him when I was little, you would have met a reactionary, hotheaded young fellow who sure knew how to slam those doors, punch holes in the walls, and pass out the spankings too. Certainly the I'm not good enough wound had been passed down to him: his father committed suicide when he was two, and his stepfather rejected him. He couldn't help but pass his wound on to me. I, likewise, as stated earlier, know that I passed it on to my young ones. It took me a good amount of time to make my way out of the I'm not good enough wound—and, unfortunately, I didn't do it before my sons were born. If you have children, you probably didn't outgrow your wounding before you had them either.

In fact, it is my experience that most people get married and have children while they are still in Lifetime One, being driven by their wounded child / their Ghost Drivers. However, the sooner parents can get into Lifetime Two, the less wounding will happen to their children. Children need and deserve adults to raise them. So, if you have children, it is essential that you do this work *now*. For my boys, my younger son said I made the shift into an emotional adult when he was eight. That made my older son fourteen. That means my older son will have more to work through than my younger one. They both have work to do but hopefully will be able to do so younger than I did. Also, if your children are fully grown, it's not too late. No matter when you do your work to become an emotional grown-up, it will help them. Think of it this way: would it have helped you at any point if your parents had become emotional grown-ups?

Make a List

Next, think about all the people who have hurt you. Write their names down. Make a list. Start with your primary caregivers and then add on everyone else: teachers, coaches, friends, perpetrators, neighbors, babysitters, exes, bosses, and so on. Write down your memories of how and when they hurt you. Add your name to the bottom of the list.

Again, go to a private place. Close your eyes and take three deep breaths. When you are ready, in your mind's eye, see the first person on your list coming toward you. They approach you and look you right in the eye and then say with sincere depth, "I am sorry for all the pain I gave you, all the pain I caused you, all the pain I passed on to you." Their eyes well up with tears. They may even start to quietly weep. They say, "I didn't know how to do it any better. I am so, so sorry." You can weep with them. Fake the tears if you need to. They didn't know how to *not* pass on the I'm not good enough wound. Think of the parenting they received.

Then they ask you, "Will you forgive me?"

Consider it and then decide: are you ready to let go of your pain, anger, and resentment concerning the hurt this person caused you? If so, forgive them. If not, tell them, "Not today."

If you have chosen to forgive this person, cross them off your list. If not, keep them on.

On another day, do the same exercise with the next person on your list. On subsequent days, do this exercise with each person on your list who hurt you deeply. Do this with as many people as you can to clean out the anger, resentment, and pain you are carrying around. But do it one person at a time / one person a day.

To really experience the vibration of love, we must find compassion for them by remembering that the I'm not good enough wound was handed to them—and the understanding that they passed on to us what was given to them. We must come to find acceptance of them, to love them as the flawed human beings that they are/were and thus forgive them at the deepest part of our being. We must release them from what they did to us with understanding and compassion for what was done to them.

Remember, everybody's behavior makes sense once you understand their history. Consider their history.

In this exercise, it really is okay if someone asks for forgiveness and you are not ready to offer it. Just tell them they'll have to come back another day because you are not ready to let go of the pain they caused you yet. Keep doing the exercise. There will come a day when you are ready to forgive.

For example, when I was last in Chicago, I visited the Mankind Project's center there. I had the privilege of eating breakfast with about fifty men from all around the country who had gone through the New Warrior Training Adventure. Before we ate, the center director asked everyone to stand in a circle and say a one-word check-in. This was the day we were all about to go and be part of the *Oprah* taping, so the words were excited, happy, grateful, adventurous, scared, open, safe, connected, and so on. At the end of the check-in, the center director then asked everyone to take two steps into the circle, go down on one knee, close our eyes, and speak our father's name out loud and welcome him into the circle.

I was shocked at my resistance. I couldn't do it! My biological father had been an alcoholic sociopath who abused me every day I ever spent with him—and I didn't want him in that safe, sacred circle. Long deceased, I didn't even want his *name* there.

I thought about this for a long time. That evening, I did another level of grieving for my little girl self and also for my father's little boy self. His behavior, of course, had come from the you're not good enough wound that was handed to him as a child. I wrote my father a letter and told him what it was like to have him as a father. I cried, and then was able to forgive my father some more, and finally was able to invite him into that circle of men. Not only to invite him but actually to welcome him.

If you are having a particularly hard time forgiving a person because what they did to you was so egregious, I suggest you go to The Forgiveness Project at theforgivenessproject.com. Read some of the stories there. Find ones that are similar to what happened to you. Take your time in forgiving the person who hurt you so much. Honor the pain but move toward the freedom that comes with forgiving.

Self-Forgiveness

Next, we have to forgive ourselves. We have to embrace ourselves with compassion, love, and forgiveness in order to thrive. We must forgive ourselves for not loving ourselves for so many years. We have to forgive ourselves for believing ourselves to be less than. We have to forgive ourselves for taking *so long* to figure things out. It takes a long time to figure out self-love because we have to get rid of that I'm not good enough wound that was given to us first. The Lie. We have to forgive ourselves for believing The Lie. Of course, we were children and believed what we perceived as truth. There was no other way, but we have to forgive ourselves for believing those things. Only then will we be able to embrace the light that we are: the amazing, capable, bright, beautiful light that we *are.*

We also have to release ourselves from being so *hard* on ourselves. For saying negative things about ourselves to ourselves. For believing all those put-downs we say/said to ourselves and for taking so long to figure out they're not even true! A friend of mine who has dyslexia used that as a hammer to beat himself with until he was forty-three years old. He hadn't been able to finish high school, he hadn't been able to go to college. This he used as proof that he was less than, not good enough, and not lovable. This man, however, is one of the best motivational speakers I have ever heard. He works endlessly at being a healing force in the world. His heart is huge. And today, at sixty-two, he knows he *is* good enough. Hallelujah.

So, we have to forgive ourselves for wasting so much time stuck in the gunk. So much of our life! Often, when people really get it and connect to the fact that they have been stuck in their emotional child their whole life, there is a deep, deep sadness that sets in. The sadness that says, "I have wasted *so* much time—I have wasted *so* much of my life feeling less than—and that's not even true!"

This is *normal*. It is humbling to suddenly be able to see what we were not able to see before, and it's not flattering. We are, sometimes in an instant, able to see the games our Ghost Drivers and wounded child have been playing.

I worked with a couple where the husband filed for divorce one day completely out of the blue. The wife was shocked and devastated. The problem in this marriage was the wife had such huge abandonment wounds from her childhood that she insisted on being in charge of *everything*. There was no room for her husband in the marriage. She took up all the space. Another way of saying this is, of course, she was a control freak. The husband was passive, went along with, had no boundaries, felt like a victim, and hated himself for being such a wimp. The wife insisted on being called "the queen" by her husband and the children, told them what to do and how to do it, and would relentlessly criticize if they got anything wrong. This was a case of trying to keep her husband small so that he didn't have the ego strength to leave her. She was trying to prevent recreating her childhood abandonment wound, of course.

When these things were pointed out to her and she was finally able to see the truth in it, she was so embarrassed. "Oh my God, I have been acting like a little girl playing *I'm the Princess*. Like I'm eight years old!" Then her embarrassment shifted to sadness as she turned to her husband in tears. "I am so, so sorry I treated you that way. And for so long! It's been thirty-eight *years* of doing that to you. Oh my God, we've wasted our whole life!"

Fortunately, no. Just Lifetime One.

To fully get to Lifetime Two, however, we need to forgive ourselves for walking around asleep for so long. Again, the reality is we do better when we know better. That's how it works. And until we know better, we are just playing out our unconscious programming ever trying to be safe, ever reacting to the wounding we got in Lifetime One.

So, forgive yourself. Forgive yourself for not knowing better sooner. You did the best you could with the information you had at the time. Now you have more information. Now you can do things differently: engage your authentic adult self to take over your life.

The Bad Stuff

But what if you did some really awful behaviors? First of all, who hasn't? A friend of mine who teaches my first book in the prison system said to me, "You know the difference between most of my prison students and me? They got caught."

You see, we all have done less than stellar behaviors. We all have done hurtful behaviors, embarrassing ones, pathetic ones. I've had clients tell me, "I can never forgive myself for …"

1. Hiring prostitutes
2. Having an affair
3. Robbing the gas station when I was a teen, seeing the terror on the clerk's face when I pointed the gun at him
4. Embezzling from my company
5. Turning my back on and walking away from my children when they were begging me to stay
6. Going along with things that I knew were wrong
7. Drinking and driving and paralyzing another man

8. Joining the military and killing people
9. Inside trading, and I never got caught
10. Doing nothing—letting my wife do it all while I stood back and did nothing. Then she got cancer and died. It's all my fault.
11. Raping that girl in college
12. Dealing coke to kids
13. Having multiple abortions
14. Lying, lying, lying
15. Being a racist, sexist pig

Yeah, some bad stuff. I don't know why it's designed this way, but it is: we all have a shadow self. We all have a part of ourselves that is capable of doing some really bad stuff. Personally, I think our adult self is capable of being in charge of our shadow self. Our adult self can shine a light on our shadow self and keep it in front of us in plain sight. Our adult self is able to make conscious decisions when our shadow self shows up. We move from doing something automatically—without much thought—into slowing the roll and looking at different options.

Our child self, however, not so much. Our child self is driven by that lie that says, "I'm not good enough, remember?" In our child self, we do things without consciously taking ownership of what we are doing. It's where we are asleep, sleepwalking with other sleepwalkers. It's where we operate out of fear, allowing ourselves to do all kinds of things, hoping to eliminate the pain we carry. In other words, when your life feels like a living hell, you will do anything to get a cup of water to ease your parched tongue.

I, therefore, do not hold people responsible for *any* of their behaviors that they did when they were asleep. Forgiven. Conversely, I hold them responsible for their *every* behavior after they are awake. That is, you get a clean slate when you start into Lifetime Two. It's time to let go of all those things you did when you were asleep, grant yourself grace and forgiveness, and move on to the authentic adult you being in charge of your life. You can safely say to yourself, "I'm not that person anymore." Because that's the truth. When we get to our adult self, we hardly recognize the self we were in Lifetime One. We no longer connect to the reactionary craziness we used to live in.

I want to underline that thought: you are not responsible for any of the behaviors you did when you were asleep. *Any* of them. That's because your subconscious was driving your thoughts, feelings, and behaviors. You, the authentic you, the real you, hadn't even shown up yet. So be gentle with yourselves for the mistakes, the stupid choices, the hurtful behaviors, the ineffective decisions, the arrogance that so often was in charge when your wounded child was driving your car. You can now safely forgive yourself *all* of your Lifetime One behavior. This is where you get to start anew. Forgive yourself your past and step into a whole new world: Lifetime Two.

It is good, too, to ask forgiveness from others whom you may have harmed. In the twelve-step programs, this is step number nine: go back and make amends to all you have harmed, unless to do so would cause them more harm. Their forgiveness of you may help you with your forgiveness of you.

Normal

I have clients all the time who are apologizing to me for being *human*, having *normal* responses to life. People apologize to me for crying when they're grieving. Why? Your mother, brother, friend, aunt, child just died —you owe me *no* apology for your God-given, Universe-given *right* to cry.

I have teenage boys who apologize to me because they can't concentrate on their studies at school because all they think about are teenage girls. Normal.

I have people who apologize to me for taking up my time and being such a problem—I'm their therapist. That's my job—walking with people through their problems and their pain. No need for apologies. Recovery from Lifetime One is a process and not an event. Your pace is normal.

We have to forgive ourselves for apologizing for just being who we are, where we are in our awakening process.

Our Parenting

We also have to forgive ourselves for not knowing any better when we were raising our children. We have to forgive ourselves for passing on the I'm not good enough wound to them. We have to come to know that if we had known then what we know now, we would have parented differently. We have to forgive ourselves by telling ourselves the truth: we didn't have the emotional tools when our children were young that we have now.

We have to forgive ourselves so that our children will be able to do their emotional work. My prayer has always been, "Please, when my children come to me and tell me everything that I did wrong in my parenting, please allow me to be centered and validate their experiences." This can only happen when the self-forgiveness has happened first and you are solidly in your adult self.

Also, once you have forgiven the holes in your parenting, you don't need to defend yourself. You can wholeheartedly admit to all of them, take 100 percent responsibility for them, and not feel diminished *at all*. You can name what you did poorly, claim what you did poorly, take complete ownership of these things without shame, and apologize for them. You can help your children heal.

I remember a man I worked with one time who asked me, "Was I really that bad?" When I replied, "What do you think?" he humbly looked me straight in the eyes and said, "Yeah, I was. I was a shitty dad."

When we allow ourselves to be humbled by the truth that we can now so clearly see, it is freeing. When we are able to completely *own* the behaviors we did when we were asleep—not beat ourselves up for them but *own* them—we are not diminished. In fact, to do so is empowering. We are then able to help our children, and anyone else we hurt, heal.

So, it's time to clean up your past—grieve it, forgive it—and grow beyond it. It's time to reclaim that pure, beautiful, lovable soul that came to the planet—to become as a child again full of unconditional love.

Chapter 20

Where the Rubber Hits the Road

So you've identified your wounds, grieved them, and forgiven those who hurt you as well as forgiven yourself. That's it? I wish!

No, the bad news is those wounds are still around. Remember those Ghost Drivers? The Ghost Drivers are ever ready to take back the wheel. They are lurking in dark places as we walk down the path in between Lifetime One and Lifetime Two. They are our triggers. They are our raw nerves that get stepped on. They are our emotional buttons that get pushed.

So this is where the real work begins. That was the easy stuff. Now comes the hard stuff. This is where we have to face our fears, silence our dragon, and keep walking forward though we are shaking at the knees.

This is where we have to emotionally grow up. And it ain't easy.

Growing up. What does that mean? Of course your body already did its part. But your psyche, your wounded child, your emotional self—how do we grow up that part?

A lot of people don't even want to. They are afraid if they grow up emotionally, they won't have any more fun in life. They think they'll be boring and that their life will be boring. They look at old, boring, stuffy people who walk around half-dead and say that's what it's like to be an adult. Then they say, "No thanks!"

Is that you? Afraid that if you grow up, you'll turn into that half-dead, boring, stuffy person?

Because nothing could be further from the truth. The reason that person is walking around half-dead is because they *never did the work to grow up*, to take responsibility for creating a fun, fulfilling life. They are stuck in Lifetime One. I worked with a client who, at age seventy-four, was stunned when he said, "I've been in my wounded child my whole life. I have been too afraid to grow up." And this was from a man who ran a billion-dollar company—yet actually stomped his feet at board meetings if he didn't feel heard and was known for firing people impulsively.

So, growing up means recognizing that your Ghost Drivers want to take over *immediately* if your circumstances are recreating the same way you felt as a child. If you feel invisible. If you feel abandoned. If you feel suffocated. If you feel controlled. If you feel dismissed. If you feel scared. If you feel ignored. If you feel trapped. If you feel unloved. These *feelings* are what trigger you into childlike behavior and thinking.

As a child, we had no power over our circumstances. We really were victims. We had the feelings listed above, and there was nothing we could do about it. For example, when a child is twelve years old and his parents say to the family, "We're moving," it doesn't matter how much he protests. It doesn't matter if he yells or cries. It doesn't matter how much he reasons with his parents that this is the first year he really feels like he has good friends and feels like he finally fits in. It doesn't matter. The breadwinner of the household got transferred across the country, and they're moving.

So, as an adult, whenever his circumstances recreate those feelings—you don't matter, you are invisible, and your needs don't count—this man will become reactionary. That is, until he wakes up and realizes he's not a little boy anymore. He has a vote. He has choice. He can do things differently.

For example, I have had clients who were military children who moved a lot and all over the world when they were growing up. They invariably will marry a person whose job begins to transfer them every other year. After two or three of these moves, my client will come in and sob because their partner got transferred again. When I say, "You don't have to move. There are other options," they stare at me as if I am speaking a foreign language. Because it *is* a foreign language to them; they have no awareness that they are no longer a child where they have no choice. They have failed to register that as a grown up, they have choice—always.

Instead, their Ghost Drivers are in charge. Time to fire the Ghost Drivers.

CHAPTER 21

Letting Go of Reactionary

To fire your Ghost Drivers, you have to slow your thought process down and think, then make conscious choices. To do this, you have to commit to letting go of reactionary.

In fact, if there is one thing that defines growing up the most, it is learning not to be reactionary and learning to be responsive. Reactionary behavior happens at lightning-fast speed, without a thought process. It is automatic. It is your wounded child screaming out. It is your Ghosts Drivers taking you on a wild ride, not too different from being in the video game Mario Cart.

In your adult self, however, you no longer let the wounds from your childhood take over. You no longer let your wounded child be in charge of your life. You fire your Ghost Drivers. You get out of that crazy Mario Cart by responding rather than reacting.

Responding is a much slower process than reacting. It involves slowing things down and thinking before saying or doing anything. It involves considering all the options and consciously choosing one. That is, you must be aware of all of your choices and, on purpose, choose the one that fits best for you.

Fight, Flight, or Freeze

These are the three ways that we react.

Fighting is usually loud. We are saying something: defending ourselves, putting the other person down, yelling F-you, arguing, hitting, throwing things, and so on. Fighting, however, can also be passive-aggressive behavior, giving the cold shoulder, lying, or guilting.

Flight is usually quiet: going into an addiction (having a drink, staying at the office), having a secret life, having an affair, or not showing up for important events. Flight can also just be silence, not responding to problems and leaving everything to someone else, or deferring all decisions by saying, "I don't know," or "I don't care."

Freeze is always quiet. It is the deer caught in the headlights behavior. It is dissociating. It is sometimes having a conversation internally but not having the ability to say the thoughts out loud.

All this is to say reactionary behavior doesn't always show. It isn't always obvious that it is going on at all. So, if you are not yelling at your partner, that doesn't mean you are not reacting to your partner. Your reaction may all be internal—but it's still a reaction. It's important to come to recognize and take ownership of all of your reactions—even the nonobvious ones.

Be Honest with Yourself

It is imperative, then, that we become aware of our reactions and when we are in our wounded child self and when we are in our centered, loving adult self. Start to look for and recognize which part of you is in charge. It can be humbling at first, for sure. Who wants to admit we are having a two-year-old tantrum? Yet awareness is key. You have to be able to see it, name it, and claim it to be able to change it. If you are reacting, admit it—at least to yourself. More advanced behavior will come later when you are able to admit it out loud to another.

I remember a man saying to his wife in a couple's session, "I quit! This is bullshit! I want a divorce!" The room was quiet as we all let that sink in. Finally he said, "That was my fear talking. I'm sorry. I didn't really mean that. I'm just scared."

Wow. Now we're getting somewhere.

So, to really make a leap in your awakening, you need to become aware of when you are acting from your child self and when your adult is in charge. The easiest way to identify whether your child or adult is in charge is simply by identifying if you are reacting or responding to a situation. This is key. If you take nothing else away from this book, take this: if you are reacting, you are in child; if you are responding, you are in adult. And remember, your reacting behavior might just be internal.

You must learn to identify *right now* who is in charge. That is, it's important to be able to identify in the moment what part of you is in charge: your wounded child or your powerful adult. Admittedly, this is advanced behavior, but that is the goal.

In the beginning, you will usually not be able to identify it in the moment. In the beginning, you will be able to identify it after the fact. Maybe hours afterward. Maybe even days. The important thing is that you identify it. Especially become aware of when your child is in charge. Then rewrite things into your adult being in charge.

For example, I recently had an email exchange with a client who was beginning to address her alcohol and sexual addictions. I very much wanted her to go to AA as a place to begin but suggested she go to all-female meetings for a while. Immediately she shot back with an enraged email saying how disappointed she was in me that I didn't have any trust or faith in her, and that if I didn't believe in her, then what was the point? She wasn't going to go at all!

Then, within two minutes, I received her next email saying, "Okay, that was child. I rewrote it: I know you love and care about me and want only good for me. I know you are advising me from your years of experience and wisdom. I trust you. I will find female-only AA meetings and start there."

I was so proud of her! It took her only a minute or so to identify that her child was in charge and to rewrite the incident responding from her adult.

You see, when our child is in charge, we often are throwing a two-year-old tantrum. That's not adult behavior. When our child is in charge, we avoid doing stuff we don't want to do. We close our eyes to problems our spouses or others bring to us. We resist, run away, defend, blame, get angry, scared, even paralyzed. We de-self when someone is upset with us. We say yes when the answer is really no. That's all child. Wounded child. It comes from the wounding your child went through in Lifetime One.

So, to make a leap toward really waking up, you have to recognize when your five-year-old has taken over driving your car. Recognize and identify that child. Try to tie what you are doing/thinking/feeling back to what happened to you as a child. See the pattern and identify what triggers you to go back into child. Question yourself, "Am I reacting or responding?" Tell yourself the truth about it.

Admittedly, sometimes it is *so* hard to see. This happens especially with emotional incest where the wounding was so thorough and began very young. It also happens where there was rage in the FOO or alcoholism. The reaction is completely automatic and happens in a nanosecond. For example, I worked with a couple where the husband was raised in a home where both the mother and father raged. He was extremely hyperaware, in tune with his wife's every breath, every movement, every tone of voice, every silence—ever trying not to get in trouble. Like a little boy. It happened so quickly and without any conscious thought process at all. If the wife sighed or even rolled her eyes, the husband was already gone—already flipped back into being a frightened little boy on guard. This was a reaction, of course, but definitely one that he had to really work to see. In therapy, I would point the flip out to him immediately when it happened. I would ask him, "What are you feeling right this second?" Usually his answer was "Trapped" or "Scared." And he was trapped—in his fear. He had to slow the roll, become aware of his feelings, learn to identify the flip, and recognize it as a reaction—and not a response. He had to learn how not to flip into his wounded child even when his wife was upset with him, crying, hurt, or judgmental. Then he had to figure out what a response would look and sound like. He had to do these things to get his wife out of the straitjacket he had her in: never able to be herself in the relationship without her husband disappearing and flipping into his child self.

Remember, responding is a slower process than reacting. Remember, too, in responding, you look at all of the options and then consciously *choose* the one you are most comfortable with. Furthermore, you take ownership of your choice. No one made you, no one forced you, no one is in charge of you. You are not in a cage, trapped, being forced to do something.

You actually make all of your choices, whether you are doing that consciously or unconsciously. The power is in learning to do so consciously. Also, the moment you make a decision, you are also choosing its consequences. Make sure you are okay with both.

So that's the goal: start looking for when your fear / your reactionary wounded child is talking. Then try to figure out what adult behavior would look and sound like. What would an adult do?

One of my mentors that I go back to over and over and over again is Gandhi. I say to myself, "How would Gandhi have handled this?" He came from peace, from love, from kindness, from nonviolence.

But not always. Because he, like every other human on the planet, had to go through Lifetime One to get to Lifetime Two. He had to wake up from being asleep. He, like all of us, had to learn how to not be reactionary.

Gandhi

It is written of Gandhi that he was a horrible husband and father. Which was true. Now, in his defense, he did get married at age thirteen through an arranged marriage. He lorded his power over his thirteen-year-old wife, who was required to ask him to do everything. When she would ask to go outside and play with her friends, he would yell, "No!" and she would shriek with fear. Into this union came a baby. And then another and another. Gandhi left his wife and children and moved to London for several years to study law. Later he got thrown into jail—a lot. He spent years of his life in jail. He was hotheaded and emotionally reactive—until he wasn't. Until he emotionally grew up. It was in a jail in South Africa that he stepped into responsibility of his life. He shifted from fear and anger into being brave enough to start walking onto the dark and scary uncharted path that separates Lifetime One from Lifetime Two. He learned how to stand up for what he believed by responding—instead of reacting.

We have to learn that too.

Taking Charge of Your Mouth

Years ago, we had a foster daughter who had been in fifteen homes and shelters before she came to us at age eleven. She had no filter at all for anything coming out of her mouth. She was completely, 100 percent run by her very wounded child and was the epitome of pure reactionary behavior.

For example, one time I asked her if she had brushed her teeth before bedtime. She said yes, she had. But when I touched her toothbrush, it was completely dry. When I mentioned this to her, she went ballistic. She screamed and yelled and called me every name in the book, cursing up a storm, using the f-bomb every other word. She, of course, felt very violated that I had touched her belonging—having learned to fight to protect her things because they were always being taken away or stolen from her.

I put up my hand and said, "You may *not* talk to me that way. You may think those things, but you may *not* say them out loud. You must take charge of what comes out of your mouth!" And then she lunged at me. She attacked me with her sharp fingernails, gouging my skin and drawing blood all the way down my arms. She went for my face next.

I grabbed her arms saying, "You may *not* hurt me!" I held her close until she calmed down.

The next day while sitting at breakfast, she asked what had happened to my arms. When I told her that she had scratched me when she was so upset the night before, she was horrified and immediately apologized. She had no recollection of the incident.

That's because reactionary anger outbursts shut down the rational parts of our brains. In other words, anger, especially rage, makes us into an altered person. We do and say things that are not congruent with who we really are. I had a client who said to me, "Anger makes me stupid. I can't think straight. I start acting like I'm in a war—and there is no war. Why is that?" Quite frankly, it's because our primitive reptilian brain takes over, and we feel like we are fighting for our lives.

With my foster daughter, that was our last physical episode. However, there were weeks of the verbal outbursts. After many, many more episodes where I gave her the same message over and over again, "You may think those things, but you may *not* say them out loud," I noticed after I corrected her one time that she went to a corner of the room where she cursed me out (I'm sure) with her lips moving one hundred miles per hour—but no sound was coming out! Ah, progress! I was so proud of her.

Later still, after much practice, she was able to hear what I had to say and only think her reactions—without even moving her lips. Eventually, she got so that she could respond out loud with a reasonable request or negotiation, "Mom, can I brush my teeth in five minutes?"

Now, for this little girl, I had 100 percent grace: she was eleven, and she had an extremely wounded child. Of course she would have reactionary behavior. Yet my experience with people who are thirty or forty or sixty or seventy is that their behaviors are just the same: split-second reactions with words coming out of their mouths that are very hurtful and destructive, and sometimes accompanied by violent physical behaviors too.

Being emotionally grown-up means learning not to do that. You may think those thoughts, but you may not say them out loud. You must take charge of what comes out of your mouth. Keep your mouth *shut* when you are in a reactionary place. Breathe, breathe, breathe. You may even think the thoughts of wanting to take someone's phone and throw it across the room, but you don't do it. Big breath. Breathe, breathe, breathe. Slow your heart rate down. Eventually, with practice, you will learn how to not even have the reactions internally for the most part. But it takes practice. Intentional practice. Practice at not saying reactionary things out loud, not doing reactionary things, and then *thinking* what would be helpful to say and do, and then saying and doing those things instead.

And I do mean practice. It is like learning to play basketball. It may take one hundred attempts your first time to get that ball to go into that basket. But the more you practice, the fewer and fewer attempts will be needed to hit the mark. What you are doing is building muscle memory. Over and over again, you are telling your body, "This is what it feels like to shoot in a way that will make a basket."

It's the same with learning how to verbally and physically respond rather than react. It's like trying to strengthen a muscle. The more you practice using that muscle, the more it will feel natural. Over and over again, you will be telling your psyche, "This is what it feels like to not react."

However, it is a process. Be gentle with yourself when you mess up. Here's a chart to help you understand how we, as humans, shift from an old behavior to a new one:

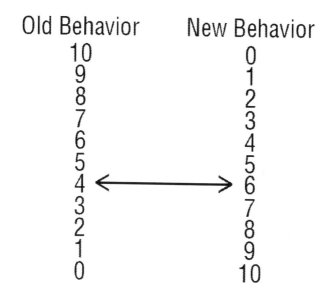

This means you start off with ten old behaviors and zero new behaviors. Then one day you are able to do *one* new behavior. Yay! That counts. However, you are still doing nine old behaviors. No worries. Try again. The next day, you are able to do *two* new behaviors. Wow! Great! But, as you see, you are still doing eight old behaviors. That's okay. Keep working. Please note, though, that when you are doing six new behaviors—six times out of ten, you are having nonreactionary behaviors—you will still be having reactionary behaviors four out of ten times. No matter. You are making huge progress. Eventually, you will be able to be nonreactionary eight out of ten times, and then nine out of ten times, and then, really, you will be able to be nonreactionary ten out of ten times—with an occasional slipup.

No one goes from ten old behaviors to ten new behaviors overnight. No one. It takes practice. You are breaking an old habit and developing a new one.

You are really rewiring the brain. In Stan Tatkin's excellent book, *Wired for Love*, the author talks about the fact that we are wired for war first and foremost. That is, we are wired for survival before all else. It is only with vast amounts of practice slowing down our process so that we can think does it become possible for us to get wired for love, and that is the goal. Said another way, we are trying to overcome our biological, natural instinct of fighting for survival by slowing down our thinking process to realize our survival is not at stake. Tatkin uses the words primitives and ambassadors rather than reacting and responding (response-able). If those words work better for you, use them. That is, we have to get our primitive self to be calm so our ambassador self can show up and be in charge. Reacting fills our brain with epinephrine and nonepinephrine (also referred to as adrenaline and nonadrenaline), and we can no longer think clearly. Remember, reacting makes our rational brain shut down. We then do and say things—sometimes even extreme things—thinking we are fighting for our lives, for our survival.

Yet we are not fighting for our lives. There is no big black bear attacking us. There is no one staring us down with a shotgun. There is no shortage of oxygen or food. We are actually just facing a very manageable problem if we slow things down, take responsibility, and let our ambassadors do the talking.

Can we ever get so we are able to calm our primitives immediately? Yes. This is done by overcoming our fear and responding from love. Ah, we've come full circle because that is our purpose on the planet: to outgrow our fear and to live in the higher-energy vibration of love.

We only become great by no longer being afraid. Gandhi was able to do all he did because he wasn't afraid. He wasn't afraid of what people thought of him, wasn't afraid of being beaten (he had been), of going to jail (he did so many times), or even of death (he would be united with his maker/God). He believed it took more courage to be nonviolent than to be violent. That is, it took more courage to sit peacefully in protest hearing the horses galloping forward with policemen wielding billy clubs than to fight back with physical weapons. Amen to that.

Likewise, it takes more courage to be nonreactionary than

reactionary. More energy. More slowing the process down and thinking.

Sometimes when I am working with a new couple, one of the partners blurts out, "I want a divorce!" When I slow the process down by having them close their eyes and take in three deep breaths, then ask the partner gently, "Really? Are you wanting a divorce or do you want your marriage to feel good again?" they answer the latter. The "I want a divorce!" comes out of the fear that it is not possible to heal their marriage. I remind them that we haven't even started yet. We haven't actually *done* the work to restore the marriage. I work to get them out of that reactionary panic.

The Reptilian Brain

However, a word about the reptilian brain.

Our reptilian brain is the most primitive part of the brain. It reacts to danger and does so immediately. There is no conscious thought process. The body just reacts in either fight, flight, or freeze. When our reptilian brain takes over, the rest of our brain doesn't work very well. For example, I had a large man suddenly grab me in the parking lot as I left a store one night. I had no thought of, *Does he have a weapon? What's my best course of action? Should I scream? Should I give him my purse? What should I say? What are my options here?* I only had one thought, *Run!* Then, with the help of a surge of adrenaline, I was able to break free and run a quarter mile—at the world-record pace I am sure. It was only much later when a friend asked if he had a weapon that it occurred to me I had no idea if he did. I never even thought about that. At the time, I just had that one singular thought, *Run*, which was shorthand for *Run for your life!*

This is the problem with the reptilian brain. When it kicks in, the rest of our brain is hijacked. Now for me, accosted in the parking lot, I was very grateful that my reptilian brain was present and in charge. It absolutely helped me stay safe and alive. However, almost *all* of our life is not a life-or-death situation. The trick is to be able to determine when it is and when it is not.

Intervention Thoughts

You have to have an immediate intervention thought that says, *My life is not in danger. I am safe*, or, *This is not about me. This is about [the other person] trying to tell me about their fear. This is not about me. I am safe*. You have to practice slowing the roll so you can accurately assess the situation and then respond to it. I don't think it's an easy process to rewire our brain from reacting to responding by any means, but it is, in most cases, possible.

I won't lie to you, though: it is extremely difficult to do. At first, it will feel impossible to do when someone is pressing one of your triggers, your buttons, that taps into a childhood wound. The Ghost Drivers are ever ready, saying, "Oh yeah? Let *me* handle this!"

Mostly, remember just don't open your mouth at that moment. Think those thoughts but slow down the process and don't say them out loud. You must take charge of what comes out of your mouth. You are 100 percent responsible for what comes out of your mouth. Remember your goal of being an emotional grown-up. What would a grown-up say? Think of the most grown-up person you know and consider how they would handle things. Then, when you are able, speak up—but with nonhurtful, nonjudgmental, nonreactionary words.

When we think of all the great leaders of the world, they always seem to pause before they answer a question. That gives them time to respond rather than react. You must learn to build that pause into your interactions as well.

This Is Not about Me

I want to underline the intervention thought, *This is not about me*. This is an extremely powerful intervention that can keep a person from reacting. Sometimes you need to say it over and over again, *This is not about me, this is not about me, this is not about me.* The reality is that's the truth. Even if someone is saying, "You, you, you!" it is not about you. It is about the suffering the other person is experiencing that they want you to validate. The other person is trying to get heard, that's all. They think you can fix their pain. And actually, you can—once you realize it is not about you. This is very important. So, too, is its corollary: as soon as you make the other person's pain about you, you cannot be helpful anymore. Instead, you go into fight, flight, or freeze mode. The key, then, is to make the intervention thought, *This is not about me*, automatic.

This is an important part of the process of emotionally growing up. Remember the child is egocentric. The child interprets the world as *Everything is about me. I cause the world. I cause the suffering.*

Learning to counteract that will help you claim your adult emotional self. The reality is it's not about you. It's about stepping into an other's world and hearing what they are trying to explain perhaps in a reactionary way. The key is not to get reactionary to another person's reactionary. Love is, really, being able to realize there is an *other* involved—not just you. It's being able to hear the other person's suffering and then being able to respond to it. It is not running away from another person's pain; it is going toward it.

To do so, you have to be okay if someone is upset with you and directing that upset directly at you. You have to be able to be strong enough to stand for what you think is right and not worry about another's disapproval. You have to be able to say no even when it's not popular. Advanced adult behavior even allows you to ease another's pain by going toward it and asking, "What else have I done to cause you pain?" You can only do these things by staying in your nonreactionary adult self. Embracing the intervention thought, *This is not about me*, will help you do just that.

Also, no one's perfect—don't expect yourself to be. Remember even Jesus raged in the temple, even Mother Teresa felt forsaken by God, even Nelson Mandela early on chose violence. Remember, too, those Ghost Drivers, even when they are shrunk down itty-bitty, would still like to drive your emotional car. Sometimes they may grab the wheel when you're not looking. Keep an eye out for them.

That is, you need to outgrow letting your egocentric inner child take over. You do this by absorbing this concept: you are not a child anymore. You must come to see it's not about you, and it never was. It's about your Ghost Drivers and the other person's Ghost Drivers crashing into each other. It's not at all about your authentic, light-in-the-world, amazing adult self, or about the other person's authentic, light-in-the-world, amazing adult self.

Keep this in mind because the moment you make the situation about you is the moment you can no longer be helpful. For when you make it about you, you start reacting out of fear, begin to defend yourself, begin to attack the other, and so on. Not helpful.

Now admittedly, believing, *This is not about me,* sometimes is extremely difficult to do. When someone is telling you it *is* about you, or is directing all their comments to you by using the word "you," then it is hard to see that, in actuality, it isn't at all about you. For example, if someone says to you, "You are such a jerk!" it is very helpful to immediately say to yourself—not out loud—"This is not about me." Let me underline, though, *do not say this intervention thought out loud.* Saying it out loud may trigger the other person, perhaps your partner, into even more reactionary. You want to help them get centered, not more reactionary. So, slow the roll and *think, This is not about me.*

It's about the other person's pain. It's about the other person trying to tell you, "That hurt my feelings—can you help me?" Or perhaps they are saying, "I have had an awful day. Everyone was mean to me. I feel like a nothing. That's why I'm lashing out. Can you help me? Can you reassure me? Can you help me get back on center? Can you let me know you care about me?" or "Can you hold me and tell me everything will be okay and that you love me?"

When one of my sons was about thirteen, and I was dressing him down about some behavior he had, he said to me in a loud, reactionary, exasperated voice, "Mom, I want you to be nice to me *all* the time!" That stunned me. I said, "You want me to be nice to you *all* the time—even when you are not nice to me? Even when you are speaking rudely to me? Even when you have not done what you said you would do?" He said, with tears in his eyes, "Yes," and then added, "I don't know what I'm doing. I'm a teenager! I'm in puberty! Life is so confusing. I'm just trying to figure it all out, and I can't! I am counting on you to stay calm and help me."

You see, his yelling at me had nothing to do with *me*. It had to do with all of the insecurities he was feeling as a young teen. All I needed to do was hear him and try to be nice to him all the time— even when I was correcting a behavior. For the most part, from that point on, I was able to see the scared little boy who was just trying to figure out this life.

In fact, that's when I started to see the signs around people's necks. They are invisible except to the heart. These signs say things like: "I am starving for love," "Please forgive me because I know not what I do," "I am not my best today because I am grieving," "Be kind to me—my heart is broken," and, my favorite, "I am acting this way because I am scared." And, of course, the teen sign says, "Be nice to me all the time: I don't know what I'm doing, and I'm overwhelmed by it all."

Suck It Up?

Take note of this as well: sometimes when people hear me say, "Don't react," they hear, "Suck it up and be silent." That is *not* what I am saying. The responding part is essential. Learning how to talk without reacting is the goal. Learning how to make a reasonable request and how to negotiate reasonably—and in a nonhurtful way—is what I'm saying. It's a slower process than reacting. It involves thinking about what to say that would be helpful and nonhurtful, then saying it.

Developmentally though, there is a step where we say nothing: Phase one: react from your wounded child.

Phase two: say nothing when you feel reactionary; keep your mouth shut and leave the situation.

Phase three: return to the conversation later and talk in a nonreactionary way.

Phase four: able to respond in the moment.

Phase two is the first time where, on purpose, you slow the roll. You just keep your mouth shut—so as not to be reactionary—then remove yourself from the situation as quickly as possible. Excuse yourself and go into the bathroom and look yourself in the eye, reminding yourself you are safe. Breathe slowly. Calm yourself down by repeating over and over and over again, "This is not about me. I am safe. My life is not in danger. I am safe. There is no big grizzly bear that is threatening me. There is only another person who is stuck right now in their reactionary child self. I am safe. This is not about me." Then *think* about a response that would be helpful. *Breathe.* Take a deep breath. You do not have to talk about the topic until you have calmed down and figured out why it is pushing your button. Remember, it is because it is recreating a feeling you had as a child: Feeling invisible. Feeling abandoned. Feeling suffocated. Feeling controlled. Feeling dismissed. Feeling unheard. Feeling scared. Feeling ignored. Feeling not good enough. Feeling criticized. Feeling unloved.

Again, it is very advanced behavior to be able to do this on the spot. You will get to that—but you don't start there. It is unrealistic to think that you will be able to respond automatically. That only comes with *lots* of practice. Really, a year.

After you have mastered the ability to stay quiet, think, and then come back to the conversation in a nonreactionary way, then you can work on having a response in the moment. Always, though, there is a time of not saying anything, slowing the roll. It could be just for a moment, but it is still there. The pause. You are able to slow things a bit to give your brain a chance to *think*.

Buy Yourself Time

Sometimes you will need to buy yourself time. Learning to say, "I'll need to think about that. I'll get back to you," or "I want to talk to you about this, but I need to think about it first. I'm just reacting to it right now. Give me an hour, and we'll come back to this, okay?" is helpful. It's reasonable to need time to process. It's reasonable to need time to get rid of your primitives and to invite your ambassadors in. It's reasonable to need time to tell your Ghost Drivers to get out of your car. All of that is adult behavior. Not coming back to the conversation, however, is child. You need your adult self to be able to show up and discuss difficult topics. Remember to say to yourself, "This is not about me."

Boundaries

In order to move from reactionary behaviors into proactive, response-able behavior, you will also need boundaries. Boundaries are simply lines. On one side of the line, it feels good; on the other side of the line, it feels bad.

Feels Good | Feels Bad

It's your responsibility to teach people in your life to stay on the Feels Good side of the line.

However, you may never have been taught boundaries. Maybe you were raised in a house where there were little or no boundaries. I worked with a client whose father had an affair when she was seven. Her mother's reaction? The day she found out about the affair—the *day* she found out—she called all the children into the room and told them all about it. She detailed who he had been with and what sex was and what an awful, repulsive father they had. No boundaries. This was sharing with children information that was completely inappropriate for their ages and understanding. Perhaps you were raised in such a house.

The point is, if you weren't taught boundaries, how could you know how to exercise them? I always say if you weren't taught to speak Chinese as a child, you probably don't speak Chinese either. It's the same with boundaries. Be gentle with yourself. You can learn about boundaries now—and need to in order to get to your adult self. Remember, the adult self takes responsibility for everything they are thinking, feeling, doing, and not doing.

For example, if someone is raging at you, you must turn the searchlight inward and take responsibility. I know that sounds ridiculous since *they* are the one who is raging, but you have a part in it. Always look for your part. They are raging at you because you have not had a boundary. You have taught them it's okay to treat you that way. And it's not okay. You are a wonderful, beautiful, amazing person, a light in the world. It's not okay for *anyone* to rage at you. But you are not a victim. You are, instead, not taking responsibility to teach people how to treat you differently.

Sometimes when I am working with a couple and I see one of the spouses, let's say the wife, individually for a session, and I focus on her need to take responsibility at every turn for all of her behaviors, she will often say, "Foul! What about *him*? What about all the outrageous things *he* is doing?"

Yes, in any system, there are at least two people. Looking at a couple, he has a part, and she has a part. However, in your own life, the only part that you have control over is your part. Are *you* in your child? Are *you* reacting? Are *you* coming from love? Are *you* coming from fear? Are you saying no when you need to say no? When we are in our adult self, our authentic self, we are, as Gandhi suggested, constantly turning the searchlight inward looking for *our* part. Remember, we are talking about *your* becoming an emotional grown-up—not your partner. How you get to your empowered adult self and move into Lifetime Two is inside of you—not outside of you. The power comes from claiming your responsibility for *everything* in your life. It is letting go of looking at what the other person is or isn't doing. It is shifting your focus to your *own* behavior.

Then the question becomes, What can I do to handle the puzzle the Universe just handed to me? Am I in my child? Am I in my adult? Am I reacting? Am I responding? If my boundaries are being violated, how can I step up to the plate from my adult response-able self and respond to the situation? I am responsible for my boundaries and for enforcing my boundaries. Nobody else is.

I will tell you a story. I once had a set of parents bring in their sixteen-year-old son because he was "out of control." When I have a session with a teen, I begin the session with the parents in the room for about five minutes. I address the teen first, telling him that I am going to ask his parents why they think he needs to be here, and then I will dismiss them to the waiting room, and he and I will talk privately. Then I check that out with the teen to see if that is okay with him. In this particular case, he said that was fine.

So, I turned to the parents and asked them what their concerns were and why they thought Johnny needed to be in therapy. The mother started to explain, but before she got past about word five or six, the sixteen-year-old yelled, "Shut up, bitch!"

Now I had never met these people before, yet I already knew: they had boundary problems. The teen's behavior was escalated behavior. On a scale of 1–10, it was a 12. This is because his parents had not had boundaries when the behavior was at level 1, a little snippy. Nor did they have boundaries at level 2, when the child refused to answer them when he was asked a question and instead walked out of the room slamming the door as he left. Nor at level 3, when the child raised his voice and refused to give up his phone when asked. Nor at level 6, when the child broke curfew and came home at 2:00 a.m. Nor at level 7, when the child punched a hole in the wall. Not even at level 10, when the child cursed them out as he grabbed the car keys and left the house.

Yes, the child had out-of-control behavior, but this was really a parenting problem. A lack of boundaries problem.

It's the same with you. If someone is yelling at you, taking up all the space, having controlling behavior, or disrespecting you, it's a boundary problem. You must practice placing boundaries when someone's behavior crosses your personal line of what feels good into what feels bad.

It is actually *your* responsibility to set and maintain the boundary.

Boundary Examples

Here are a few examples of what boundaries can look like.

1. It can be putting up a hand in the stop position and saying, "Please don't talk to me that way. I am not talking to you that way, and I don't want to be talked to that way."
2. It can be removing yourself from the room. Close your mouth, walk away.
3. It can be saying, "I can't talk about this right now because I am not calm. I will talk to you about this after I calm down."
4. It can be saying, "I will *not* be talked to this way. I respect myself too much to allow myself to be talked to this way. When you calm down, I will be available. But until then, I will not be." Then get up and leave the room.
5. It can be saying, "You are being verbally abusive to me right now. Stop it."
6. It can be saying, "Do you want to get your needs met? If so, then you have to stop talking. You are taking up all of the space."
7. It can sound like "No."
8. It can sound like "No, I'm not interested in doing that," or "No, I won't be able to do that," or, "No, thank you. That won't work for me."

9. It can be taking away privileges from a child when they are disrespectful.
10. It can be deciding to leave a job where the boss is critical and rageful, and after several attempts to change the situation, you consciously decide to quit putting energy into it and instead put your energies into getting a different job.
11. It can sound like "If you are not willing to get sober, that's okay, but I am not willing to be exposed to the toxicity of your drinking anymore," then taking the children and leaving when your partner gets drunk again.
12. It can sound like "Stop putting me down. I am valuable too. I want a relationship where we both speak respectfully and lovingly to each other."

Of course, there are hundreds of ways to have boundaries—these are just a few. The main point is, as an adult, *you* are the person who has to set boundaries that are comfortable to you.

Saying No

If you have problems saying no, practice in the car. Really. Say it out loud when you are driving. You can practice saying it softly, saying it loudly. You can practice saying it with conviction: "No!" You can practice saying the boundary out loud: "No, that won't work for me. No, I'm sorry, I won't be able to do that. No, no, no, no, no!" Sometimes when I am working with a client who has poor boundaries, I stand across from them and tell them to say no to anything I say. I then ask things nicely of them, then beg them, then guilt them, then get angry at them, and so on. If they crater, they are then able to figure out what causes them to crater. This increases their awareness. You must do the same. Increase your awareness of what causes you to deself, and then, in the car, practice saying no to that.

Boundaries with Yourself

It's important to recognize, too, when you are slipping into victim, blaming others for behaviors you are actually in charge of.

For example, a client who is trying to lose weight said to me the other day that she broke her diet by going to a buffet where "they encourage you to overeat." Really? She is the one who chose the restaurant, and she is the one who kept returning to the buffet for seconds and thirds. Actually, there was no one encouraging her to overeat. *She* made all of her choices, including not having boundaries to stay within her diet. Take responsibility for *your* behavior. Tell yourself the truth.

Take ownership of the choices you are making. Whether you are choosing intentionally or not, you are still choosing. You are choosing *all* of your life.

CHAPTER 22

Taking Ownership

You have to take ownership of your behavior in order to take ownership of your life. It's no good to pretend your behavior is—and was—different than it is and was. Then you just become fraudulent, unable to really and truly love yourself because you are rejecting the truth about yourself. So, to take charge of your life, you have to take charge of your behavior. To do that, you have to become aware of it. You have to get honest with yourself and see what your behavior really is. For example, if you are constantly trying to people please and get others' approval, own that. Say, "Yes, I do that." Really take that in at a cellular level.

In the twelve-step programs, this is called step four: take a fiercely honest look at yourself. See all the warts, see all the ugly, see all the arrogance, see all the avoidance. Then, take *ownership* of it. Look at the mistakes you've made and say, "Yeah, I did that." Look at all the embarrassing things you've done and say, "Yeah, I did those things." Look at the problems that are currently happening in your life and say, "Yeah, I helped create that. I have a part."

The trick is not to beat yourself up when you are owning your behaviors or lack thereof. It's not about shaming yourself. This is about being neutral. It is about being able to take in the truth about your life without judgment. The judgment isn't necessary, isn't helpful. The honesty, however, is necessary and helpful.

For example, I have a teenaged client who came home one night smelling of cigarette smoke. Her parents confronted her and took away her phone. They then went through her phone and found much, much more than smoking going on. Her father called me and told me everything he'd found: drugs, alcohol, promiscuity—including a sexual relationship with a forty-year-old man. Of course this had to be reported to the authorities. The next day, we had a two-hour family session. The father began by saying his goal was to help his daughter not feel stressed, and then she wouldn't have to smoke.

What?

Of course, this lack-of-honest approach would never have worked. The daughter could never truly feel loved until she knew her parents knew *everything*—the good, the bad, and the ugly—and that they still loved her. So, I insisted we put everything on the table and look at it in a nonreactionary way. Then we could talk about and heal the real issue—her not feeling loved and her acting out because of it.

It's the same with you. If you want to heal the real issue—conquering the *I'm not good enough* fear dragon—you will need to have *everything* on the table and look at it in a nonreactionary way. You will have to *own* it.

The amazing part of this process of ownership is that it gives you a sense of relief. No more secrets. No more pretending. No more rationalizing. No more running away from the truth. It's just looking at everything in a neutral light, saying, "Yeah, I did a lot of crazy things when I was asleep." Take heart and know everyone does. When I was in my early twenties, I climbed over an eight-foot-high locked chain-linked fence one time so I could sneak into my boyfriend's house while he was out of town to see if there was any evidence of his cheating on me. Yeah. We all do crazy things while being driven by our wounded child. So be gentle with yourself when you are claiming ownership of *all* your behaviors.

Don't try to talk your way out of your behavior. Don't try to excuse yourself. Don't try to minimize things. Take full, unadulterated ownership of behaviors you've done in the past and ones you are doing presently. You can make amends for behaviors that have hurt others. Take ownership, express remorse, ask for forgiveness, and then move on. Or not. Mostly you have to get honest—completely—with yourself.

A Word about Privacy

However, some people confuse honesty and privacy. *Some people think, If I don't tell everything to everybody, then I am being dishonest.* Not so. You have a right to privacy. Think of it like this: the behaviors you did while you were in your wounded child are classified information. It is sacred information. Don't share it casually. Don't share it with unsafe people. Don't share it with people who will use it against you.

But *do* share it with a therapist, with a trusted friend, with a trusted sponsor in any of the twelve-step programs, with your partner.

Let me give you two examples.

First, if I had a huge argument with my teenaged child right before I came into a session, and you asked me, "How are you today?" the honest and private answer would be, "Well, I've had better days. How about you?" If I said, instead, "Oh, I just had this ridiculous argument with my son. He did this and this and this, and then he said this and this and this—and then I said this and this and this …" that would be treating sacred information casually. That would be having no boundaries. Some people would call that being honest; I would call that being inappropriate. However, if you asked me how I was, and I gushed and smiled and said, "Great! I am just wonderful!" that would be being dishonest—and you would trust me just a little less. You might not even be aware of trusting me less, but you would. Why? Because our bodies know when we are lied to. In fact, research has shown over and over again that a person's muscles go weak when they are being lied to. Just a little bit, but at some level, we are registering the dishonesty.

So, the goal is to be 100 percent forthright and to own *all* of your behaviors but not to do so casually. You have a right to privacy. You don't get a pass to be dishonest though. You must commit to being honest and keeping your privacy when it is prudent.

Here's the second example. I worked with a couple after a crisis had occurred in the family: the husband was at a company function, severely overdrank, blacked out, and woke up in a coworker's bed the next morning. The coworker confirmed they had had sex. My client had little memory of any of the night's events.

Not unexpectedly, the wife was out-of-her-mind upset. She felt angry, betrayed, and hurt. Of course! Yet one of the things I recommended to her was not to share the information with too many people. She asked whether she should tell her parents, and I asked whether she thought they would ever forgive her husband or forever hold it over his head. After some thought, she said, "No, they would never let go of it. They would encourage me to leave him. They would bring it up incessantly." So, she and her husband decided only to tell her parents that they were having a hard time and were working through some marital issues. They decided, together, to keep the information private. They decided, together, that it was *their* issue to work through and not the whole family's.

Checking in with Self

Taking ownership of all you are doing, thinking, feeling, as well as not doing, also means being able to hear other people's opinions as just that: opinions. They are not the right answers; they are another person's opinions. You must learn how to hear another's opinion and not discount your own. You *are* good enough. Trust yourself.

I remember when one of my sons turned eighteen, and I was wanting to hand over the authority of his life to *him*, I said to him, "Remember, son, whenever I am giving you a piece of advice or telling you my thoughts on something, I am only giving you my *opinions*. I am not judging you—I am only offering my opinion.

You get to decide whether you agree with it, disagree with it, or find yourself somewhere in the middle with it. It is *your* life, and you get to make all your own decisions—including disregarding any opinions I might offer you. You are responsible for your life—not me. I will love you no matter what decisions you make, including totally disregarding my opinion about whatever. It's *your* journey. Take hold of it. If you want my advice on something, I will be glad to give it to you, but know that it is not the *right* answer. It is only an opinion. After you gather people's input and opinions, then make your own decision. Your opinion is the only one that matters in running your life. What you decide is the right answer."

Let me give you an example. Let's say someone says to you, "You should improve your customer service—it's awful!" The first response is to realize that is just an *opinion*. One person's opinion. You have an opinion too. Other people's opinions are not better than your opinion. Evaluate what they are saying to you by, in this example, looking at your customer service. Is it at the level *you* want it to be? One of my friends who is an artist says, "Yeah, my studio's a mess, my customer service is a mess, but, hey, I'm an artist. If people like my artwork, they buy it. If they're hung up on the messiness of my studio, they don't. Fortunately, most of my customers couldn't care less about that, so I'm happy, and I'm eating." She then is able to dismiss the other person's opinion as just that: an opinion. If however, she heard the other person's opinion and it confirmed what she was already thinking, she could take ownership of the way her customer service was and decide to implement some changes. The point being, she needs to change her customer service only if *she* believes it needs changing—not what someone else believes.

That is, she needs to neutrally own the truth of it: my customer service is not good. Then she needs to decide if that works for her—or not. If not, then she has to pick up the reins, take responsibility, and change things.

Remember, nobody can make you do anything. You are in charge of how your life is.

CHAPTER 23

Letting Go of Blame

Therefore, since you are in charge of your life, emotionally growing up means you can no longer throw down the victim card:

- You did this to me.
- You made me do it.
- I had to (fill in the blank).
- It's not my fault.
- It's your fault.
- I got fired because my boss is an idiot.
- Well, I couldn't do anything—I'm not in charge!
- I can't get a job because the market is bad.
- My marriage is awful because I'm married to a jerk.
- I did it because everyone was doing it!
- I can't play with my kids because I have to work eighty hours a week.
- I don't have any money because you always spend it all.
- Of course I don't talk to you—you're a bitch!
- I have to go home, or I'll get in trouble.
- You're always controlling me.
- I have to defend myself—you're attacking me.
- I can't pursue my dreams because the kids take up all my time.

- Nobody likes me—I don't have any friends.
- I have to drink to calm down.
- You make me feel this way!
- I can't start a company because no one's honest.
- I'm trapped. I'm suffocated. There's nothing I can do.
- I can't be a stay-at-home mom because my husband won't let me.
- You control what comes out of my mouth.
- I can't leave my job even though I hate it.
- I can't go out with my buddies because my wife won't let me.
- I can't change jobs because I'm too depressed.
- I'm fat because you drive me crazy!
- I'll die if you leave me.
- *You* are the problem.
- I don't know what I'm feeling.
- I don't know what I want.
- I need them to love me to be okay.

And so on.

No. Growing up is being able to *respond* to *any* problem that is handed to you by the Universe and not blaming someone else for your words or behaviors or lack thereof. Growing up means relinquishing your victim card, giving it up, turning it in.

Giving up your victim card means the difference between living in pain and suffering, and living in joy and empowerment. It is saying, "I will be in charge of my life now. I will drive my own car." It is *the* difference that has to happen to move from Chernobyl to Glacier National Park.

Think about what I am saying:

1. You are in charge of everything you are doing—or not doing. You are alone in your boat, and everything you are doing or not doing is completely up to you. You are responsible for *every* word that comes out of your mouth and *all* of your

behaviors, including your inactions. Nobody can make you do or say *anything*.

2. You are in charge of everything you are thinking. If you don't like the way you are thinking, you can respond and change the way you are thinking. It is up to you to do so; there is nobody else who can do it for you. You need to ABC things (Action, Belief, Consequence) and change your beliefs.

3. You are in charge of everything you are feeling. If you don't like the feeling you are having, you are responsible for either embracing it, learning from it, or changing it.

4. You are responsible for your *life*. You are responsible for creating the life you want to live; no one else is. *You* are. No one—*no one*—can prevent you from creating the life you want to live.

5. You are not a victim.

For example, I meet many people who are in painful, unfulfilling marriages who come to therapy and want me to change their partner. I can see what they can see: their partner is stuck in their child ego state, in Lifetime One. In fact, they have been stuck there for years. In the meantime, the person who initiated the therapy has grown, has been moving on down the path between child and adult. They are tired of being married to a child. This is the scenario I most often see in my practice: one of the partners is stuck in child, while the other has grown up, at least considerably.

One indication of this is looking at the couple's sex life. When it gets down to nothing or practically nothing, it is a good indication there is an imbalance of "emotional age" going on. Why does it show up in the bedroom? Because we don't have sex with children. We are not interested in having sex with children. The inner taboo that says *do not have sex with a child* kicks in, and we are no longer attracted in that way to our "child" partner.

Marriage as the Crucible

But here's the trick about marriage: when we get married, we marry our mother, our father—all of their worst characteristics—and a child. Our partner, likewise, marries their mother, father—all their worst characteristics—and a child. That is, both partners bring their wounded child into the marriage. Then one of them begins to grow up. I believe, in fact, that a marriage is actually designed to help us grow up. It is a crucible in which the work can be done. Or not.

Because remember, most people are asleep. They don't even know about Glacier National Park. Most people remain asleep their whole lives. Even if they find out about Glacier National Park, most people are too afraid to do the work of taking responsibility for *everything* that is or is not happening in their lives. My father died at seventy-two completely asleep, having never grown up. Why? Because it is so much easier to blame others, the circumstances, the weather, the job, the neighbors, the boss, our parents, our kids, the politicians, the in-laws—our partners.

Remember, to get to your empowered, amazing self, you have to get out of victim. If your partner is stuck in Lifetime One, it is important for you to face your biggest fear: what if they never get it? *You* are responsible as an adult, after all, to create the life you want. Does that mean leaving your partner? Does it mean accepting that this is as grown-up as they might ever get and that's okay? Do you feel this relationship is holding you back from being your fully alive, powerful adult self? Are there other things that you would like to be doing but are not doing, and then blaming your partner for that? What keeps you from doing them?

There's the rub. This is where the victim card is usually played. Our fear steps in, and we then blame our partner for restricting us. Yet here's the truth: we are the only ones who can restrict us. The rest is just an illusion. A paper tiger. There is no entrapment, there is no "I'm not allowed to," there is no "I can't because my partner won't let me." There is only you limiting you—and blaming your partner.

Remember the goal is to outgrow your fear. What are you avoiding? What do you need to take responsibility to do to become fully alive?

At one point in my life, I found out my eighty-five year old stepmother with Alzheimer's had tons of money in the bank. She had told me for years she wanted to leave her money to her immediate family: me and my brother, and her sister and brother. Next I found out she had no will and that her sister had arranged for all of my stepmother's money to transfer to her and her brother upon my stepmother's death. After the initial shock of the betrayal by my aunt, I began to think to myself, *What if it was different and you would inherit the money? What would you do with it?*

I thought I would use the money to cut back at my busy practice, allowing me more time to write and speak, giving me a chance to share my message with a larger population. Then it struck me: I don't need her money to do those things! What I need is courage. That has nothing to do with money. I need to start stepping in the direction I want to go.

It is the same in marriage. If your partner refuses to grow up, refuses to do the work, then it is *your* issue. You have to decide what to do and take action. You have to practice responding: slowing the roll, looking at all of your options, picking one, and doing that. You will have to face some hardcore fear probably, but it is yours to face. Turn in your victim card.

So let me tell you my bias. As a therapist, I am very pro-marriage. I think it is the crucible needed to push us into growing up. If children are involved, I triple my efforts to get both people to grow up emotionally and take responsibility for *creating* an adult-adult relationship.

Secondary Gains

However, it doesn't always work. Sometimes people are quite content with getting the secondary gains from being a victim. What are secondary gains? They are indirect benefits we get from our behaviors. For example, let's say you have a good job. A primary gain may be that you are paid well and get to live in a nice house, travel, and buy beautiful things. Examples of secondary gains from the job might be you get to feel important, you get to be in control, or you get to avoid going home and dealing with your unhappy partner.

So sometimes people are not willing to grow up emotionally because they are content with their secondary gains. They *want* to be the victim; they are not interested in giving it up. Ever. Remember, it's easier to stay in that victim, "it's not my fault" child place.

Here's an example of wanting to stay in victim. I owned a rental property that had old galvanized piping in it. This meant that the pipes would spring pinhole leaks every once in a while, ruining the sheetrock, paint, and so on. After about the third leak, I had had it. I decided to replumb the whole house so as not to keep dealing with the same problem. It was the early part of December when I came to this conclusion. I called a plumber who told me they could do the replumb the week of December 9 and that it would take four days. I said I would have to check with my tenant since it was the holidays.

So, I called my tenant, saying I wanted to replumb the house, the plumber was available on the ninth, and that I was not wed to that timing. I said she could wait until January or February if she preferred since it was the holidays. She said she'd rather do it right away and get it over with. I asked her, "Are you sure? Are you having guests for Christmas?" She replied that she was sure, she wasn't having guests, and that they were going out of town for the holiday.

So, I booked the plumber. He then spent four days listening to my tenant say, "I can't *believe* Patti is making us do this at Christmas! I can't even get a tree! It's ruined our whole holiday! I told my husband *next* year we are having a *real* Christmas!"

Really?

Take responsibility. *She* chose the time but then blamed *me* for the decision. This is child/victim behavior. She was going for the secondary gain, however. She was hoping for sympathy and understanding of how hard her life was. She was hoping for someone to see how much suffering she was going through—and therefore receive some comfort for it. All of this, I'm sure, was done subconsciously.

Now, there is nothing wrong with my tenant. She is a lovely fifty-year-old woman. Unfortunately, she is stuck in her child self, trying to get her needs met. However, the power is in adult. The ability for us to really get our needs met is in adult. The ability to get out of pain and suffering is in adult. Taking ownership of "I have choices, and *this* is what I choose" is in adult. How much better her life would have been if she had been able to say, "Really, Patti, I don't want to go through that during the holidays. Let's wait until January," or "Yes, I'm fine with their coming now. I know it will be a little messy, but that's no problem. I'll just dust at the end of each day for a few minutes. Don't worry about it. It's not going to be a big deal—and the pipes will never leak again! Thanks for investing in new pipes. I really appreciate it."

The power is in adult. The power is in letting go of "I am a victim."

Options

Once you commit to letting go of being a victim, this is how life works. The Universe hands you a situation. Any situation, big or small. You can react to it from your child self / victim self or you can respond to it from your adult/nonvictim self. Your child self says, "I don't know what to do! What should I do? I can't deal with this!" And that's the end of it. Your child self doesn't take responsibility; it plays the victim card. Your adult self gets handed the problem and says, "I don't know what to do, *but* I am smart and capable—I can figure it out. What are my options here?"

Then the adult self brainstorms. Guesses. Adults do not *have* the answers; they have to figure them out. Figuring out means naming all the possible responses to a given situation. It's acknowledging "I *always* have a choice"—and figuring out what those choices might be. Brainstorming for options means there are no incorrect answers. Name everything that could possibly be an answer to the question. Then pick one. Pick the one that resonates with you the most. Then do that one.

Here's an example. I am working with a woman who hates her job. Her child self says, "I can't quit my job because we have a large house payment." Victim.

Her adult self brainstorms:

1. I could change my attitude about my job.
2. I can ABC it: rewrite the story of why I am in this job at this point in time. (A is the action that happens, B is the beliefs we carry about the action, and C are the consequences from holding those beliefs. If you want a different consequence, go back to B and change your belief.)
3. I could put my résumé on Monster and other job-seeking websites.
4. I could talk to a recruiter.
5. We could downsize our house. We could move.
6. I can take out a school loan and go back and get a more marketable degree.
7. I can open the boutique that I have always wanted to open.
8. To do that, I can get investors. I can get a loan. I can downsize my house and get a loan.

What my client decided to do was change her attitude about her job by taking steps in the direction of actually opening a boutique. In focusing on her boutique, she stopped focusing on feeling trapped in her job. Therefore, she was able to keep her income up, which she was grateful to have, as she gradually took steps toward changing careers. Each day, she just figures out one small thing she can do to take her closer to having her boutique. I have every faith she will get there.

Now sometimes all of the choices are, as my one client said to me, "shitty choices." If that's the case, which it sometimes is, I say pick the least shitty and do that. Take responsibility for the situation by *deciding* on an option, then doing the necessary actions to follow through on that option.

If, once you get into the situation, you notice your choice isn't going so well, step back, brainstorm again, and pick a new option. That is, just because you made a choice one way to begin with doesn't mean you have to stay that course. You are certainly allowed to change directions whenever you see that as needed. After all, *you* are in charge of your life. *All* of it.

Remember, the power is in adult. The good stuff is in adult. Fully alive, happy, creative, joyful is in adult. We *cannot* get to it in child. We cannot get to it by being a victim and blaming others. We cannot get to it by avoiding scary things.

I had a client who once said to his wife, "I only flip back into child when I am around you—no one else—so that means you are doing it to me!" No, not so. He is just fully embracing the "I am a victim because you make me flip back into my child." He is playing his victim card. I had him look at the first part of his declaration to his wife, "I only flip back into child ..." He had to come to complete ownership of "I am flipping back into child" in order to change *his* pattern. He had to slow the roll and recognize the second he flipped into reactionary, then take responsibility to do it differently.

So, to review a bit. To make the shift from child to adult, you must first really decide to do so. Next, you have to do your family of origin work by looking at what actually happened to you growing up, identify your Ghost Drivers, and be willing to grieve. After grieving, you need to work toward forgiveness—of those who hurt you and of yourself.

Then the rubber hits the road. The work of taking responsibility begins: calling your Ghost Drivers out when they show up to drive your emotional car. Letting go of reactionary and replacing that behavior with responding. Cultivating the ability to respond to all scenarios. That is, taking responsibility for all you are doing, thinking, feeling, as well as what you are not doing, no matter *what* the Universe hands you. Turn in your victim card.

Next, you must learn to step toward your fear.

CHAPTER 24

Step toward Your Fear

Stepping toward your fear is stepping toward conquering your "I'm not good enough" dragon. You can't run away from it; you have to confront it. The work in this chapter is about stretching your comfort zone. Remember, the goal is to get to the place where you live without fear. You have to go beyond where you are currently comfortable to get there.

What are you afraid of? Wouldn't it be nice to get rid of all that?

Your fear—all of our fears—of course, boil down to that universal lie: that you are somehow not good enough, that you don't have what it takes, that you are somehow less than, that you are not worthy of the good stuff, that you are not worthy of love. This manifests itself in a thousand different ways, but it really just boils down to facing that one *lie* that you were given and have believed throughout your life. I am here to tell you it is a *lie*. Remember, our thoughts are crooked: we think it and so believe it as true. In reality, there is no trap, no suffocation, no abandonment, no victim to deal with in adult. You only have to stop believing the *lie*. It is not true. You actually are good enough to take over the reins of your life and create the life you want. Who better to run your life, after all? You know yourself better than anyone else knows you. It's time to start trusting *you*.

In order to get rid of your fear, then, you have to let go of what other people think about you. You have to realize your decisions don't have to make sense to anyone but you. You don't need anyone else's approval. After all, it's your life and your happiness.

One way to get rid of being ruled by what others think or what others will say is to embrace the concept of "I'm not that important." Again, it's the egocentric child part of us that thinks the world will stop if we get a divorce, if we move to another state, if we start a business and it fails, if we run away with the mailman. In truth, the world will not stop.

I often read the news headlines on the home page of my computer, and what I've noticed is that today's top story is rarely tomorrow's top story. Even huge things—the beheading of a journalist, the death of a superstar, the kidnapping of a child, the invasion of one country by another—rarely stay at the top spot more than a few days. Then there's another top story.

To me, this is somewhat reassuring. I look at my own little life and think, *You know, it's not big news if I decide to do something and it doesn't work out. I'm not that important. I need to stop living as if when I make a mistake or a wrong turn, that it is life and death. It is not.*

Another thing that can help you step toward your fear is learning to trust yourself by doing scary things. In other words, if something seems scary to you, you probably need to at least think seriously about doing it. Let go of worrying about what other people think and step toward your fear.

One of my children was valedictorian of his high school graduating class. This was no small feat since he has dyslexia. That means his reading and writing are extremely slow and arduous. When he began college, on a full scholarship, he struggled and struggled. Too much reading. Too much writing. I sent him notes and cards every few weeks to encourage him, yet he was suffering.

One day, I sent him one of my favorite quotes from Danny Thomas, as said to his daughter, Marlo:

> I raised you as a thoroughbred, and
> thoroughbreds run with blinders on.
> They don't compare themselves to the other horses.
> They look straight ahead and run their own race.

I told my son, "Stop comparing yourself to others and run your own race."

About a week later, three days before Thanksgiving his freshman year, he asked me to meet him to talk. He said he was really scared and needed my support. I said, "You've got it!" So I met him. This is the profound thing that he said to me:

"I've been thinking about what you have been saying to me all of these years—that we have to outgrow our fear in order to be free. I think that's true. So, I've been thinking, what is the scariest thing I can do? I've decided it's dropping out of school. I know people will be aghast. I know they will judge me. I know they will think I'm stupid and making a horrible mistake. But, Mom, I also know that's the only way I can claim my life. I have to outgrow worrying about what people think of me. I can't spend my life being determined by other people."

That's what conquering the "I'm not good enough" fear dragon looks like. It's letting go of what other people think of your decisions and looking inward to make sure *you* are good with your decisions. Always there will be people who will judge you and tell you that you are wrong. Don't let those people run your life. *You* need to run your life.

My son dropped out of school. He walked away from a four-year scholarship. He is finding his way in the world, and most importantly, he feels good about himself for being true to himself. He said to me recently, "For the first time in my life, I feel free."

You learn to trust yourself by listening to yourself. Yes, you can gather other people's thoughts and opinions on any given decision, but ultimately, it is what *you* think and decide that is important. As Tennessee Williams said, "There is a time for departure even when there's no certain place to go." We must be brave enough to step in the direction that sometimes doesn't even make sense. Remember, you will be able to connect the dots backwards.

So, silencing the "I'm not good enough" fear dragon often means stepping into the unknown. This much I know is true: as long as you take yourself with you, you will be okay. That is, be very present in each moment of your life, listen to your gut, listen to your truth, and you will be fine. Remember, life is an adventure with many twists and turns, thrills and spills. It's all good / it's all God. Step toward what scares you. You will be pleasantly surprised when you walk through your fear and find out, "Hey, I did it! That wasn't so bad!"

This is the next thing you need to do to conquer your fear dragon: realize you are afraid of paper tigers. We build up our fears to disproportionate levels. We believe something big and drastic will happen. We believe it is beyond our capacity to go into our fear without dying. Yet this isn't true. Remember, fear is False Evidence Appearing Real. We are afraid we cannot face the big and scary Wizard of Oz, who is just that little man behind a curtain pushing buttons and pulling levers. He's putting on the big act because *he's* afraid. The more you walk toward your fear—and then through it—the more you will begin to see other people are even more afraid than you are! We are all afraid of illusions that we have made up in our imagination.

Often, I am amazed when I walk toward my fear and find out, "I was afraid of *that*?" I find out it was just a paper tiger—an illusion. That's the most amazing thing about moving into Lifetime Two. You will realize you have been restricting yourself by a piece of paper that simply has "Roar!" written on it.

As a child, we cannot differentiate between real and fantasy. If we see a monster on television, we think that monster really exists. As an adult, though, we know that wolves don't really dress up in granny's clothes and talk. So why so much fear as an adult? Because we are letting our child self be in charge. To get to our adult self, we must go closer to our fear and see that we are really only facing an illusion and that we are quite capable of standing up and shredding the piece of paper that says, "Roar!"

It's like when the Supreme Court building in Washington, DC, was being renovated. It was covered in scaffolding. To prevent visitors from seeing this eyesore, the powers that be constructed a full-sized picture of the courthouse and set it up in front of the actual building. That way, visitors could still have their pictures taken in front of the Supreme Court. It was an illusion. A very well done one but an illusion nonetheless. That's how our fears are. They aren't even real.

For example, years ago when I was in my child self, I had a sun window put into my meditation room. The contractor was an older man, nice, married with three children, and very sure of himself. The only problem was his workers had put in the sun window crooked. When I pointed this out to him, he told me yes, they had done the best they could, and that if I couldn't live with it that way, it would require them to start the job all over again, breaking the sun window at great expense, perhaps needing to move the studs, getting him behind on the other jobs he had lined up, and so on. He also told me it wasn't that bad and that it added character to the room.

I reluctantly agreed to leave it as it was, and I paid him for the job. I was too afraid of inconveniencing him. I was too afraid of insisting that it be done correctly because he might get mad. I was too afraid of trusting myself over his expertise. I was afraid, too, of hurting his feelings even. After all, he was trying his best, right? I was so afraid of bad things happening. I also thought, *Who am I to ruin this poor guy's day?* So much fear—over nothing. He left, and I never saw him again.

That's when I realized he went home and didn't have to see the crooked sun window in my house ever again. I had to see it daily. I took care of *him* and not *me*. I never had that sun window corrected.

I decided to leave it exactly as it is to remind myself of when I was willing to de-self to please someone else and avoid a conflict.

Do you do that? Do you say yes when the answer really is no? The "I'm not good enough" dragon tells us that we have to go along with to not rock the boat.

Willing to Rock the Boat

But to conquer the dragon and take over your life, you have to be willing to rock the boat. You have to be willing to walk toward the conflict and stand strong, knowing there really is only a paper tiger to face.

Today, as my adult self, I would simply have said to the contractor, "Yeah, I'm sorry it's going to be a hassle and an expense to replace, but I need you to do that. It was put in incorrectly." Now I know, because I'm not that important or powerful, the moon would not have fallen out of the sky.

Standing for what you feel is right, saying no when the answer is no, and stepping toward the conflict in a nonreactionary way will all lead to your empowered, capable, competent adult self and the feeling of freedom.

So, when you are afraid of doing something, that's a good indication of where you need to go next—toward whatever you are afraid of doing. You are not trapped. You are not a victim. You are just restricting yourself by making the circumstances bigger than they really are. Remember, all big tasks are really just a lot of small tasks glopped together. All you have to do is figure out the next step.

As Zig Ziglar says, "We don't have to wait until all the traffic lights are green before we leave our house." Just get in the car and start driving toward your fear. If you get to a red light, stop. Think. Then proceed when the next step becomes clear to you. As you go from step to step, letting go of what others might think, trusting your gut, remembering the intervention thought, *I'm not that important,* you will find your fear dragon shrinking.

Most importantly, you will find that what you were afraid of, *I'm not good enough*, isn't even true. It's been an illusion all along. You *are* good enough to figure out whatever problem the Universe hands you. You have actually already been doing that your whole life. You are very capable. It might take some time to figure things out, and you will make mistakes along the way, but so far, even all your worst decisions have not made the sun fall out of the sky. No matter the darkness, the light always returns.

Step toward your fear. Stop avoiding doing the hard stuff that will lead you to the life you were born to live. Because the reality is the only way to get out of fear is to go through it. Fear is an illusion that keeps us trapped. Step up to it and say, "Love is greater than fear, and I love myself enough to not let fear blackmail me anymore." Just say, "Back off, fear. You're in my way."

I have a client who got her degree in philosophy. Admittedly, not too marketable. So, after graduation, she moved back home and got a waitressing job. She was miserable. This is not how she wanted her life to be. When I asked her what it was that she had passion for, she knew right away, video games. Hmmmm ... what to do with that? I asked her if there was a way for her to make a living with video games, and again, she knew exactly the answer, "Yes, I want to make video games. I have wanted to make games since I was a little girl. I have made games my whole life!" It turns out she went to college because her parents insisted she go to college. She even went to the school they selected for her—which didn't have a video games department. Her mother was a control freak and a rager, so my client just went along.

So really, let's look at this. Her mother would get mad if she pursued a career in video games, but she was always mad anyway. Her mother would express her disapproval of a career in video games, but she expressed her disapproval of everything my client chose anyway. My client, therefore, wasn't avoiding the mad or the disapproval by de-selfing—she was only getting depressed.

We outlined what it would be like to walk toward her fear—to live out in the open and say, "This is who I am, and this is what I want to do with my life." She practiced saying it in my office. She practiced saying it loudly and with conviction. She practiced saying it in her car. She practiced saying it looking into the mirror. Then one day she was surprised when she realized she didn't even have to say it to anyone at all. What she needed to do was take action in the direction she wanted to go.

It turns out she was further along her path than she had realized. Over the years, she had taken several free animation classes online. She had a dozen story lines already outlined. She had taken free programming classes online. She had made friends with kids at college who loved video games and played around with building their own ones. She, therefore, had a support group of peers who could help her brainstorm. She had spent hours and hours and hours researching and learning, researching and learning. She was actually pretty good at exactly what she wanted to do.

Then she figured out her next step: put together a portfolio to search for a job in the field she wanted to be in. She also decided to continue to develop some of her story lines. She expressed to me that she felt so much freedom since she wasn't afraid of her mother's anger or disapproval anymore. When she realized she would get the anger and disapproval no matter what she did, she was no longer controlled by it. She was taking claim of *her* life. She knew it wasn't going to be easy to figure things out, but she was willing to start. One step, then one step, then one step. As the Chinese say, a journey of a thousand miles starts with one step.

I encourage you to take one step in the direction of living the life you were born to live as well. Don't worry about what other people think: follow your bliss. Let yourself fall down. Risk. Try again. The main thing is to start listening to *you*. Are you living the life you want to live? If not, it is up to you to take over driving your car and drive in the direction that feels congruent with who you really are. Not who you are supposed to be but who you are.

Remember, to get over your fear having power over you, you

227

must do the things you are afraid of. In fact, look around for something hard to do, and do that. It doesn't have to be a big thing, just something.

I have a client who has a natural talent for comedy. At the end of our sessions, I often feel like I should pay *her* for her time because I have laughed so much at her twist of words and the tilted angle in which she sees the world. A stay-at-home mom, married with three kids, living in a conservative neighborhood, I asked her what kept her from pursuing comedy. Her response? "I might get laughed at!" Then she cracked up because isn't that the point?

Her fear, like the rest of ours, is "What if I'm not good enough?" Her childhood messages were, "You're too much! Put a lid on it!" I told her, "You have a *talent* in comedy. Use it." Remember, the goal is to take what happened to us as a child and transform it, along with our talent, in such a way that we become part of the solution in the world. Being raised in the Bronx, my client realized all the messages she was given as a child could actually be turned into stand-up material. Unknowingly, she had been given a treasure trove of real-life situations that could be used to help us all laugh at our own foibles.

All she had to do was figure out her next step. She bought a notebook and started writing down things she could build into stand-up material. She was inspired by Joan Rivers having card catalogues of jokes. She decided not to discuss her plans with anyone for fear she would get discouraged.

Next, my client designed her own outrageous Halloween costume for the neighborhood party. Not surprisingly, she was the standout. She let herself be over the top and *not* put a lid on it—and the crowds loved her. She is well on her way to claiming her life, firing her Ghost Drivers, as she feels the fear but does it anyway.

It truly is like the Wizard of Oz when Glinda, the Good Witch, says to Dorothy, "You've had the power all along."

The power is inside of you. You are a light in the world—let it shine. What is the scariest thing you can do? Do that.

CHAPTER 25

Update Your Image

Updating your image simply means shifting your image of yourself from who you were in the past to who you are in the present.

For example, I have a client who married young, age twenty. He married his wife because she was so outgoing, so comfortable in crowds, and could "talk to a rock, and it would answer." My client said he'd been attracted to her because he was the exact opposite: shy, tongue-tied, with "no social graces." Now, thirty years later, his wife was a raging alcoholic who had been to rehab dozens of times and decided she had no intention of ever getting sober. My client said he had shut off his feelings for her years and years earlier. He was miserable but felt stuck with her since he had a job that demanded a lot of social engagements with clients, and she would be the life of the party while he saw himself as not good at socializing at all.

Yet here are the facts:

1. He spent two hours with me, talking easily the whole time, expressing himself clearly, cracking jokes, being very articulate and aware of his thoughts and feelings.
2. He was an executive at his company, traveled a lot, and went to many social occasions without his wife when he was out of town and did just fine.

3. His job required him to teach classes and to do quite a lot of public speaking—both of which he did very well. People loved to work with him and found his classes both informative and inspiring.
4. He was well liked and had many friends both at work and outside of it.

It was time for him to update his image. It was time for him to realize he had evolved from his twenty-year-old socially awkward self into a quite socially capable fifty-year-old self. When I said this to him, he was shocked. He realized his behaviors *had* changed over the years, but he never really registered it.

That's what updating your image means: you don't have to change anything in the present moment. The change has already happened—and you just didn't notice it.

Another example is from my own life. I have a brother who is two years older than I am. While we were growing up, he and his friends found it hilariously funny to call me "Fatty Patti." They would taunt me with the nursery rhyme:

Fatty Patti two-by-four, couldn't fit through the bathroom door, so she did it on the floor, Fatty Patti two-by-four!

Then they would laugh hysterically. Their pet name for me was Hunker.

I remember. My brother doesn't remember. My parents don't remember. But I remember. It started me on ten years of an eating disorder. It started me on ten years of feeling shame about my body. I knew—in my head—that at 105 pounds I *wasn't* fat, but I *felt* fat. I wouldn't eat. I wore baggy sweatshirts to hide my body. In ballet class, I wore warm-ups over my tights and always had a sweater tied around my waist. I was embarrassed by my size, thinking people were repulsed by it.

Then there was the day. I had just finished an hour and a half warm-up class before the actual dance class would begin. Everyone was taking a ten-minute break to get some water and catch their breath. As I was leaving the studio, the instructor was standing talking to another dancer. As I walked by, she said, "Well, we all can't be as tiny as Patti." That stunned me. I quickly went through everyone in the class and confirmed: I was the only Patti. I ran toward the mirrors and really, really looked at myself. I remember thinking in utter shock, "I *am* tiny! I am a tiny person!" I couldn't believe it.

Suddenly, in an instant, I was able to update my image. I was able to change the way I saw myself, as Fatty Patti, into what I actually was: Tiny Patti.

You will need to update your image too. In stepping into your adult self, you will need to shift your thinking from how you were to how you are. You will need to shift your thinking from *I am a less than* to *I am an equal*. You will need to shift your thinking from *that was then* to *this is now*, from *that's who I used to be* to *this is who I am*.

I worked with a man who was addicted to porn. When his wife found out, she wanted to end the marriage. Instead, I convinced her that the problem wasn't porn, but rather, the problem was that her husband was stuck in his child self. Often, when men don't feel powerful in their marriage—for example, if their wife is ultracontrolling or hurricaning at them—they will turn to porn to "have some power over women." In other words, porn is just a symptom. Porn is a symptom of a much larger issue—the need to grow up. Of course, ultracontrolling is a symptom too—of the need to grow up. So, I began to work with this couple, encouraging each one of them to emotionally grow up.

With the husband, as he gained self-confidence and his authentic adult self by working his twelve-step program, SAA, Sex Addicts Anonymous, he responded to his wife's fear that the addiction would return with these words, "I can promise you I'm done with that. I'm not that person anymore."

That's what updating your image looks like, really claiming,

"I'm not that person anymore." Because that's the truth: the more you respond instead of react, the more you take ownership of your mistakes and allow yourself to be human, the more you address every problem that is handed to you, and the more you walk toward your fear, the more you will come to know, "I have evolved. I have changed. I'm not that person anymore. I am now my empowered, authentic adult self—not my reactionary, wounded child self."

Here are some thoughts you need to claim—really take ownership of—in order to see that who you used to be is not who you *are*.

1. You are capable. You have made decisions your whole life and will continue to. However, as an adult, you have the ability to make conscious decisions—ones that you actually participate in.

2. You are enough. You don't have to be any bigger or better than who you are—just *be* who you are. Whenever I write a book or an article, I remind myself that I don't actually have to write something I don't know: I can just write what I do know, and that is enough.

3. You are an equal. Other people don't have better answers than you do. You know yourself better than anyone else does. Listen to yourself. After all, you have everything it takes to be a human being bungling along, trying to figure out life—just like the rest of us. Remember, there are no less thans. There are only imperfect human beings, some awake, most asleep. You can be one of the ones who are awake by realizing the goal is not to be greater than but to allow yourself to be equal to. Trust your own answers. Yes, you can ask other people's opinions, but then take those in, digest them, and decide for yourself what works best for you. You have a good brain—consciously, on purpose, use it. Stop deferring decisions.

4. You are not alone in not being perfect: we are all the walking wounded, imperfect human beings. Do the best you can, and that is good enough.

5. You are supposed to be on the planet at this point in time with the history you have, the brain you have, the talent you have, the gender you have, the nationality you have. Claim your space. I once heard someone say, "There is enough money on the planet for every human being to have one million dollars. If you don't have yours, go get it." It's the same with claiming your space: there is enough space for everyone on the planet. Claim yours. As stated in the Desiderata, written in the 1400s, "You are a child of the Universe: no less than the trees and the stars, you have a right to be here."

6. Life is a river, not a lake. That means *your* life is a river—it is ever flowing, ever changing. *You* are actually ever flowing and ever changing. You really are outgrowing who you used to be—your wounded child—and are evolving into your beautiful, amazing, authentic adult self. Give yourself credit.

So today, look in the mirror and really *see* yourself. You are a work in progress: beautiful and amazing, lovable and enough. You're not who you used to be: you are who you *are* right now, right here, today.

CHAPTER 26

Putting It All Together

Ready to fly? Here we go!

Problem/Trigger

The Universe wants you to get out of your fear and into your love. It will hand you a problem to encourage you to evolve in that direction. The problem might be big, might be small. The problem may come in the form of a loss, a trauma, a challenge, a surprise. The problem may come as a trigger leftover from unresolved issues of your childhood. It may come in the form of someone else's unexpected behavior. It may come as a financial problem, a relationship problem, a medical problem. Whatever it's form, it's been handed to you.

Slow the roll. Look the problem over. Look at it from different angles. Don't react.

The Truth

Tell yourself the truth about the problem. It has come to you to help you somehow. It has come to urge you to address your fear. It has come to encourage you to love more than you think you can. It has come to teach you that you are capable. It has come to push you into transformation—sometimes whether you like it or not. Befriend the problem. You will learn and grow from it if you are open to it.

Even if the problem you've been given is a massive loss, walk with yourself as you go through your grief. Tell yourself the truth: everyone has to take a turn at the impossibly, gut-wrenching hard stuff. Tell yourself the truth about yourself. You are capable. You are smart. You can figure the problem out. In fact, not only can you figure it out, you will figure it out. You have moved past all of the other problems that were handed to you in your life thus far. You will move past this one too.

Tell yourself the truth about taking control of your emotional car. Kick your Ghost Drivers out if they show up. *You* are responsible for your life: everything you are doing, saying, feeling, or not doing. You are responsible for getting out of your child self. Turn the searchlight inward. Look for your part and what you can do to solve the problem. Use your voice.

Tell yourself the truth about fear. False Evidence Appearing Real. It's not real: it's a paper tiger. Walk in the direction of your fear. Keep going.

The only thing that's happening is you've been handed a problem. What are you going to do about it? Shrink it down. Tell yourself the truth: it's up to you to deal with it. Take responsibility. The problem has been handed to you on purpose. It's yours. Take ownership of it even if you don't want it. Because whether or not you deal with it, it's still there. Deal with it when it's small, or it will have to come back bigger to get your attention.

Choice

Remember, always, always, always, without exception, you have choice. In Viktor Frankl's book, he speaks about his time in concentration camps during World War II. He was amazed when he realized that he had choice about his attitude. He realized the

Nazis could house his body but not his soul. He realized the Nazis could not control his thoughts—only he could. This discovery of choice—and his willingness to embrace suffering as valuable—allowed him to not only survive his experiences but to thrive from them afterward.

Always, always you have choice. Choose responding over reacting. Choose it again. Choose to ABC the problem: write new beliefs about it to make it manageable. Choose to be on your own side—working for yourself instead of against you. Choose to shrink the problem down so it doesn't overwhelm you.

Brainstorm. What are possible ways to deal with the problem? What are your options? Lay them out and look at them all. Even the bad ones, even the far-fetched ones. Throw in thoughts of how to respond in the most loving way. Try those on. Could you really respond that way? How would that feel to you? Which one feels the best to you? Do that one.

If you choose that one and it becomes clear you are off track, go back and brainstorm again. Look at all of your options. Choose another one. Do that one. Remember, so much of life is trial and error. We guess—the best we can—and that is good enough.

Choose to give yourself grace when you make mistakes—because you will. Be gentle with yourself. Life is messy. We become wise by getting things wrong and then readjusting our thinking.

Courage

Remember, the goal is to outgrow your fear. I mean outgrow it. Not have it. Not be run by it. That cannot happen without calling forth your courage. As A.A. Milne wrote in *Winnie the Pooh*, "There is something you must always remember. You are braver than you believe, stronger than you seem, and smarter than you think." That is true about you: you are braver than you believe, you are stronger than you seem, and you are smarter than you think. Don't forget that.

Be braver than you think you can be.

Or as George Danton says, "Be bold. Boldness and more boldness and always boldness."

Action

You must step in the direction you want to go. It doesn't have to be fast, but it has to be. Personally, I am the tortoise. I take solace knowing every time I read that story, *The Tortoise and the Hare*, the tortoise always wins. One step and then one step and then one more. You will be shocked when you get to the other side of doing whatever you were afraid of doing and find out that you no longer have that fear—it's gone.

Be proactive. Don't wait for someone else to tell you what to do. *You* need to tell you what to do. I read an article one time about how to survive a plane crash. First, when you get in your seat, look around and find the nearest exit. Then visualize yourself quickly getting out of your seat and going to that exit. That's it. So often, the people who do not survive the crash are the ones who never got out of their seats. They were waiting for the flight attendant to come onto the loud speaker telling them what to do. Tell yourself. Trust yourself.

Do the action you decided fits best for you from your brainstorming. Don't wait. Life is short. You are older today than you were yesterday. Do it now. If it's not working well, that's okay. Brainstorm again. Choose something else. I tell my children, "If you can't think of anything to do, do something. If you can't think of anything to say, say something. Even if it's completely off, it will get you unstuck and get your brain juiced up again so that you can figure out your next step."

That's it. That's what it takes to exercise your adult muscle: problem, truth, choice, courage, action. Repeat.

You must develop a strong adult self to get to Lifetime Two. Keep practicing.

Problem, truth, choice, courage, action. Repeat.

CHAPTER 27

Step toward Love

Remember our purpose on the planet is twofold: first to outgrow our own fear and emotionally grow up, and second, to become part of the healing force of the world by living in the higher love vibration and helping others wake up as well. This is the advanced lesson. It's hard to do—at first. Then it becomes clear it is the only way to live.

But you may be thinking, *Heal the world? It's such a mess!* What I've noticed is when people think in terms of "I have to heal the world," their immediate reaction is, "I can't do that!" So, they get paralyzed and do nothing.

Remember, though, you are having a human experience on this planet and not a god experience. So the good news is you don't have to heal the world. All you have to do is heal yourself. After that, you can become part of the healing force of the world. That will be enough. I call it shifting from healing "I," the self, to developing a Healing Eye. After you have done your own work to heal yourself, you will then be able to see others' wounds clearly. You will then be able to see where your love is needed.

Remember, almost everyone you meet is being driven by their unconscious wounding from their childhood. They are angry, scared, prideful, ashamed, and reactionary. They are depressed, anxious, addicted, and starving for love.

Starving. Our world is starving for love. That means every time you put a drop of love into it, it matters. Personally, sometimes the best I can do is do no harm. Sometimes the best I can do is visualize sending golden light to someone and wrapping them in the light. Sometimes I can just offer silence. Or a silent prayer. The point is, whatever you can offer, if it's given in love, that's enough. Do the best you can. The goal is to be part of the solution. You don't have to be the whole solution—you just need to do your little part every chance you get. Like in football, do what you can to move the ball down the field. No heroics, just consider being kinder, more loving. As Plato is quoted as saying, "Be kinder than necessary, for everyone you meet is fighting some kind of battle."

Admittedly, though, some people are easier to love than others. I believe, however, that we are not charged with just loving people who are lovable, but that we are charged with figuring out a way to love people who are not lovable—people who are porcupines and will stick us with their quills. There's the rub. How do we love them?

I once had a client who was a police officer. He did not want to be in therapy. He was there because his wife had threatened to leave him and take his children with her if he didn't get help. He was a very, very angry man with rage that seeped out of his every pore. He was unpleasant and disagreeable. He was offensive. Our first session went something like this:

Him: I don't give an F (think of all of these F's as having the full word attached because they did) what you think! I don't give an F what you have to say. I think it's best if you just keep your F-in' mouth shut. I F-in' kill people—do you know that? I F-in' shoot them *dead*. I'm an F-in' badass. I'm your F-in' worst nightmare."

I let him talk. I sent him warm, healing light. I said to myself, "Oh, this poor man! *So* much pain and suffering in him." I asked him to tell me more about killing people.

"That's my F-in' job! Are you F-in' stupid? I go in with my gun pulled, and I shoot bastards. I F-in' love it!"

I continued to send him love silently. He went on and on with all the F-in's. Finally he took a pause, and I said quietly, "I think behind all your bravado, you have a lot of pain. I think it's a cover-up. I think underneath you are hurting, and you use all that stuff to keep people away."

"You got that F-in' right!" he said.

Thus the therapy began. I fall in love with all of my clients. I see their light almost immediately. With this guy, it took me a little longer. But I got there—and then he was able to get there. But I had to get there first. I accepted him as a gift from the Universe to me. I accepted him as an opportunity to practice loving more. He was my opportunity to stretch into a higher level of love. He was my opportunity to practice nonreactionary behavior. He was my opportunity to practice the golden rule: treating him gently as I would like to be treated.

You will be sent such opportunities too. They might come in the form of a person, they might come in the form of an event, but they will come. Just remember when they come not to be judgmental. You used to live in Lifetime One too. In fact, you will go back and visit there sometimes—each time you let your Ghost Drivers take over the wheel. So be gentle with the people in your life who are still stuck in Lifetime One. I always say, "I can't judge you for being in your wounded child because I know you—I *am* you. I have a wounded child too. In fact, I lived in Lifetime One ruled by fear for a long time."

Let go of your judgments of other people's fear. Try to get to compassion and gratitude instead. When I meet someone who is entrenched in reactionary Lifetime One, I immediately say a prayer of gratitude, "Thank you, God/Universe, for helping me wake up. I am the luckiest person in the world. Thank you, thank you, thank you. I am so very, very grateful that I can see with different eyes now. I am so lucky that I can see through the eyes of my heart. Thank you." It's an automatic prayer, a habit now. I believe living in Lifetime Two is a privilege, and I am grateful I have been let into the club.

You are allowed into the club too. See with your heart. See the pain, the fear, the suffering. See the signs around people's necks that say, "I am starving for love," and give just a little love their way. Step toward love over and over and over again. As Mother Teresa said:

> People are unreasonable, illogical, and self-centered. Love them anyway.
>
> If you do good, people may accuse you of selfish motives. Do good anyway.
>
> If you are successful, you may win false friends and true enemies. Succeed anyway. The good you do today may be forgotten tomorrow. Do good anyway.
>
> Honesty and transparency make you vulnerable. Be honest and transparent anyway. What you spend years building may be destroyed overnight. Build anyway.
>
> People who really want help may attack you if you help them. Help them anyway.
>
> Give the world the best you have and you may get hurt. Give the world your best anyway.
>
> For in the end you will find, it was never about them anyway.

That's the amazing part: it was never about them anyway. It's about you. It's about your personal spiritual evolution. It's about your shifting out of your fear and into your love. They are just opportunities for you to do so.

This I know is true: if you step toward love at every opportunity you get, you will experience a life full of joy and peace and happiness. It's worth it. You're worth it.

I promise you: love is not a big deal; it is *the* deal.

CHAPTER 28

A Little More about Marriage

I believe that marriages have the opportunity to go through two lifetimes too. The first lifetime of a marriage is run by our wounded child, of course; the second, by our adult self.

That is, in the first lifetime of our marriage, all of our unresolved issues from childhood show up—and we act like children! We think in terms of *me* and getting *my* needs met. We try to pull love toward us instead of giving love from us. We stomp our feet and demand to be loved. We become reactionary and throw temper tantrums. We get our feelings hurt, we cry, yell, shut down, and eventually feel like *I married the wrong person.*

However, this is not the case. You have just come to the wall between the first life of a marriage and the second life. It is similar to running a marathon. Every marathon runner will tell you that, at some point, they hit a wall during the race. They feel like they can't go on. They want to quit. Their legs and feet are screaming in pain. Yet, also, every marathon runner will tell you that they have learned to overcome the part of the brain that says, "No more!" and to keep pushing themselves through the wall.

That's what has to happen in order to get to the second lifetime of a marriage as well. Nowadays when people hit the wall, they file for divorce and look for another partner who won't be as awful as their first spouse. But they will be. For most marriages start with love, respect, and hope. Then that wounded child shows up, and everything flip-flops. The person who used to be my best friend has become my worst enemy. We hit the wall again—with every person we try this with. And that is why our divorce rate is over 50 percent in our country. We quit at the wall.

So, how to do it differently?

First of all, it helps to know there is a wall, and you are going to hit it. I think maybe that's why older married people cry at weddings: they know this sweet innocence is going to end, and this couple, like all others, will hit the wall.

Sometimes a crisis happens when a couple hits the wall: one or the other will have an affair, start Facebooking an old flame, get caught at a topless bar, lie, hide money, hide spending, and so on. All of this, of course, keeps the marriage in the first lifetime. So this is step number one in doing things differently: when you hit the wall, which you will, don't panic and do stupid things. That is, don't be impulsive, reactionary, and hit the divorce button.

Because, if you want to really get to love, you've got the opportunity right there in this broken marriage—it's your partner. They are the angel who has come to help you. If you can love them, you can love anybody. In my own life, I got the nonreactionary ability to love everyone on the planet but two people: my mother and my husband. Then I got my mother. My husband was the last one I got. Why? Because he and I had recreated all of my and his unresolved childhood wounds. Our wounded children were in charge of the relationship.

So, the next thing you need to do is realize—when your heart is in excruciating pain standing there at the wall—that the Universe just handed you an opportunity to wake up to a higher level of loving. You have been wrapped in a chrysalis and now must do the very hard work of breaking out of it to become the beautiful butterfly that you actually are. You, your partner, and your marriage are in a metamorphosis process. So, in Lifetime One, you and your partner were both caterpillars. Then each of you, individually, got all wrapped up in a chrysalis where your original body, your original self, pretty much melts away. In the chrysalis, a new you was formed. Actually, a beautiful you. A more authentic adult you who is capable of doing the very hard work of getting out of that hard-shelled chrysalis.

All this is to say there is no way to move from Lifetime One marriage to Lifetime Two marriage without working hard. Remember those fairy tales? The first scene introduces the lead characters who are wonderful; the second seen introduces the villain who is dreadful. The third scene, the lead characters outwit and slay the villain, and then finally, they live happily ever after.

However, there is one major difference between the fairy tale and real life. That big and dangerous thing that has to be conquered is inside of you. That's right; the work is inside of you. Why do we always think the work is inside of our partners? Well, wouldn't that be easier? If *he* or *she* needs to do a lot of work and I, on the other hand, don't? Unfortunately, it doesn't work that way. Each and every one of us has to go into our very own chrysalis, melt away the old self, and form a beautiful, new adult self. We each have to move from our wounded child self into our adult self. We can scream and yell, rant and rave at our partners, thinking they will save us somehow from having to do our own breaking out of our own chrysalis, but to no avail. *You* have to face the hard stuff inside of *you*. Nobody can do it for you.

Marriage, you see, is a wonderful crucible where the work can be done. Marriage pushes us to the wall faster than if we stayed single. Our wounded child shows up alive and well and starts to act out—blaming our partner for our suffering. Sometimes it takes some more time, but usually, couples hit the wall by their seventh anniversary. Then they either do the work of emotionally growing up—or not. If they don't do the work, the marriage gets worse and worse. They might stay together because of the kids, of course, but the love dwindles. They often end up feeling more like roommates than partners—or they may end up just hating each other.

So what to do?

As stated earlier, we need to move out of our wounds from our childhood—out of our fears of not being good enough, worthy enough, or lovable enough—and into loving ourselves even though we are imperfect human beings. We have to move out of our fears into our humanness. That's right; we have to let go of this perfection idea and realize we all came from caterpillar stock. I did, you did, your partner did. You and your partner are just human beings trying to figure out how to get to happy.

So, we get married as little caterpillars. Then we hit the wall and build a hard chrysalis around us, trying to protect our hearts. We are in that chrysalis grieving, melting away our resistances to love. I think part of that process involves feeling the pain of our little child for all the times we got the message "You're just a worthless caterpillar!"

Remember, when we connect to what happened to our little child, that's when we have to do our best to let the tears flow. Have a good belly sob. Embrace the idea that "Yes, I was a caterpillar—and that was enough! I needed to be a caterpillar before I could become a butterfly!" Cry, cry, cry as much as you can and get it out. Next comes the work of breaking through the chrysalis and becoming our true, beautiful butterfly self.

It is here, stuck in the hard-shelled chrysalis, where the tendency is to turn *against* our partner. We get mad at them for not getting us out of this predicament. We get mad at them for not being there for us. We expect them to make everything all right, and they're not!

No, they're not, because the work is *inside* of *you*. They can't make everything all right by saying some magic words or having some magic behavior. No, only *you* can slay your very own dragon, remember? So, the trick, then, is in times of despair, turn toward our partner. Use them as the place you go to fall. Use them for comfort. Now, if they are not comforting you the way you would like—and they won't—I suggest you simply learn these words: "Could you just sit quietly and hold me?"

Then sit quietly and let yourself be held. For at least five minutes. Breathe into your partner's arms. Envision atoms from their skin jumping over to yours and vice versa. Trade some atoms. Relax into the embrace. Let some time pass and then simply say, "Thank you." That's enough. Remember, you are an adult and not a bottomless pit.

Then as your butterfly self emerges, start to notice what a beautiful butterfly you have turned into. Your caterpillar days are over, and now you can fly! Really notice the talents you have, the things you do well. Really notice how, when you put your mind to something, you can get it done. You are so capable, so amazing. You have a unique and beautiful journey on this planet that is yours, all yours. Step up and claim it. Time to kiss that quest for perfection goodbye and admit, "I am human, and I will never get it all right. In fact, I don't have to! I am free, and I can fly!"

Then, once we know in our core that we are enough in spite of being human, then we can take 100 percent responsibility for having gotten our relationship to the place that it is. We can admit wholeheartedly everything we have done that was hurtful when we were stuck in the first lifetime of our marriage. We can beg forgiveness without diminishing ourselves *at all*. We can name what we did wrong, claim what we did wrong—that is, take ownership of it without shame and apologize for it—and then change what we did wrong.

There is no need for defensiveness. We can face the truth.

We can say things like, "Yes, I *did* totally abandon you emotionally. I got so mixed up in just making money and getting accolades at work. No wonder you didn't feel safe!" Or, "Yes, that was absolutely my issue that came out of my childhood, and I am so sorry I kept throwing it on you! No wonder you haven't felt loved!" Or, "I am so, so sorry I raged at you. I didn't know a better way. Now I do." Or, "Wow, I have been so stuck on all these stupid little things: keep the house clean, make me dinner, wear different clothes! I cringe to think I beat you up about those things. I got totally lost on the love part. I love you so much, and I'm sorry you haven't had the experience of feeling loved by me."

Also, when your partner says, "You did this to me! And this! And this!" Validate that by just saying, "I know! I did! I am so sorry!" Name it, claim it, change it. You can even ask your partner, "What else have I done to hurt you?" Hear it *all*. Is there more? Own it. Validate it. Apologize. Apologize again. Heal it by responding instead of reacting.

And then you can begin to love. So many times, couples come to me completely in the quagmire of the first lifetime of their marriage, and they are surprised to hear, "The love hasn't even begun yet." But it hasn't. It can't begin until you break out of your childhood wounds and grow into your butterfly self. Remember the old saying that we have to love ourselves before we can love someone else? It's true.

But what if you do this metamorphosis and your partner doesn't? Because almost always two people in a couple do not do this evolving at the same rate. And that's the test: how to love when your partner is still living in a reactionary way. It is very hard to do. It is discouraging.

I always say there has to be a hero in the relationship though. This is the person who gets it before the other person does. With your newfound loving self, it is now time to go back and own up to everything, *everything*, you have done hurtful in the marriage as stated above, and it is time for you to ask forgiveness. It is time to do all of this expecting nothing in return. It is time to lay down your sword unconditionally. Not "I'll lay down my sword if you do." No. It's "I lay down my sword. I am so sorry for how I have hurt you. Can you forgive me?"

In the Bible, Jesus said only one prayer, the Lord's Prayer. One prayer in the whole Bible. And in that prayer, he said, "Forgive us our trespasses as we forgive those who trespass against us." This is when you ask your partner, "Is it possible for you to ever forgive my trespasses against you?"

Hopefully your partner will be able to say, "Yes, I think I can. With time." And then you have to *be* the change you wish to see in your marriage. Respond; don't react. Go inward when you feel fear instead of glopping all that stuff on your partner. Work hard to make sure your partner has the experience of love. One of my colleagues says it this way: Loving your partner is not enough; divorce courts are filled with people who love each other. Instead, your partner must experience *feeling* loved.

That's what Lifetime Two in a marriage is all about: both you and your partner get to experience the feeling of loving and being loved almost always. Why not always? Because we are human, there is no perfection, and we all have a bumbling part of us that shows up at the most inopportune times.

Remember, we love people who make us feel good about ourselves. Are you doing that with your partner? Or are you chip, chip, chipping away at the love with constant criticisms and directives?

After you get to your authentic, adult, loving self, one of two things happens in your marriage: either your partner evolves too, or you outgrow the marriage.

Learned Helplessness in Marriage

Just like the dogs in Martin Seligman's experiments demonstrated learned helplessness when they came to believe no matter what they did, they would get shocked, so it is sometimes in marriages. I see it most frequently when a partner bullies their spouse. When a partner is subjected to a daily dose of toxic criticism, they can, and often do, slide into learned helplessness. What this leads to is their inability to take action. They become passive, having lost their belief in themselves to change their circumstances.

Are you doing this to your partner?

Denial in Marriage

Also, sometimes it's so hard to see our behaviors because our denial system is full on. We have to learn to be nonreactionary so that we can actually hear what our partner is saying. They can see exactly where we need to evolve.

Often in my practice, people tell me their stories, and sometimes the issues they need to resolve are so blatantly obvious to me on the outside but invisible to one of the partners. For example, I have a couple who I am working with now where the husband is outraged that his wife doesn't trust him. He yells at her when he finds out she has looked at his phone or read his emails. He feels violated and outraged. But his behavior? He is an alcoholic who sometimes has one-night stands when he is drunk. He stays out all night with another woman and then feels like a victim when his wife is checking up on him.

Wow, this husband needs to wake up to a lot more honesty in his relationship, or it will not heal. If you don't have trustworthy behavior, it would actually be pathological for your partner to trust you. If you want to be trusted, you must tell yourself the truth: trust comes from consistent trustworthy behavior. And we can't grow up by pretending or lying to ourselves.

So what does trustworthy, adult behavior look like? Here is a transcript from part of another couple's session where the transformation took place:

Husband: We are now putting the couple first. We have decided we want a good life together. We are willing to do whatever it takes to get there. I can see so clearly now I was aloof, dragging my feet, I didn't do the effort to get a job to provide for my family—I was waiting for a miracle. I was very, very passive. I wasn't fully committed to my marriage.

[Wife agrees.]

Husband: Being alone was very important to me. I didn't know how to join and hold onto myself at the same time. My mother was overbearing, and I projected that onto my wife. I was hiding stuff from her; I was not sharing; I was too afraid. Now, it's strange, but I feel like a grown-up. Now I am sitting at the table—not just wishing that I was. Now I am not afraid—I know my abilities. I speak up. All my life, I tried to stay out of harm's way. Now I am much more proactive, and I don't have to do that anymore. I found out I like challenge!

Wife: It's so nice now that I have an *adult* for a husband. I love it. He's not defensive and running away anymore.

Husband: I thought my wife was better than me; I slowly withdrew, and she took over everything—she got more and more capable with practice, and I got less and less so. I was afraid to make a mistake and upset her. I slowly gave more and more to her to do—*my* responsibilities. I was such a child. When someone criticized me or my work, I didn't take it well. I made it about *me* and would have a temper tantrum and then withdraw into silence.

Wife: He is much more honest now—and confident. I need to encourage him and not do everything for him. That's emasculating! I can see that now. Then I was just really, really controlling because everything felt so out of control. Like he couldn't answer a direct question—it had to be five questions back to me.

Husband: Sometimes I didn't grasp what she was asking because I was so busy trying to come up with the right answer. I didn't want to get in trouble or yelled at—like I was a little boy.

Wife: Yeah. Also, I believe you now when you tell me something like when I am talking too much. But do you believe me? Can you hear me saying I can take no for an answer but not *no* answer? I get so reactive the moment you start sitting there silently. I know I need to work on that. That's when my little girl shows up—when I feel ignored.

Husband: I know. I am so sorry I did that to you. Man, it's unbelievable—I don't even recognize my old self. I feel and act so differently now. I feel powerful. It feels great.

It really is possible to get to Lifetime Two in a marriage—and it really is worth it. There is nothing better than being loved by someone you love.

The Postwork

CHAPTER 29

Do Meaningful Work

Now it's time to fully step into your empowered adult self.

I don't know if there is anything like recycled souls. I don't know if what the Hindus believe is true: that God loves us so much that we are given as many lives on this planet as we need to get rid of all of our karma and become part of the universal healing love force. Maybe it's true. I don't know that it's not true. All I know for sure, though, is that we have this life. So, what are you going to do with your one precious life?

Make it count.

To do this, you must get in touch with what your talent is, what your passion is, and do that. So many people tell me, though, they have no idea what their passion or talent is. So maybe that's the wrong question. A better question is, What's important to you? The reality is you are here on the planet for an undetermined amount of time and have 1,440 time tokens (minutes) a day to spend. Some of the time we spend is in doing things that are important to us. The rest of the time we spend is doing things that are not really important to us. What I have discovered is this: when we are spending time doing things that are important to us, it increases the meaning of our life and our happiness. When we spend our time doing things that are unimportant to us, we mostly are just killing time. So the question becomes, What is important to you? Are you spending some time doing it?

For example, what's important to me is world peace. I don't know why it is important to me, but it is. So, when I am working toward that end—teaching healing self, teaching love, teaching about the two lifetimes—I feel fully alive. I feel I am living the life I was born to live.

So, what's important to you? Are you spending some time doing it?

It doesn't matter if you do it for a living, but it matters that you do it. Things that could be important to you might be the environment, education, laughter, fun, dancing, children, poverty, gardening, sports, flowers, art, kindness, being in shape, nutrition, music, helping others, equal rights, eradicating hunger, and so on. It doesn't matter what it is; it just matters that you spend some of your time doing it.

One of my son's friends wants to be a stand-up comedian. His mother wants him to be an engineer even though math doesn't make sense to him. She doesn't know yet that he needs to be a stand-up comedian. He will have to claim his life as his own and take over driving his car to become who he was born to be. You see, when we become who we were born to be, everything falls into alignment. So, be open to discovering that about yourself.

If you don't know what your life work is right now, that's okay too. There is a psychology theory called the acorn theory. In this theory, we are all born with a tiny acorn inside of us that will, one day, grow into an oak tree. For some people, the acorn starts to grow when they are very young. Mozart, for example, was a child prodigy musically, playing for the king at age five. For others, the acorn bursts open much later in life. Colonel Sanders of Kentucky Fried Chicken fame, for example, opened his first restaurant when he was sixty-five. Mary Kay Ash started her Mary Kay Cosmetics when she was forty-five. There is a time for you too. In Ecclesiastes

3:1, it is written, "To every thing there is a season, and a time to every purpose under heaven."

So don't worry if your path isn't clear to you right now. Just keep stepping toward doing things that are important to you. If you do this, the doors will open, the coincidences will happen, the people you need to meet will show up. I am often amazed that this happens, and I certainly don't understand it except to believe Einstein's statement that we are all interconnected. Yet, regardless of my little understanding of it, it is still true. Move toward doing what's important to you—whatever it is—and you will find you are on the right track by noticing the synchronicity that begins to happen all around you.

Consider Dr. George Lombardi. In medical school, he did a rotation where he worked with hardened drug addicts. He struggled as he tried to get IVs into their collapsed veins. Giving good care was important to him, though, and so he worked hard at getting good at successfully finding the veins. Years later, when he was starting his own practice, hoping his phone would ring and he would get some patients, he was stunned when he was asked one day to immediately fly to India to heal a dying patient: Mother Teresa. When he arrived in Calcutta, Mother Teresa was dying from septic shock, an infection caused by the pacemaker in her chest. She needed massive amounts of antibiotics pumped into her system and the pacemaker removed. The problem? She was severely dehydrated, and nobody had been able to get an IV into her veins. But because he had practiced doing what was important to him years ago—delivering good care to every single patient—Dr. George Lombardi did. Mother Teresa lived another eight years after his intervention.

Be true to the things that are important to you. Spend at least some of your time doing them. You never know how the work you do now will be transformed later.

Think about this too: What will they say about you when you die? Will they say you contributed to the healing of the world? And in what way?

CHAPTER 30

Walk in Integrity

There are two definitions in *Webster's Dictionary* for integrity:

1. the quality of being honest and having strong moral principles
   Synonyms: honesty, honor, good character, decency, fairness, scrupulousness, trustworthiness
2. the state of being whole and undivided
   Synonyms: unity, unification, coherence, cohesion, togetherness, solidarity

It seems to me that one leads to the other. That is, being honest and having strong moral principles leads one to feel whole and undivided.

So, you must define your own values and principles: What do you stand for? What are your values? I believe it is your responsibility—to yourself and to the world—to figure these things out. Here are some values to consider: honesty, kindness, not harming others, protecting the environment, being fair, not stealing from others, fidelity, family, and so on. Take what you like from this list and add to it to form your own list. Once you have done this, defined what you stand for, then you only have to measure your potential behaviors against your own standard. It makes life much simpler.

A close friend of mine's value code is simply this: do not violate another. The great actor Anthony Hopkins's life code is this: "I expect nothing, and I accept everything, and it makes my life simple." Many choose the golden rule as the standard they will live by: I will treat others the way I would like to be treated. The main thing is to figure out what works for you.

One of my standards that I try to always live by is *do the right thing*. Our gut usually tells us if it's right or not. If you have a feeling of doubt about something—should I or shouldn't I?—that is your gut telling you, "Don't." Learn to trust it. For example, when I was making copies of this manuscript for others to proofread, the clerk at the copy center said she would give me the military discount since I had a lot of printing and it was their biggest discount. I said to her, "But I'm not military," to which she replied, "Oh, that's okay." But it wasn't okay with me. It didn't matter that I wouldn't get caught. It didn't matter that no one would know. I would know. I politely declined the discount. It cost me twelve dollars extra for every copy of this book I made. It was worth it. I felt empowered. Doing the right thing helps us be a person of integrity.

I had a worker come to my house one time to clean my chimney and put a chimney cap on it. He charged me seventy-five for the whole job. I said to him he could have charged me more because I had no idea what the going price was. He told me, "I don't do anything I can't tell my daughter. That's my criteria. Yeah, I could rip you off, but I couldn't look my little girl straight in the eye. Money's not worth jeopardizing her trust in me."

So set your own standard and be true to it.

Tell the truth. Mostly to yourself. How are you doing at staying in your adult self? What are you doing to take care of yourself? What have you done today to move your life in the direction you want to go? Tell yourself the truth.

Keep your word. To yourself and others.

I support a foundation called Because I Said I Would. This movement was started by a young man, Alex Sheen, whose father died from cancer when Alex was in his twenties. When writing the eulogy, he tried to think of the largest lesson his father had taught him. Alex realized it was making and keeping promises. Today, Alex sends one hundred promise cards at no charge to anyone who requests them, encouraging people to make promises and keep them. This is the standard by which he lives his life. I encourage you to watch his TED talk.

It is a value that has been lost by so many today but is essential in order to stay in your adult, authentic, empowered self. Don't just talk the talk—walk the walk.

CHAPTER 31

Have Adventures

Our time on the planet is short. Enjoy it. It's time to do things that you want to do. Do things that you are afraid of doing, because as the singer Anna Nalick reminds us, "Life's like an hourglass glued to the table," and "no one can find the rewind button." We don't get back time we have wasted.

So, write a bucket list. Write down all of the wild and crazy things you would like to do before you leave the planet. Then do them one at a time. Yes, you will have to be brave, but remember the goal is to outgrow fear. Even with fun adventures, you must walk toward your fear. Doing adventures helps us be less afraid.

Last year, I traveled to Nepal by myself to stay in a remote village where the student I sponsor lives. People were aghast, saying things like, "You are traveling by yourself? You are a woman traveling halfway around the world—by yourself? Are you sure that's safe?" No, of course I wasn't sure. But I was sure of what Richard Bach wrote in his brilliant book *Illusions*:

Here is a test to see if your mission on earth is complete: if you're alive, it isn't.

Why be afraid? I am going to be here until my mission is complete, and then I won't be. It's the same for you, so live your life. Live it fully. Live with your arms wide open, taking in as much as you possibly can, spreading love everywhere you go. Remember, once you have let go of fear ruling you, you are free.

Or as the poet Mary Oliver said:

> When it's over, I want to say: all my life I was a bride married to amazement. I was the bridegroom, taking the world into my arms.

I recently read about a woman, Roz Savage, who, at age thirty-two, quit her job and quit her marriage and rowed across the Atlantic Ocean—by herself. With no chase boat. In doing so, she had to confront lots and lots of fears. The end result? Her fears were tamed—and she went on to row across the Pacific Ocean as well. By the time she had finished that and decided to row across the Indian Ocean, her fear dragon was nowhere to be found. Be brave. Be bold.

One of the most thrilling experiences in my own life happened in Nepal. I decided to paraglide down from a mountain in the Himalayas. I flew in tandem with a pilot, of course, trusting his expertise. I will always remember his words to me, "When the parachute gets air in it, run as fast as you can to the edge of the cliff—and jump."

Yeah, do that. It's worth it.

CHAPTER 32

Give Back

Contribute. Certainly it's a given that you need to practice loving every single person who you come in contact with, but it's also important to figure out some way to give back. When I think of giving back, I think of practicing random acts of kindness and senseless acts of beauty. Yes, you can contribute by giving money to worthy causes—that counts—but I also think it's important for you to get involved in goodness guerrilla warfare as well. What can you do today to do something nice for someone—anonymously?

We have to watch that our giving isn't about our ego. That's where the anonymous part comes in. Do simple things. Here are a few ideas to get you started:

1. Leave quarters at the car wash for the next person.
2. Drop pennies and quarters on the ground for others to find. I had a client who lived on the streets for three years as a teenager. Each day, he would go to a large parking lot and look for thirty-eight cents in dropped coins so he could afford to buy a package of Ramen noodles for his dinner. It matters that we share.
3. Pay for the car behind you in the drive-through line.

4. Leave a ten-dollar gift card on someone's windshield in the parking lot.
5. Send flowers anonymously to an elderly person.
6. Make a flower garden in your front yard so people can enjoy it as they walk by.
7. Always stop and buy lemonade from children.
8. Leave a note of encouragement to the person at your office who is most starved for love.
9. Tie a balloon onto the back of a chair at the mall.
10. Write a thank-you note to someone today.
11. Let someone cut in in front of you while driving.
12. Wave a thank you to the person who let you cut in on the freeway.
13. Give someone your seat on the bus.
14. Give someone a smile.
15. Always say thank you.
16. Be fully present when someone is talking to you, looking them in the eyes.
17. Show up for someone's special day.
18. Say a prayer for the world to heal.
19. Give hugs.
20. Think of the other, work for justice.
21. Volunteer to help at an event; Google "volunteer [your city's name].org (for example volunteerhouston.org).
22. Be a mentor.
23. Write a large "Thank you for doing such a good job!" sign to the trash collector.
24. Throw flower seeds along the side of the road.
25. Sing in the choir.

Of course there are thousands of other examples of things you can do. Get creative. The important thing is to remember to be kind to one another, to care for one another at every turn, and to never, never violate another. First do no harm.

Remember, too, those in Lifetime One have yet to see that we are one, all wanting the same thing. Help them. Be generous with your praise. Tell them about the light that you see in them. Remember, love is *the* deal—everything else is just details.

CHAPTER 33

The Awakening Is Happening

I believe the world is awakening. I believe the Universe wants us all to wake up. I believe we must get to the tipping point—where more people are run by love than are run by fear—to get to world peace.

I am convinced this shift is happening.

I have had the privilege of traveling a lot in my life, but on my first trip to Nepal, I was shocked. I was shocked to see prayer flags everywhere, urging people to pray for peace. There were many temples along the roads where children knelt—praying for peace. There were even small pieces of painted wood hung on trees far from the city that said, "Pray for peace." I was shocked at all of the kindnesses that were extended everywhere we went.

At one point, my son and I decided to take a flight up to the Himalaya Mountains to see Mt. Everest. We were given our boarding passes, having no idea where we were sitting. I got lucky: row two, a window seat. I looked around for my son, who had gotten lucky too: row one, across the aisle, window seat. I was so happy that we both got window seats so we could have a good view of the mountain range.

And then I noticed: they only sold the window seats. Every single window seat was taken. The rest of the plane was empty. Buddha Air evidently does this on purpose—so everyone can have a good experience.

So we took off and headed for the mountains. When they came into view, the flight attendant asked me if I wanted to go into the cockpit. Incredulous, I said, "Excuse me?" Then she asked me again if I wanted to go into the cockpit since the view was so much better there.

Really? I thought to myself, *Who* are *these people?*

So, I went into the cockpit, where I was greeted by the pilots saying Namaste to me. Namaste: the sacred in me greets the sacred in you. They explained each mountain to me as we flew by them. The view was amazing. After about five minutes, the flight attendant tapped me on the shoulder and motioned me out so my son could come in and see. I wondered if we were getting this special treatment since we were the only Americans on the plane. No. Every single person on the plane got to go into the cockpit, as the pilots flew up and down the mountain range making sure everyone had a good experience.

Wow. The awakening is happening.

Some clients of mine went to Africa this year to go on a safari in the Serengeti. They watched as a cheetah chased down and killed a gazelle. Their tour guide told them, "You see, we have lessons from the cheetah. They never take more than they need. They do not kill for killing's sake. They kill only when they must, to eat."

Then there is the internet where we can see Kid President telling us, "Hey, we're all on the same team, right? So we need to start acting like it."

Then there's the internet, where we can download the movie *I AM*, directed by Tom Shadyac. Tom Shadyac, the director of such movie hits as *Bruce Almighty*, *Liar Liar*, and *Patch Adams*, was in a in a devastating accident that left him severely depressed and even suicidal. Before he died, though, he decided to take a camera crew around the world and find out what was wrong with the world and what we needed to do to fix it. What he discovered, however, was what is right with the world. Everywhere, people loving and supporting one another, extending kindnesses. He discovered that John Lennon was right: all we need is love.

I see it everywhere. More and more people are waking up. More and more people are seeking answers to how to get to happy. Kindness is multiplying exponentially. I promise you, the shift is happening.

And I invite you: be a part of it.

Acknowledgments

I would like to thank all the people who loved and supported me through the birth of this book. You are too many to name: all my family, all my friends, all my clients, all of the people who helped me in the publishing process, my colleagues, my mentors, all those upon whose shoulders I stand. To all of you, I humbly say thank you.

ADDENDUM

I Believe

Here are some more of my beliefs: a summary and some more things to ponder. But the big question is, What do *you* believe?

Remember, this has been my story. Take what you like and leave the rest.

More importantly, now it's time for you to write your story.

If any of my beliefs resonate with you, then take them as your own. That is, take them and own them. Write them into your story. Conversely, if any of my beliefs don't resonate with you, feel free to discard them. Write your story—what works for you.

My story works for me, but this book is really about you. Ponder what I've said and then define *your* truths.

1. I believe peace is the way to peace.
2. I believe there is no need for blame and that, actually, it is not helpful and prevents the shift from Lifetime One to Lifetime Two.
3. I believe in forgiveness.
4. I believe I am you and you are me, and therefore, I can't judge you.
5. I believe we all have a Jesus and a Judas self: a light and a shadow self.
6. I believe we always have choice.
7. I believe we can always use A>B>C, Action>Belief>Consequence.

8. I believe you are a light in this world. Take your candle—go light your world.

9. I believe we are responsible for what we are doing, thinking, feeling, saying, not doing, not saying.

10. I believe those who grieve well live well.

11. I believe loss is an integral part of life, so there is no need to fear it.

12. I believe there are angels that come to help us shift from Lifetime One to Lifetime Two: they are often disguised as difficult people.

13. I believe we are too busy.

14. I believe it is necessary—and possible—to create win/win.

15. I believe the good guys should have the money.

16. I believe money is only a vehicle.

17. I believe we can draw money to us.

18. I believe we must give money away.

19. I believe your children deserve to have two adults to raise them.

20. I believe God is love.

21. I believe if the only prayer you ever say is thank you, that is enough.

22. I believe love is more powerful than anything else, including fear.

23. I believe there is a bias toward healing.

24. I believe the good stuff is in adult.

25. I believe adult is learning to respond rather than react: response-able.

26. I believe the lyrics to "Climb Every Mountain" are profound. **

** "Climb every mountain, ford every stream, follow every bi-way, 'til you find your dream: a dream that will need all the love you can give, every day of your life, for as long as you live."

27. I believe every journey is sacred—even those with sociopathology, addiction, special needs, handicaps, and so on. They are exactly perfect and are necessary for the awakening of the world.

28. I believe it's all good—even the hard stuff. Put the label of blessing or lesson on everything. For example, if after my dad died, he met God, I believe God would say to him, "You were a great sociopath; you played your part well. Thank you."

29. I believe part of the lessons on this planet are trauma and challenge. These are not things to be afraid of; expect them.

30. I believe there is nothing to be afraid of: Jesus said so many times, "Fear not."

31. I believe our soul continues after this earth experience.

32. I believe lifetimes are different lengths and people live their whole lifetime.

33. I believe love is the healing force on the planet.

34. I believe everything can be reduced to either love or fear.

35. I believe we are the only one with ourselves twenty-four seven.

36. I believe enabling is not helping.

37. I believe the media is stuck in fear and encourages it.

38. I believe most religions are stuck in fear and encourage it.

39. I believe you can outgrow fear, and then you are free.

40. I believe the human experience is that we are imperfect.

41. I believe we must have the courage to love ourselves as imperfect to get to Lifetime Two.

42. I believe Jesus—and Gandhi—got it and were trying to teach us Lifetime Two.

43. I believe we must become as children to enter the kingdom of God/Love, which is right here surrounding us.

44. I believe the word God confuses people and can be better understood by the word love; that is, put God first—put love first.

45. I believe we are all interconnected, and therefore, we are never alone. Abandonment is an illusion, a paper tiger.

46. I believe these are the most exciting times to be alive.

47. I believe we are in an individual evolution as well as a global evolution.

48. I believe most of the world is still asleep.

49. I believe we each have a boat and are floating down the river of life on an adventure.

50. I believe each one of us comes to the planet on purpose.

51. I believe people are afraid to grow up.

52. I believe that we need to call upon our courage more often.

53. I believe people come to the planet fully equipped with everything they need to get to Lifetime Two: lovable, capable, intelligent, talented.

54. I believe that we can transform the bad/sad that happened to us in Lifetime One and *use* it in Lifetime Two to add to the healing of the world.

55. I believe we are here to contribute to the healing of the world.

56. I believe I don't know why it's designed this way, and that that's okay, because we don't have to understand the why.

57. I believe in optimism; I am optimistic about the world.

58. I believe everything is part of Divine.

59. I believe there is a higher order than me.

60. I believe our mission is to emotionally grow up.

61. I believe there are movies that tell about Lifetime Two: *Field of Dreams* (ease his pain), *Avatar* (from fear to love), *Black Swan* (from child to adult), *The King's Speech* (from child to adult), *Star Wars* (follow the light).

62. I believe we can learn to recognize when our wounded child is driving our car and when our adult self is.

63. I believe we are all wounded as children—some more, some less.

64. I believe the goal is to be who you were born to be—the authentic self.
65. I believe the authentic self exists only as a small child and then in Lifetime Two as an authentic, nonreactionary, ruled-by-love adult.
66. I believe we are addicted to short-term gratification because of fear.
67. I believe Lifetime Two means telling yourself the truth.
68. I believe we have to use the golden rule and do the right thing.
69. I believe every baby is born with the need to be loved and never outgrows it.
70. I believe we can learn to see the signs around people's necks who are crying out for love.
71. I believe life is short and that, therefore, we must make good use of our time.
72. I believe there are no less thans or greater thans—only asleep or awake or on the path in between the two.
73. I believe you are a sacred, beautiful, amazing, lovable human being.
74. I believe you have what it takes, you are enough.
75. I believe love is *the* deal on the planet—the rest is just details.

May you open your heart, become an emotional adult,
see with healing eyes, and enjoy your journey.

Recommended Readings,
Links, and Movies

Books

Boundaries by Henry Cloud and John Townsend
Broken Open by Elizabeth Lesser
Feel the Fear and Do It Anyway by Susan Jeffers
Getting the Love You Want by Harville Hendrix
Iron John by Robert Bly
Hold Me Tight by Susan Johnson
Love Busters by Willard Harley
Man's Search for Meaning by Viktor Frankl
Mao's Last Dancer by Li Cunxin
The Emotional Incest Syndrome by Pat Love
The Emotionally Unavailable Man: A Blueprint for Healing by Patti Henry
The Life You've Always Wanted by John Ortberg
The Music Is You by Rosita Perez
We Love Each Other, But by Ellen Wactel
Wired for Love by Stan Tatkin
You Can Heal Your Life by Louise Hay

YouTube

Kid President
Ronny Edry, TED Talk
Lizzie Velásquez, TED Talk
"Because I Said I Would," Alex Sheen, TED Talk

Brave, Sara Bareilles
T-Mobile Welcome Home, You Tube
The Automatic Thanking Machine, YouTube
Kids Solve World Hunger Problem

Movies
I AM
Avatar
Field of Dreams
Happiness
Selma

Link
Bob Hoffman's Negative Love Essay, http://www.institut-hoffman.com/articles/the%20negative%20love%20syndrome.pdf.

Index

Symbols

1 Corinthians 13 6

A

AA 33, 103, 185
ABC 100, 101, 102, 105, 106, 107,
    109, 129, 212, 217, 236
Abu Ghraib 59
Albert Einstein 50, 133
Albert Ellis 100
Anger 3, 28, 29, 39, 68, 78, 80,
    102, 122, 162, 163, 168, 171,
    172, 188, 189, 227
Anna Quindlen xi
astronaut 26
athleticism 57
Avatar 18, 272, 276
avoidance 69, 74, 75, 83, 84,
    164, 205

B

birthday cards 70, 71
Boldness 237
Boundaries 25, 77, 118, 158, 174,
    199, 200, 201, 202, 203,
    204, 207, 275

Broken Open 3, 275
bucket list 258

C

Cancer 32, 36, 122, 140, 176, 257
Candid Camera 5
caterpillar 243, 245, 246
challenge 9, 40, 46, 75, 92, 99, 107,
    110, 117, 118, 119, 122, 234,
    250, 271
Chernobyl 4, 5, 10, 32, 79, 85, 211
comfort zone 33, 75, 78, 117, 220
conscious choice 36, 37, 40, 41,
    140, 183
C. S. Lewis 90

D

Dante's Inferno 6
Dan Zadra xi
Denial 57, 164, 248
Desmond Tutu 169
Dr. George Lombardi 254
Dr. Seuss 7

E

E. E. Cummings 46
egocentricity 145, 149

Elizabeth Lesser 3, 275
EMDR 160
emotional incest 141, 142, 143,
    144, 145, 186, 275
Encouragement 9, 82, 131, 261

F

FAA 50
Fear Dragon 48, 49, 82, 85, 135,
    206, 222, 223, 225, 259
Field of Dreams 17, 272, 276
Finding Nemo 41
FOO 150, 151, 186
Forgiveness 103, 150, 163, 166, 167,
    168, 169, 172, 173, 176, 177,
    178, 207, 218, 246, 247, 269

G

Gandhi 38, 52, 187, 188, 192,
    200, 271
Ghost Drivers 137, 138, 139, 140,
    141, 142, 143, 144, 145, 147,
    148, 149, 150, 152, 157, 158,
    159, 160, 161, 162, 164, 166,
    170, 174, 180, 181, 182, 183,
    194, 196, 199, 218, 228,
    235, 240
Glacier National Park 5, 32, 79, 85,
    211, 213
good finder 96

H

Habits 81, 191, 240
Hawkins, David 58
Henry Ford 69
Hitler 124
Hoffman, Bob 44, 276

Hoffman Process 163
Holocaust 112

I

I AM ix, 4, 17, 25, 27, 28, 30, 33,
    37, 38, 39, 47, 50, 54, 55, 57,
    58, 59, 68, 76, 81, 82, 84,
    90, 91, 92, 93, 95, 99, 105,
    107, 108, 118, 119, 120, 121,
    122, 127, 129, 130, 131, 132,
    141, 142, 144, 145, 148, 157,
    161, 168, 171, 175, 182, 193,
    194, 197, 198, 200, 201, 202,
    203, 207, 208, 211, 214, 216,
    217, 218, 220, 223, 227, 230,
    231, 232, 237, 240, 241, 246,
    247, 249, 250, 253, 254, 258,
    263, 264, 269, 272, 276
Illusions 213, 223, 224, 226,
    258, 272
Intervention Thoughts 194, 195,
    196, 225

J

Jiddu Krishnamurti 100
John F. Kennedy 51

L

Las Vegas 34
Learned Helplessness 159, 248
loss 7, 111, 122, 123, 124, 125, 153,
    234, 235, 270
Louise Hay 141, 275

M

macro level 124
Mankind Project 126, 127, 130,
    131, 163, 172

Marianne Williamson 24, 96, 169
Mario Cart 183
marriage 19, 77, 78, 79, 81, 128,
        141, 143, 144, 168, 174, 187,
        193, 210, 212, 213, 214, 231,
        242, 243, 244, 246, 247,
        248, 249, 250, 259
Mayan Calendar 60
media 65, 66, 67, 68, 85, 145, 271
micro level 124
Mother Teresa 38, 52, 132, 169,
        195, 241, 254

N

no shortcuts ix, 31
Notel 67

O

Oprah 92, 126, 127, 128, 130, 131,
        132, 172
options 23, 37, 41, 104, 119, 176,
        182, 183, 187, 193, 214, 216,
        217, 218, 236

P

passing tones x
Pippin' 92
Power vs. Force 58
primary relationship 77, 78, 142
Princess Diana 124
privacy 207, 208
PT Barnum 49
PTSD 113, 160

Q

Qur'an 27, 37

R

reactionary 22, 26, 29, 37, 56, 77,
        83, 106, 170, 177, 181, 183,
        184, 187, 188, 189, 190, 191,
        193, 195, 196, 197, 198, 199,
        218, 232, 238, 240, 242,
        243, 247
red deer 54
religion 15, 16, 19, 25, 29, 51, 125,
        128, 271
Reptilian Brain 193
responding 25, 41, 60, 183, 184,
        185, 186, 187, 188, 192, 194,
        197, 201, 214, 218, 236, 247
Ronny Edry 59, 275
Rumi 11, 107
Rush Limbaugh 66

S

saying no 24, 200, 203, 225
saying NO 24, 200, 203, 225
self-forgiveness 173, 178
self-honesty 79, 93
self-talk 68, 85
seminary 72, 73
Siddhartha 6
Socrates 80, 137
Spong, Shelby 15
Stan Tatkin 191, 275
Starving for Love 53, 197, 238, 241
Steve Jobs 113, 139, 141, 144
sun window 224
Susan Boyle 27

T

talent 27, 32, 56, 57, 84, 92, 97, 98,
        99, 228, 233, 246, 252

Thich Nhat Hanh 38, 52, 164
Thoreau, Henry D. 132
transition 39, 42, 44, 48
trauma 7, 36, 65, 110, 111, 112,
        113, 114, 115, 116, 117, 156,
        157, 160, 161, 163, 234, 271

U

Universal Wound 79, 136, 140, 145

V

victim card 210, 211, 213, 214, 216,
        218, 219

Viktor Frankl 235
Voice Dialogue 88

W

Wild 93, 183, 258
Wired for Love 191, 275
Wizard of Oz 167, 223, 228

Z

zero days 84, 85

Would you like a consultation with the author?
Call Patti Henry's office directly to arrange a time and payment:
713-977-9397
Other services available:
Heal Your Marriage Intensive
Individual Therapy
Couple's Therapy
Public Speaking Engagements
Radio/TV Interviews
Professional Seminars

For more information, call 713-977-9397,
or go to www.patti-henry.com
email: patti@patti-henry.com

Printed in the United States
By Bookmasters